THE ANCIENT-FUTURE VISIONARY:
SELECTED SHORTER WRITINGS
BY ROBERT E. WEBBER

The Ancient-Future Visionary

SELECTED SHORTER WRITINGS
BY ROBERT E. WEBBER

✢

ROBERT E. WEBBER

EDITED BY
Keith Call

FOREWORD BY
Karen Burton Mains

CASCADE Books • Eugene, Oregon

THE ANCIENT-FUTURE VISIONARY
Selected Shorter Writings by Dr. Robert E. Webber

Copyright © 2025 Keith Call. All rights reserved. Except for brief quotations in critical publications or reviews, no part of this book may be reproduced in any manner without prior written permission from the publisher. Write: Permissions, Wipf and Stock Publishers, 199 W. 8th Ave., Suite 3, Eugene, OR 97401.

Cascade Books
An Imprint of Wipf and Stock Publishers
199 W. 8th Ave., Suite 3
Eugene, OR 97401

www.wipfandstock.com

PAPERBACK ISBN: 978-1-6667-8949-2
HARDCOVER ISBN: 978-1-6667-8950-8
EBOOK ISBN: 978-1-6667-8951-5

Cataloguing-in-Publication data:

Names: Webber, Robert E., author. | Call, Keith, editor.

Title: The ancient-future visionary : selected shorter writings by Robert E. Webber / Robert E. Webber, edited by Keith Call.

Description: Eugene, OR: Cascade Books, 2025 | Includes bibliographical references.

Identifiers: ISBN 978-1-6667-8949-2 (paperback) | ISBN 978-1-6667-8950-8 (hardcover) | ISBN 978-1-6667-8951-5 (ebook)

Subjects: LCSH: Robert E. Webber, 1933–2007. | Public worship. | Historical theology. | Evangelicalism.

Classification: BV15 W686 2025 (print) | BV15 (ebook)

To Bob Webber, Bob Jones Sr., Bob Jones Jr., Madeleine L'Engle,
Leanne Payne, St. Cyril, Hudson Armerding, Georges Florovsky,
Alexander Schmemann, Martin Luther, and William Perkins,
all singing, all dancing, all praising in that
great ring of pure and endless light, all calm as it is bright

Table of Contents

Acknowledgments ix
Foreword Karen Burton Mains xi
Introduction xiii

1). The Silence of God 1

2). The Tragedy of the Reformation 10

3). The Trinity 18

4). A Critique of Popular Evangelical Christianity 25

5). Is Our Worship Adequately Triune? 34

6). Church Buildings: Shapes of Worship 41

7). Behind the Scenes: A Personal Account 48

8). Are Evangelicals Becoming Sacramental? 66

9). Ecumenical Influences on Evangelical Worship 71

10). Bring Them In: Three Models for Evangelism Through Worship 78

11). Evangelism and Christian Formation in the Early Church 86

12). Narrating the World Once Again: A Case for an Ancient-Future Faith 99

13). Ethics and Evangelism: Learning from the Third-Century Church 112

14). From Jerusalem to Willow Creek: A Brief History of Christian Worship 118

15). Let's Put Worship into the Worship Service: And Let's End Gospel Pep Rallies and Sunday Morning Variety Shows 131

16). Praise and Worship: From Its Origins to Contemporary Use 134

17). Living in the World 139

18). Easter: Reliving the Mystery 147

19). From Modern to Postmodern: Worship Changes During the Twentieth Century 154

20). The Road to the Future Runs Through the Past: Reviving an Ancient Faith Journey 171

21). Symposium on Witnessing Through Worship 176

22). Enter His Courts with Praise: A New Style of Worship Is Sweeping the Church 187

23). The Future Direction of Christian Worship 197

24). A Call to an Ancient-Evangelical Future 218

25). What We've Learned Along the Way: Reformed Worship Through Twenty Years of Liturgical Change 223

26). Christ the Victor, Christ the Center 229

27). Worship Like You Mean It: Interview with Sally Morgenthaler and Robert E. Webber 233

Bibliography 243

Acknowledgments

The editor humbly bows in gratitude to the competence,
encouragement, and guidance of
Rodney Clapp, Laura Kelly, and David Osielski.
Thank you most kindly.

Foreword

Karen Burton Mains

DR. BOB WEBBER BROUGHT his significant intellect and historical knowledge to our Mainstay Ministry broadcast when we mounted a national emphasis on worship. At the time we aired a daily radio outreach, The Chapel of the Air, over some five hundred Christian stations. My husband, the Rev. Dr. David Mains—also a Wheaton College graduate—was passionate about stimulating spiritual renewal (often called "revival") in the local church. After ten years of pioneering many of his ideas in a church planted in the inner city of Chicago during the years of "white flight," daily broadcasting presented him with other challenges.

Over a decade, with the input of literally thousands of local pastors, Mainstay Ministries developed the Fifty-Day Spiritual Adventure, which was broadcasted nationally during the Lenten season and utilized by some four thousand churches yearly with an eventual cumulative total of some twenty thousand churches. At the time, we were not aware of any other national radio ministry that put an emphasis on developing growth tools for the local church.

All this to put into context our deep appreciation for the theological/historical emphasis Dr. Webber brought from his scholarly studies. In time we worked with him on our own media event titled "Worship." What is worship? How is it manifested currently in local churches? What is the evangelical role in the development of contemporary worship? What is the historical context of worship throughout centuries of church development? The participation of an informed and scholarly theologian was invaluable to us.

The following compilation of essays reviewing Bob Webber's career is invaluable, revealing his own learning curve about church history, particularly as related to the development of and eventual influence on contemporary evangelicalism.

Reading through these pages is a cumulative retrospective, particularly as related to the evangelical church. These papers are also almost a memoir of learning, written by a master of this particular study. I found that the more I read of Webber's journey—even if the topics of church history were not a major interest to me—the more I became involved, grateful for the breadth of his comprehension and analysis.

And as a casual friend with the Webbers, I am grateful for this collection. We all too often forget the influence, the laughter, the exchange of ideas of those who have slipped into the afterlife before us. This reading has been a valuable reminder of Bob Webber and his theological passions.

Some personal notes. When two of our young adult sons became intrigued by the history and contemporary ministry of the Eastern Orthodox church, I attended their introductory classes. At that time I was exposed to the existence and outreach of Orthodoxy. My evangelical Christianity has always been expanded in ways positive and beyond my expectations by exposure to the various branches of Christian faith. Travel through some fifty-five countries of the world has also introduced me to the amazing ecclesiastical expressions of the followers of Christ, and to the faithfulness of Christ's disciples under often wretched and restrictive conditions.

Learning about the multitudinous proclamations of Christian faith throughout the centuries is always humbling. That, also, I believe, is a lesson of Dr. Bob Webber's life. The more we know, the more there is to know.

Introduction

Richard C. Leonard,
Dean of the Institute for Worship Studies, 1999–2001

IN THE PERIOD FOLLOWING World War II a liturgical revival took place in the "mainline" churches of North America. Under the influence of the "neo-orthodox" or "neo-Reformation" movement, several denominations began to recover the fourfold pattern of worship that had been the legacy of the ancient Christian church: Entrance, Service of the Word, Service of the Table, Dismissal.

Churches with a heritage from Europe or Great Britain—Lutheran or Anglican bodies—had largely retained the traditional forms of worship that characterized their pre-American life. But communions such as the Methodist, Congregational, or Presbyterian bodies which had taken shape during the expansion of the American frontier, and which lacked a pronounced continental influence, were only then—in the 1950s and 1960s—recovering something of the ancient fourfold pattern. They compiled and published new hymnals and service books for the use of their congregations, highlighting a recovery of the traditional church calendar from Advent through Pentecost. Clergy garb and vestments began to appear in the place of business suits, as worship leaders sought to visualize the return to tradition that was taking place. Kneelers, robed acolytes, and other traditional features added to the visual impact.

But this postwar liturgical revival was limited to the mainline denominations, and did not affect churches that identified as evangelical, fundamentalist, or Pentecostal. In these bodies the weekly worship gathering retained the form inherited from the frontier camp meeting or revival: a song service, focusing on devotion to Jesus, followed by preaching aimed at the conversion to faith of the sinning congregants—with the altar call to climax the event. The Lord's Supper, or Holy Communion, took second place to preaching and, in many groups, was observed only infrequently. The historic fourfold sequence of Entrance, Word, Table, and Dismissal was not in view when leaders planned for their worship gatherings.

It is the legacy of Robert E. Webber that this historic fourfold pattern has been reintroduced to the evangelical Christian community, promoted through his teaching as a member of several faculties and through the institution he founded in 1998, the Institute for Worship Studies (now renamed the Robert E. Webber Institute for Worship Studies). Additionally, Webber urged the return to the traditional full sequence of worship through his many publications. His books included *Evangelicals on the Canterbury Trail* (1985), *Worship Is a Verb* (1992), and *Worship Old and New* (1994). He edited the multivolume *The Complete Library of Christian Worship* (1993-94) incorporating contributions by a range of Christian worship leaders and scholars.

With his advocacy of the revival of ancient and traditional patterns in worship Webber was something of a gadfly within evangelical circles, and provoked some criticism from those who believed he had departed from biblical norms. To the consternation of many of his colleagues, he was confirmed in the Episcopal Church. As instigator of the influential "Chicago Call" of 1977 he urged evangelical leaders to shift the focus of worship away from a merely intellectual appreciation of the faith, or from the felt needs and sentiments of the worshiper. Instead, the focus must be on the action of God himself:

> We call for public worship that sings, preaches and enacts God's story. We call for a renewed consideration of how God ministers to us in baptism, Eucharist, confession, the laying on of hands, marriage, healing and through the charisms of the Spirit, for these actions shape our lives and signify the meaning of the world.

Though a committed evangelical Christian, Webber mounted a critique of evangelicalism from within, touching concerns other than that of worship practices alone—as the writings collected in this volume will illustrate. Regarding the "Chicago Call" he wrote:

> What is happening to us is analogous to the growth process. The adult still has the same identity as when a child, but the child has grown outside of himself. So we are still evangelicals, but

evangelicals in the process of growing out of our previous narrow strictures. ("Behind the Scenes: A Personal Account")

In his critique of evangelicalism Webber identified three "cultural narratives" that have influenced how evangelicals think and operate. He saw them as anti-historical, meaning that instead of taking into account church history leading to the present they tend to "start over again" based only on their present reading of Scripture. He viewed evangelicals as committed to reason and science to "prove" the Bible instead of allowing the Word to stand on its own as the source of truth. And Webber saw evangelicals as committed to a pragmatic approach to ministry; that is, their practical expression of Christian faith is shaped more by cultural conditions and dictates than by the "divine narrative" of historic Christian theology. (See "Narrating the World Once Again: A Case for an Ancient-Future Faith.") Worship, he stressed, must be theologically driven and not shaped by priorities derived from the surrounding culture or personal inclinations.

Webber's response to his analysis of the current state of evangelical Christianity was to advocate, with passion and incisive expression, a return to the faith and life of the early church. As an avowed evangelical he saw this also as a return to the Bible, because the formation of the creeds and practices of the ancient church was intermixed with the formation of the canon of Scripture. (See "Evangelism and Christian Formation in the Early Church.")

Thus Robert Webber stood forth as the "ancient-future visionary." Outlining the history of Christian worship and the prospects for its future, he wrote:

> In the future I see a return to early Christian worship—rooted in the death and resurrection of Jesus Christ; having balance of both Word and Table; seeking both intimacy and theater; and involve the people in a more participatory way. (See "From Jerusalem to Willow Creek: A Brief History of Christian Worship.")

The writings compiled in this volume reveal Robert Webber as an astute and perceptive observer and analyst of the state of worship and church life in, especially, North American evangelicalism. But, more than this, they reveal him as a visionary for worship that restores the impact of the ancient church's celebration of the gospel—worship that tells the story, and brings the worshiper into that story, of what God, through Jesus and the Holy Spirit, has done, is doing, and will do for his people.

1

The Silence of God

WHEATON COLLEGE CHAPEL, NOVEMBER 5, 1969

THE FIFTEENTH CHAPTER OF the Gospel according to St. Matthew relates the story of a young Canaanite woman who came to Jesus and cried out for mercy and help. St. Matthew records the words of Jesus' answer which may be regarded as some of the worst, most terrible words in Scripture. "He answered her not a word."

Eric Hoffer, the longshoreman, is quoted as having said, "At one point in history, God and the priests seemed to become superfluous, yet the world went on as before."

The secularization of Western culture has brought us to the place where God is indeed superfluous. Humanism, which proclaimed man to be the measure of all things, has brought about the collapse of God, of man, and all human values. The tools involved in this secularization were science and rationalism. They promoted the attitude that only that which could be proved would be believed. In the eighteenth and nineteenth centuries it was discovered that one could not prove God's existence; one could not prove that God had created; one could not prove that God had revealed himself; one could not prove that man was made in the image of God; one could not prove that Jesus was a historical person; when this was understood, Nietzsche, who really understood it, said, "God is dead."

In the early part of the twentieth century, [Adolf von] Harnack, the theologian of the liberals, attempted to build a new theology on the basis of the rationalism that had destroyed Christianity in the nineteenth century. He said, "We must reinterpret Christianity; we cannot let it die; the essence of Christianity is to be found in the fatherhood of God and the brotherhood of man and love."[1]

With World War I and II, it was discovered that liberalism did not work; it was not the answer; it was not Christianity. The irrationalists filled the gap by proclaiming the need to return to the ideas of the Scripture, even though they were destroyed in the nineteenth century, and could no longer be believed as historical truth. They taught that truth was in the symbol. It was Julian Huxley who said, "Even though God does not exist, we must live as though He does exist, because it is better to live that way."

But the irrationalists' theory is now on its way out and one knows the poverty of that view, too. Now there has fallen upon us a sense of nothingness. God is dead and man is dead.

In 1966 there appeared in the news magazine *Der Spiegel* the following statement written by several students:

> *Deceased after a long illness, God the Lord.*
> As we hear the war in Vietnam continues with unabated harshness; napalm bombs drop on the civilian population; Hitler follower General Ky is further supported by America; and more soldiers die daily.
>
> As we read, men are starving continually in India, China, and Algeria; seed is rotting in Western grain silos, and church congregations take collections for a new section for the cemetery fence. As we see, in the kingdom of God, ever more people are tortured, murdered, victimized by violence, stabbed, burned, or allowed to starve. In our opinion, our conclusion is forced on everyone who thinks honestly, that God who over all things so wondrously reigned, who my soul praised, who led me in green pastures, is absent, sick on a journey, dead. God who orders all for the best in Auschwitz, the Warsaw ghetto, Vietnam and the Negro section of New York, no longer exists. He has not finished His work
>
> His position is open. He must be replaced. The future is open.

The most significant result of the death of God in the twentieth century has been the death of man. Everywhere we are surrounded by the death of contemporary man. [Samuel] Beckett, one of the writers in the theatre of the absurd, really understands this. An article appeared in *Time*

---

1. Harnack, *What is Christianity?*

magazine a few weeks ago. Beckett's view that man is dead emerges as the central feature of his plays. The author wrote:

> Waiting is the real activity of all Beckett's seemingly totally passive characters. As in an electricity blackout one waits for the light, so in Beckett's metaphysical and moral blackout, one waits for new gods and values to replace the old. So the two tramps in *Waiting for Godot* Estragon and Vladimur wait. To pass the time they play games. Games become a substitute for life and the loss of purpose. They are contretemps of clowns. The clown is the only entertainer who consistently draws laughter through his own self-abasement. And Beckett's ultimate position is that man himself is the clown of the universe. But he is a clown for whom Beckett weeps. And that is Beckett's saving compassion.[2]

Martin Esslin, writing in "The Theatre of the Absurd," explains the position of man without God. He writes:

> Ultimate purposes cannot and never will be known. We must therefore be able to accept the fact that much that earlier metaphysical systems, mythical, religious, or philosophical, sought to explain must forever remain unexplained. From this point of view any claim to systems of thought that provides or purports to provide complete explanations of the world and man's place in it must appear childish and immature and a flight from reality into illusion and self-deception.[3]

[Albert] Camus in *The Myth of Sisyphus* wrote:

> The certainty of the existence of a god who would give meaning to life has a far greater affection than the knowledge that without Him one could do evil without being punished. The choice between these alternatives would not be difficult, but there is no choice.[4]

And that is where the bitterness, the bitterness of life begins. There is no choice, for there is no God.

Esslin continued:

> But by facing up to anxiety and despair in the absence of divinely revealed alternatives, anxiety and despair that result from the loss of God in our society can be overcome. The sense of loss

---

2. "Nobel Prize."
3. Esslin, "Theatre of the Absurd."
4. Camus, *Myth of Sisyphus*.

at the disintegration of facile solutions and the disappearance of cherished illusions retains its sting only while the mind still clings to the illusions concerned. Only when they are given up, (that is, the illusions), then we have to readjust ourselves to the new situation, and face reality itself. And because the illusion we suffered from made it more difficult for us to deal with reality, their loss will be ultimately thought as exhilarating. In the words of Democritus that Beckett is fond of quoting, "Nothing is more real than nothing."[5]

Do we understand what is being said? Do we understand that because there is no God, man is dead, we are dead. There is no love, there is no friendship, there is no communication, there is nothing left but nothing! How long can man go on that way? Not very long!

Beckett knows this. The author of the *Time* article sums it up with the concluding words of *The Unnamable*, which he regards as an epigraph in courage that knits Beckett to his task and to buffeted and bewildered men everywhere. "Where I am I don't know. I'll never know. In the silence, you don't know. But you must go on. I can't go on. I'll go on." The truth of this statement is now being experienced by modern man.

The theatre of the absurd, and the concept of despair, is rapidly becoming a philosophy of the past. Yet the concern for the future is deeply entrenched in the concept of despair and nothingness reflected in the absurdist philosophy. It's a new optimism but it is an optimism that is built on despair. A good example of this despair-optimism is Peggy Lee's song "Is That All There Is?" The words are nihilistic, but the music is bubbly, cheerful, and optimistic.

> I remember when I was a little girl,
> Our house caught on fire;
> I'll never forget the look on my father's face as he gathered me up into his arms
> And raced from the burning building onto the pavement;
> I stood there shivering in my pajamas
> And watched the whole world go up in flames
> When it was all over, I said to myself,
> "Is that all there is to a fire?"
> Is that all there is? Is that all there is?
> If that's all there is, my friends, then let's keep dancing,
> Let's break out the booze and have a ball,
> If that's all there is.

---

5. Esslin, "Theatre of the Absurd."

When I was twelve years old,
My daddy took me to the circus,
greatest show on earth;
There were clowns and elephants and dancing bears and
A beautiful lady in pink tights flew high above our heads as I sat there watching;
I had the feeling that something was missing; I don't know what
But when it was all over I said to myself,
"Is that all there is to a circus?"
Is that all there is? Is that all there is?
If that's all there is, my friends, then let's keep dancing,
Let's break out the booze and have a ball,
If that's all there is.

And then I fell in love with the most wonderful boy in the world;
We'd take long walks down by the river, just sit for hours gazing into each
other's eyes;
We were so very much in love;
Then one day, he went away, and I thought I'd die;
But I didn't, and when I didn't, I said to myself,
"Is that all there is to love?"
Is that all there is? Is that all there is?
If that's all there is, my friends, then let's keep dancing,
Let's break out the booze and have a ball,
If that's all there is.

I know what you must be saying to yourselves,
If that's the way she feels about it, why doesn't she just end it all?
Oh no, not me, I'm not ready for that final disappointment;
Cause I know just as well as I'm standing here talking to you,
That when that final moment comes, and I'm breathing my last breath,
I'll be saying to myself,
Is that all there is? Is that all there is?
And if that's all there is, my friends, then let's keep dancing,
Let's break out the booze and have a ball,
If that's all there is.[6]

In preparing this message, I came to this point and asked: "What must evangelicalism do in the 1970s to confront the problem that God is dead and the subsequent belief that man is dead?" I said, "Evangelicalism must take at least a thirty-year leap in history and move from 1930 and

---

6. Peggy Lee, "Is That All There Is?"

1940 up into 1970." I said, "Evangelicalism must rid itself of its legalistic ethics." I said, "Evangelicalism must rid itself of its legalistic piety." And then I asked, "Do we have something positive to say once we've done that?" I began to look at my theology. I said, "Yes, of course we have something positive to say. We can say that Christianity is not rational, but it certainly is reasonable. Give its assumptions; stack it up against any other worldview, any other position in this world and we will find that it's the most reasonable position in all of the world, and that it's the only position that can give meaning and sense to life." I said again, "Christianity must not be irrational, we can say that. There is truth behind the idea; an idea has no significance or meaning unless there is fact behind it." And then I said, "Yes, we can say that God is. God is alive. God has created the world. God has made man in his image. Man has fallen and sinned. Jesus Christ has come to die on the cross and to suffer for the sake of mankind so that through him there might be a renewal and a recreation of man." And then I said, "Having been renewed and recreated in Jesus Christ, we must go back into culture and bring all of culture under the submission of Jesus Christ." I said all of that to myself. I put it down on a piece of paper.

I came back the next day and looked at the answers. I looked at them and cried, *"NO, these answers don't answer."* Then there flashed before my mind the faces of so many of you that I had talked to. You who have said, "I have no reality in the Christian faith." And I remembered that I had polished up the answers and had given them back to you and said, "Here it is." Then I picked up the answers from my desk. I threw them into the wastebasket. I said, "The answers don't work." I cried out in my anguish and said, "Oh, God, what is the answer? Why don't the answers work?" In that moment as I cried out in my anguish, I was met with utter silence. I was met with the silence of God. I discovered that the silence of God was more real than his presence.

Then the Scripture came to me. Of course God is silent, he has withdrawn himself from us. God is not dead, but he's silent; he's withdrawn his mercy; he's withdrawn his grace; he's withdrawn his kindness; he's withdrawn his benevolence. He's withdrawn it from all of culture, and man is crying out for something, crying out, "Help!" And yet there's no answer. We preach the gospel to them and nothing happens. And then I remembered Romans 1. Three times Paul states, "God gave them up. God gave them up. God gave them up!" He gave them up because the creature worshiped the creature rather than the Creator and God gave him up to their passions, and said, "Go on and live in this world without me." God removed himself from our world; God is not here. And then the awful truth; the awful, terrible, judgmental truth came to me that not only has God left the world, but in Romans 2, God left the religious people. The religious people who are so proud—proud of their piety, so proud of their prayers, so proud of their legalism, so proud of their goodness, and Romans 2 implies: Who are you, O man, to judge, for God has left you, too.

It's not something new, it happened before in history. In Genesis 6, when God looked at the strife and the sin of the world, God said, "Will my spirit strive with man forever?" And in Genesis 9 man is destroyed. The northern kingdom of Israel, so proud of their piety, so proud of their covenant, so proud of their works, but the Assyrian hordes came down and destroyed them. The southern kingdom of Israel, so proud—it had the law, the works—but the Babylonian army came and slaughtered them and took them into captivity. Then the silence of God reigned till the coming of Christ. When Christ came he did not go to the Pharisees, nor to the religious leaders, because they could not understand him. They rejected him! They were caught up in their legalism! They were caught up in their pharisaism! They were caught up in their rules! They were caught up in their piety! They were caught up in themselves! And they did not know the Son of God when he came to them. His judgment was upon them. He left the people of Israel and went unto a people who were not his people. These were the irreligious people of the first century who turned to Christ in faith.

Throughout history this has happened again and again. The rise and fall of monastic movements: the fall of the Catholic Church in the late medieval period. The movement of God in the Reformation brought the Spirit of God and love, and reality was felt among the people. But by the seventeenth century that spirit of love and reality was gone as it capitulated to Protestant scholasticism. In the eighteenth century in England, there was a dearth, a deadness, a culture which had turned from God and where God was not present. Then with the preaching of Wesley and Whitefield there was an outpouring of the Spirit of God and a turning of people to God. In the first part of the twentieth century, the evangelical movement was one that was raised up by God himself and the Spirit of God was in it. But the Spirit of God is gone from the evangelical movement today. We have learned all the phrases; we have learned all the right words; but all those good things have become cliches for so many. Now there is a perpetuation of phoniness—the same words, the same ideas, but the power is gone—because we are phony.

What must we do? I tell you the first thing we must do is stop preaching the gospel. Our gospel is cheap. Our answers are not answers at all and there are so many people who know it. Our gospel is twisted into the cheap concept of the love of God that loves all people and the cheap concept that all you have to do is turn to God and grasp on to these answers, and that there's power in the answers and that one will find reality and faith there. This is wrong! We must stop preaching that gospel! This is not a day for the preaching of that gospel! We must stop! God is silent and God will not use that gospel! That's why so many are turned off again and again by the preaching of that gospel.

What we must preach today is the judgment of God. The judgment of God is upon us, for the silence of God is upon us. We are under the curse. God has left us; he has withdrawn himself from us, and we are under the curse. Then perhaps we will turn back to God and perhaps we will say; "Oh, God, we cannot live this way," and then maybe God will break his utter, his awful, his unspeakable silence, and come to us again. May I apply God's silence to Wheaton?

There are those of you here who believe. What I am saying should not shake you at all.

There are those of you who believe that you believe. What I am saying and what God is saying in his judgment and the silence of God (if it is upon you), should shake you—because it should expose your phoniness.

There are those who want to believe, but can't. I shall read just part of a letter I received from a student yesterday. "I get depressed at the lack of success in my attempts to love and in the poor quality of love that I show. It has made me wonder sometimes if there is any such thing as love, and whether I can ever experience it. Last night I lay in bed for several hours thinking; I began to realize that what I had to talk to you about was much greater than my lack of reality and love. It also dealt with my lack of reality in Christianity. I hang tenaciously on my intellectual beliefs, and I insist that I have encountered God in a meaningful way, but is he really real in my life?" I say that's what so many of us have done. We've polished up the intellectual answers to Christianity and we say, "Yes, that's the answer; I'll grab hold of the answer," and nothing happens. It's because the answer is not the answer; God only is the answer, but God is silent. And because he is silent, we are filled with an emptiness, with a lostness.

There are many of us here today who must come to the end of our phoniness. We must recognize that we cannot grasp on to the answers. We must recognize that only God can turn us to himself!

May I say this one final thing? To those who are experiencing this emptiness and loneliness, let us be reminded that there is hope in that, for we are indeed participating in that greatest emptiness and loneliness that ever confronted anyone in history. That is the loneliness and despair of the cross, when Jesus himself was forsaken by the Father, and in his despair turned and cried, "My, God, My God, why have You forsaken Me?" If we feel that forsakenness today, we are participating in the cross of Christ, in his suffering, which ended in the victory and the glory of the resurrection. This is our only hope, if God himself in resurrection victory should break his silence and turn toward us in love and mercy and grace.

Let us pray. "Oh, God, break your awful silence. Amen."

Three Notes:

1. The silence of God refers in particular to Western culture and application is made to the effect of his silence in the evangelical church.

2. The reference throughout is to a gospel spelled with a small "g." The True Gospel of the Scripture includes both the judgment and the grace of God. It is my conviction that evangelicalism has been preaching only the second half of the Gospel—which because of its omission of the first half of the Gospel must be regarded as a perversion of the True Gospel. The God of Scripture is silent toward those who have only been fed on grace. A continuation of preaching which only emphasizes the second half of the Gospel can only result in the continued silence of God and an increase of phoniness among those who continue to disregard the judgment of God that leads to true repentance of the human condition and acceptance by God's grace in Christ.

3. The reference here is to the belief that reality in the Christian life is obtained by mere intellectual assent to propositional faith.

2

The Tragedy of the Reformation

WHEATON COLLEGE CHAPEL, OCTOBER 24, 1974

ON OCTOBER 31, 1517, Martin Luther strode across the courtyard and tacked on the door of the Wittenberg Church his ninety-five theses against medieval Christianity. That event marked the beginning of the Reformation. Today I want to talk to you about what Jaroslav Pelikan calls the "tragic necessity" of the Reformation. I'm sure, as Protestants, all of us are very familiar with the necessity of the Reformation. We believe the secularization of the medieval period necessitated a reform—a fresh outpouring of the Spirit in the rediscovery of New Testament faith and practice. Out of the turmoil of these sixteenth-century events, then, emerged the basic principles of "protesting" Christianity: the authority of the Word of God in matters of faith and practice; the sufficiency of grace; the primacy of faith; and the centrality of Jesus Christ.

In 1521 Martin Luther was called before the Diet of Worms to recant these basic protesting views, as well as other principles that he had enunciated in his pamphlets, and told that he must either recant these views or be excommunicated by the church and banned as a fugitive from the Empire. In a tense moment, Luther stood before Charles and said:

> I cannot and I will not recant
> Since it is difficult, unprofitable, and dangerous indeed
> To go against one's conscience.
> God help me. Amen.

There is another side of the Reformation that is less dramatic and perhaps more unfamiliar, and that's the tragedy of the Reformation. What is the tragedy of the Reformation? Is it something moral? Is it something social? Is it something political? Is it something religious? What is the tragedy of the Reformation anyway? Primarily, the tragedy of the Reformation is their failure to understand and to implement the relationship between the church and the Holy Spirit. Let me explain. A study of the Bible indicates that our Triune God has revealed himself to us in three mighty acts. As Father, he has revealed himself in the act of creation. As Son, he has revealed himself to us in the act of redemption. As Spirit, he has revealed himself to us in the act of creating the church, and filling it with his presence.

In the second and third centuries in the debates between the Gnostics and the polytheists, the Christians clarified and affirmed in the words of the Apostles' Creed that God the Father is maker of heaven and earth. In the sixteenth-century Reformation, in the debate against indulgences and the problem of works, the Reformers clarified that Jesus Christ is indeed our redeemer, and they stated "sola Christus"—in Christ and in Christ alone—is man made acceptable before God. But nowhere in the history of the Christian church—not in the ancient church, not in the medieval church, not in the Reformation church, not in the modern church—has the church ever clarified the doctrine of the Holy Spirit; and the tragedy of the Reformation is that they, like their predecessors, failed to push on until the role of the Spirit in the church was clarified.

The most immediate evidence of the Reformation's failure surfaced in the second generation of Christians after the Reformation who, instead of carrying on the spirit of the Reformation, froze the forms of the Reformation and perpetuated them. This is the problem of form without spirit, words without meaning, creeds without understanding. It is the same problem that Moses foresaw. God had just brought the people of Israel up out of the land of Egypt. He had given to them the statutes and the commandments, he had acted mightily on their behalf, and his presence with them was real and fresh; but Moses foresaw the day when the reality of that activity of God in their lives would be lost, and then those statutes and those commandments would become mere empty, fixed formulas without meaning. Moses cautioned the Israelites to be always concerned about their meaning, about the truth that stood behind them.

The heirs of the Reformation, like the Israelites, lost the meaning of their forms. The spirit that stood behind them was lost. Because these forms lost their meaning, several tragic developments resulted. First of all, deep divisions occurred within the church. I speak of the spirit of denominationalism—"I'm of Luther," "I'm of Calvin," "I'm of Zwingli," "I'm of Menno Simons," "I'm an Episcopalian," "I'm a Presbyterian," "I'm a Baptist," on and on ad infinitum. Perhaps one of the greatest problems with that aspect of denominationalism is not so much that people were broken up into different groups, but the fact that some people began to consider belonging to a particular denomination as being more important, at least in practice, than being Christian.

This is a clear case of taking that which is secondary and making it appear primary, and therefore, taking that which is really absolutely primary and making it appear secondary. Thus, out of this particular division, there grew a judgmental spirit, a haughty spirit, filled with pride, which says something like, "My church is better than your church because—because we don't baptize infants, or because we have a liturgy, or because we worship three times during the week." And then, as a result of these divisions, of this spirit of division that was created in the church, the church lost the sense of what it meant to be a real, living body. Instead, the church became a fractured and divided entity.

The second tragic result, then, was a formal Christianity with the loss of power. When the Spirit is gone, and all that is left is a hollow, empty form, then those who seek to perpetuate the form do so only in their own power. Specifically, this has occurred, I think, in the area of worship—singing, praying, preaching in our own power; in the area of witnessing—declaring the sufficiency of Jesus Christ to other people in our own power; in the area of ministry—attempting to help others, to meet their needs, in our own power; and in the area of confronting evil. The Apostle Paul tells us that our struggle is not against flesh and blood, but it's against rulers, against powers, against world forces of this darkness, against the spiritual forces of wickedness in the heavenly places. And I ask you, how is it possible to meet that kind of power with human power?

Basically, what I'm saying is that Protestantism has lived to see its own death—both a liberal Protestant Christianity and a conservative Protestant Christianity that seek only to perpetuate the forms of their faith are dead! And although the problem is somewhat cyclical in nature, it also seems to be linear, in the sense that the church by the middle of the twentieth century has ground to a screeching halt. The Reformers themselves knew the inevitability of this, and they suggested a corrective: that the church must always be reforming itself. By this they meant that the Spirit, which is the animating principle of the church, must always be reforming the church. [But] somehow, they themselves failed to clarify and implement their own principle.

We must ask ourselves the question: Where are we now? Where are we today?

What's happening? First, I believe we are in the midst of a new, worldwide revolution that is greater in proportion than the sixteenth-century revolution. We are living in a time of upheaval, a time of hunger and starvation, a time of political uncertainty, a time of violence, corruption and hate, a time of global change, a time when death and suffering stalk our world. But also, I believe that we are living in a time of unprecedented religious change and reform, a time when the Spirit of God is being poured out on the world in unusual proportions, a time when the old lines of demarcation are being broken down and replaced by the new, a time when a dead and lifeless church is being brought into question, a time when old wineskins are being filled with new wine, a time when, I hope, the tragedy of the Reformation is being reversed,

Whether this is one of those cyclical experiences like the pietistic movement, or the Wesleyan revival, or even the early stages of fundamentalism, will only be known through the passage of time. But right now, new and refreshing things are happening in our time—a slumbering church is being awakened. There are signs of the new order all around us. These signs are the Catholic renewal, the lay renewal movement, the charismatic renewal, the renewed interest in biblical scholarship, and the devastating critique of social issues made by the Evangelicals, as seen in the Chicago Declaration and the Lausanne Covenant.

Now, we must ask ourselves, "What are the results of this new reform that is occurring?" First of all, I believe that we are moving toward the clarification of the understanding between the church and the Holy Spirit. Luther said that the church is to be found wherever the Word of God is rightly preached and the sacraments rightly administered. To this, Calvin added discipline, and to this Menno Simons added discipleship, love, non-resistance, and suffering. So we had seven marks of the church coming out of the Reformation: the Word of God, the sacraments, discipline, discipleship, love, non-resistance, suffering. But I think we are beginning to realize today that without the Spirit, all of these expressions of the faith, these symbols of the faith, are dead. For we're looking back at Acts, chapter two, and we're beginning to recognize the fact that when the Spirit came, the church was born. And so, now, the primary mark of the church is the Spirit. Where the Spirit is, there is the church! You can have everything else, but if you don't have the Spirit, that which you have is dead, empty, hollow, and meaningless.

Second, we're beginning to discover that the life of the Spirit brings unity. I think, all around us in the world today, the old lines of denominationalism are breaking down. I'm not talking about the emergence of one structure, one organization, but rather I'm talking about the emergence in our time of a body, a community, a people who are joined together in their confession of Jesus Christ and animated by the life-giving principle of the Spirit. And because of that, we are beginning to recognize that we need each other. I think of Corinthians, when the debate was going on between those who said, "I'm of Paul, I'm of Apollos, I'm of Peter;"[1] and the Apostle Paul wrote back to them and said, "Wait a minute. 'All things belong to you. You belong to Christ, and Christ belongs to God.'"[2]

What we are beginning to discover in the latter part of the twentieth century is that we really do need each other! Protestants need Catholics and Catholics need Protestants, traditionalists need the progressivists and the progressivists need the traditionalists. We need each other. Lutherans need the Episcopalians, and the Episcopalians need the Lutherans. We need each other. You need the administration and the administration needs you. I need Dr. Armerding,[3] and Dr. Armerding needs me. There is a new sense of love and unity, a new sense of the Spirit of our togetherness that is beginning to emerge in the church today.

As a result, we are beginning to discover that the life of the Spirit brings power. We're beginning to sense the reality of the power described by Paul in Romans 15: "May the God of hope fill you with all joy and peace in believing, that you may abound in hope by the power of the Spirit." It's the power that seems to be described and experienced by the early church expressed in Acts, chapter two, where they had the power to declare Christ. They declared him with boldness, with courage; and it says, "They did not stop speaking of him." They had the power to worship. It was not just a mere humanistic worship, but the Spirit within the community, causing them to worship and lift their hands to God in praise. They had the power to minister to each other, to take care of their needs. They were beginning to discover the reality of what Jesus said to Peter when he said, "To you and the church I will give the power to loose

---

1. See 1 Corinthians 1:12, New American Standard Bible. Hereafter cited as NASB.
2. 1 Corinthians 3:22–23, NASB.
3. Dr. Hudson T. Armerding was president of Wheaton College from 1965 to 1982.

and to bind." And they were beginning to discover that power in their midst.

They were also beginning to discover the power to confront evil. I say to you that there is nothing worse than a humanistic church, a church that feels it can do everything in its own power—witness in its power, pray in its power, worship in its power, minister in its power, or confront the evil forces of the world in its power. Just this past Friday, I spent the evening with my friends from the *Post-American*,[4] and we were talking about what God has been doing in our lives recently. And every one of us without one omission said, "God is leading me to be concerned about the Spirit of God that brings power in my life. And we're coming to recognize the fact that we cannot concern ourselves about the moral, social, and political evils of our world in our own power, but only in the power of Jesus Christ through the Holy Spirit."

Now, the question is, how does this apply to us here today on October 24, 1974, at Wheaton College? I must admit that I had the greatest deal of difficulty with coming to some kind of a conclusion with this message. Late last night and early this morning I struggled to know how to say that this applies to you. What I'm going to say, some of you are going to misunderstand; but I hope that you will not, because I'm going to say it in love. But it seems to me there are three groups of people here on the campus of Wheaton College, and I need to make an application of this to each one of you. First of all, there are those of you who say, "I've got it all together." You're like the Pharisees who had a quick answer to every question, an easy rule for every situation, a neat little box in which to put God. You think of yourself as so spiritually mature that you check out your roommate, or your professor, or that person you just happen to meet, to see if they use the right words, read the right books, subscribe to the right magazine, or go to the right church. You, I think, are hung up on the forms. Just as the Pharisees were hung up on the forms, you are perpetuating a dead and lifeless and empty Christianity.

Listen to what Jesus said to the Pharisees: You "tie up heavy loads and lay them on men's shoulders;" you "do all your deeds to be noticed by men;" your long prayers are a pretense; "you tithe mint and dill and cummin, and have neglected the weightier provisions of the law: justice and mercy and faithfulness"; "you are like whitewashed tombs which on the outside appear beautiful, but inside they are full of dead men's bones;"

---

4. Later known as *Sojourners* magazine.

"you serpents, you brood of vipers, how shall you escape the sentence of hell?"[5] Then in the end of that very chapter in which all these denunciations appear, Jesus in tears cries, "O Jerusalem, Jerusalem. . . . How often I wanted to gather your children together just as a hen gathers her brood under her wings, and you would not have it!"[6] For those of you who think that you have it all together, the only thing that I can do for you is to declare and proclaim the gospel, the gospel that everything that ever needed to be done to make you acceptable to God the Father has been done in Jesus Christ. And I challenge you to rest in that truth, and stop being so proud and boastful of your understanding and your own self-righteousness.

The second group is the "I couldn't care less" group. You're the people who have been through it all. You have a pound of Sunday school pins. You've put your faggot in the fire a dozen times or more, you've longed for intellectual satisfaction from the Christian faith and never found it, you've longed for an emotional high that would last for more than a week, you've tried it all. You've been down the aisle, you've prayed, read your Bible, dedicated your life. But now, you say, "There's nothing there." To you I want to say, maybe there's nothing there because all you've ever known are the forms, the hull, the shell. Maybe what you have known is what Paul describes as "a form of godliness, denying the power thereof." Maybe what you've given up is not real Christianity, but only an empty shell, a counterfeit. Listen to the words of Paul: "Your faith should not rest on the wisdom of men, but on the power of God. For the kingdom of God does not consist in words, but in power." To you I say, be open to the power of the Spirit who, as Jesus said, does not come upon whom he must, but upon whom he will.

Finally, there are those of you who are serious about discipleship. You are the ones who may consider yourselves weak in the faith. For you the lines are not very clear-cut. You have a hard time putting things together. You know the sorrow of looking through a glass darkly, both intellectually and emotionally. You often feel dissatisfied with yourself. You wish you could pray more fervently, read the Word more diligently, follow Christ more freely, care more about the needy people of a chaotic world. But deep down inside yourself, you are absolutely serious about your faith. You want to learn, you want to grow, you want to feel, you

---

5. See Matthew 23:4, 5, 14, 23, 27, 33, NASB.
6. Luke 13:34, NASB.

want to be open to whatever the Lord has for you. To you I say, the future is wide open. There's much yet to learn. We are living in the era of the Spirit—a time when God appears to be doing a new thing in his world. Out of the old order a new order is emerging. You are living in a time when you may yet see what Paul described as "the whole building, being fitted together, growing into a holy temple in the Lord, in whom you are being built together into a dwelling of God in the Spirit." You may yourself experience the community of love, joy, power, described in the early chapter of Acts. You may experience in the church the power of binding and loosing given by Jesus to Peter and the church. For you, life is open-ended, God is moving, and you are waiting on him to see what happens.

In the meantime, let me suggest a stance for you. Let me suggest that you stand with one foot in the old order, and another in the new—with one hand clenched into a fist and the other hand stretched upward and outward. The clenched fist represents your anger, your disgust, your contempt for dead forms. It says, "I will not play religious games. I will not tolerate the inauthentic. I will not desecrate my integrity." But it's a fist that's raised with fear and trembling, and a fist not raised without tears. The open hand represents your openness, your readiness, your willingness to be touched by the Spirit. It says, "I want more knowledge, I want more love, I want more power." But it is a hand that is lifted without demand, only expectancy. Then I say to you, if you're willing to lift the fist and lift the hand, be prepared for the consequences. For the fist you may be misunderstood, for that hand your whole life may be turned upside down. God help us—Amen!

3

The Trinity

WHEATON COLLEGE CHAPEL, OCTOBER 13, 1980

WHY BOTHER TALKING ABOUT such an esoteric subject? Why bother when there are people who need to be saved? Why bother when there's a world that needs to be changed? Why bother when there's a life that needs to be lived? Why bother with such a subject that is so clearly associated with how many angels can dance on the head of a pin? But if someone had walked up to me and said, "Hey Webber, do you believe in the Trinity?" I would have thrown back my head in self-righteous indignation and I would have said to him, "Of course I believe in the Trinity," and then I would have proceeded to lay on that person. My Sunday school theology, you see, it's like this: take water and oil and vinegar and put them together, and what do you have? A single liquid substance with three parts. It wasn't until I went to graduate school that I first began to have any kind of doubts about the Trinity.

It's interesting, but it was a professor in a Christian college who first created within me some doubt about the Trinity. He said to me, "I cannot think of one good reason to believe in the Trinity." Later I found out that the word *Trinity* was not in the Scriptures and that, as a matter of fact, the word *Trinity* was never used until the end of the second century. I also discovered that some of the passages in Scripture that refer to Father, Son, and Holy Spirit were really, indeed, subject to different kinds of interpretation. I was also told that it was very possible that the whole conception of the Trinity was a result of the synthesis between a thesis and antithesis, the thesis being Hebraic monotheism, the antithesis being Hellenistic polytheism, and the synthesis being the fourth-century conception of the notion of eternity. It wasn't until much later, when I became acquainted with the Fathers of the early church and with the whole conception of classical theology that I began to discover the reason why the Trinity is an indispensable aspect of the Christian faith.

Now when I'm finished this morning, I suspect that some of you are going to say, "Webber did not give us an explanation of the Trinity," and that's right. I'm not going to do that because that is not possible. Someone is quoted as saying, "If you try to understand the Trinity, you'll lose your mind; but if you don't believe in the Trinity, you'll lose your soul." I am going to address the second part of that. If you don't believe in the Trinity, you'll lose your soul. I want to go back to my early doubts, because I also questioned, "Why Trinity?" And what I want to try to do this morning is to give you a reason to believe in the Trinity. Now to do that, I'm going to follow three things.

First of all, I want to talk about the origin of the concept of the Trinity in the fourth-century debate. Second, I want to talk to you about the impact which Trinitarian dogma made on classical culture. And third, I want to speak to you briefly about the relevance of Trinitarian dogma for us today. Now, in order for me to get into this whole issue of the fourth-century debate about the Trinity, I have to tell you a story. I find that Wheaton students always like stories.

The occasion and setting for this story takes me back to the end of my first year in seminary in Philadelphia, City of Brotherly Love. It was one of those summers when it was very difficult to find a job. You probably know the feeling. So I decided, along with a couple of other seminarians, that I would become a salesperson. Well, every good sales program starts off with a kickoff program. So we all went to the boss's house in Ardmore. Big, beautiful house, swimming pool and of course that's the essence of selling, to get you to think that someday you might have that kind of material blessing. So I headed right for the swimming pool. And I was in the swimming pool doing a backstroke, when all of a sudden I heard this voice. Now it didn't come from heaven. It was a local voice, and it said, "Somebody tells me you're a seminary student." Now I kept swimming. "Yep." The voice said, "I'll bet you study a lot of church history in seminary. I'll bet you believe in the Nicene Creed."

Just about that time I thought to myself, "Hey, something's going on here." Now, for those of you who don't know what the Nicene Creed is, let me tell you the Nicene Creed is the church's universal statement on the doctrine of the Trinity, and in part it reads, "We believe in one Lord

Jesus Christ, the only begotten Son of God, begotten from the Father before all time light from light, true God from true God, begotten not created, of the same essence of the Father." Now I want you to notice that that statement is a description of a relationship that exists between the Word and the Father, and describes the Word as the only begotten from the Father before all time as the same essence of the Father. So I'm still swimming, and I said to him, "Yeah, I believe in the Nicene Creed." And all of a sudden, that voice became an angry sound, and he said "You're wrong. You're wrong. The whole church is wrong. The greatest mistake that the church ever made in history was to accept the Nicene Creed." I said to myself, "Good grief, what have I got here, some sort of heretic?" I immediately stopped swimming, went to the side, jumped up on the ground and looked around for a match so I could burn him at the stake right there and then.

Instead, I stood against the person, and I said, "What do you mean, the Nicene Creed is wrong?" And he said, "Jesus is not God." I said, "Where do you get that?" He said, "John 1:1, 'In the beginning was the Word, and the Word was with God, and the Word was a God.'" All of a sudden, I realized that what I had on my hands was a Jehovah's Witness, and that's the same point of view taken by the group today known as the Way. He said Jesus is not God. Now, immediately in my mind flashed the fourth-century debate between Arius and Athanasius. I knew you would like that. Arius was a presbyter in Alexandria in the fourth century, and he was trying to deal with this whole issue of what is the relationship between Jesus and God.

And he said four things. One, "God the Father alone is God. Jesus or the Word is therefore a created being. Thus there was a time when the Word was not." Now, in order to get that across, let me give you a little caricature of what that could look like. It's like this: God is sitting up there in his heavens, relaxed on his throne, drinking a ginger ale, saying to himself, "It's really lonely up here. What shall I do? I know what I will do. I will make me a son." So, boom! Ex nihilo, out of nothing, there is a son. And God stands back and he looks at his son and he says, "Hey, I like it. I like my only begotten son, my first begotten, my first creative act. I like him so much that I will say to him, 'You are a god by divine favor.'" You see, he is not of the same essence, but God by divine favor. Athanasius came along and he said, "There are two problems with the Arian point of view."

First of all, it makes nonsense of the liturgical tradition. Now you know I'd get that in there, didn't you? What does it mean to say that that makes nonsense of the liturgical tradition? Simply this, and it's a clue to an understanding of the origin of the Trinity. The origin of the Trinity is not some metaphysical notion, not some metaphysical speculation determined by an armchair theologian, but the origin of the Trinity lies in the historical action of God, who was present in history in Jesus Christ and the church recognized by revelation that this Jesus Christ was God, and therefore in her preaching, in her baptismal formula, in her doxologies, and in her benedictions, the church immediately worshiped Jesus as God.

The second thing that Athanasius set against the Arian position was that only God can save. Now I want you to notice the meaning of this. Athanasius was trying to deal with the revelation of Scripture. He was trying to stand in the tradition of St. John, who said, "The Word became flesh." And that was interpreted and understood in the church, as Irenaeus says, "That the Word was born by his own created order, which he himself bears." Now follow, because this is the clue to understanding the Trinity. God himself, who in the person of Jesus the Word created the world, actually entered into his own creation and received from the womb of the Virgin Mary his own creation, and he bore that creation in the flesh of manhood. He lived in that creation. He was crucified in that creation. He was buried in that creation. He was raised from the dead in that creation. And the church proclaimed that this Jesus, who lived among us, was indeed God.

Now do you see the problem with Arianism? The problem with Arianism is that it says that a creation saved the creation. Then you don't have a Trinity. But with the Athanasian formulation that remained consistent with revelation of Scripture and with the worship of the church, it insisted that God did not save his creation by some intermediary being, but that God himself entered the creation and destroyed the dominion of sin and death and the power of the devil, himself re-created the creation. Now I have to take you back to my story, because I haven't concluded it yet. When I stood there before this fellow who said Jesus is not God, I must confess to my shame that I did not have an answer, and I did not have an answer because I did not understand what I've just told you. If Jesus is not God, then God has not saved you and this creation. But because the church declares, and has always believed in her very bosom, passed down in her worship, that Jesus is indeed God, then there's a sense in which from that historical angle we move up into the heavens and say, "Move over, God. There's somebody else up there with you." Do you see? Recognizing Jesus as God recognizes that there is plurality in the

Godhead. And so the church, in the same way, affirmed that the Holy Spirit is God, and thus affirmed the paradox that while there is only one God, this God is known to us in three distinct persons, Father, Son, and Holy Spirit, and affirmed the mystery of the Trinity known to us in history and experienced by us in the life of worship and in our own personal salvation. Now that's my first point.

The second point, and I'll have to go through this very quickly, is the impact that it makes on classical culture. First of all, I want to say that it shattered the pagan philosophical notion that God and creation were separated by a gap that could not be crossed. The problem in paganism is the fact that material and immaterial do not come together. The immaterial is there, the material is here, and there is no way that the immaterial can meet the material. Now you see this is the problem of Arianism. Arianism was actually buying into the classical paganism, because it was saying the only way in which God can reach man is through an intermediary.

But Trinitarianism did two things. First of all, it insisted that God became flesh. And second, it insisted that because God became flesh, our flesh is taken up into God. Look at your hands for just a minute, and if you dare to turn to that person next to you and look right square in the face of that person. Maybe I shouldn't have asked you to do that. What you saw was human flesh. But I want to tell you that the human flesh that you saw has been lifted up into the Godhead. The cherubim does not have it. The seraphim does not have it. The angels do not have it. But God wears your flesh, because God in Jesus Christ assumed your flesh, and in the glorified body ascended into heaven so that God himself wears your flesh.

Second, it shattered the pagan notion of experience. Paganism insisted that God could not be experienced, but Trinitarianism insists that God himself, in the person of Jesus Christ, has experienced our existence, so that now we can experience God. Third, it shattered the pagan notion of man. Paganism insists that man has no ultimate reference point from which he derives his meaning, but Trinitarianism teaches that the man Jesus is the express image of God. This paved the way for the radical notion that man himself is made in the image of God, that the ultimate reference point for our self-consciousness, the ultimate reference point for our will, the ultimate reference point for our morality, is found in God himself, and therefore raised the dignity of man to recognize that man was indeed made in the image of God.

This whole sense of the immaterial God coming and taking part of the material world, therefore, is a revolutionary notion that, as a matter of fact, paved the way for the whole Christian worldview, which in turn revolutionized and converted the Roman Empire. Now what is the relevance of Trinitarian dogma for today? First of all, let me say as preface that we live in the context, I believe, of a new paganism that today's secularistic humanism is not that much different from the paganism in which Trinitarianism first came. And I should like to suggest then that the impact that Trinitarianism made on the classical culture is an impact that it can still make on our culture today, for it flies in the face of secular humanism and insists that there is an ultimate reference point to life itself. The second aspect of the relevance of Trinitarianism for today is it says that God himself has entered into our suffering.

I was recently speaking to a person who said, "I can't believe in a God who would make a world like this. All of the suffering, the despair, the war, the hate, the greed, the death, the hunger that stalks our world. I cannot believe in a God who would make a world like this." And I said to him, "All of that is a result of sin. But beyond that? The God who made this world actually entered into this world in the person of Jesus Christ and took the suffering of the world into himself. And I tell you that the suffering of Jesus Christ on the cross is a suffering that reached up into the Trinity in the moment when Jesus cried, 'My God, my God, why have you forsaken me?' There was a split in the Trinity, a break in the relationship between Father and Son. There was a wrenching. There is a sense in which that suffering reached up into the Trinity, and I can say to you that God in Jesus Christ suffered on behalf of you and suffered on behalf of the suffering of the whole world. He participated in our suffering."

What should this whole sense of Trinitarianism do for you? I think, first of all, it should lead you to faith. I tell you, do not trust your mind. Do not trust your senses. Do not trust your wisdom. Do not trust your wealth. But trust only in Jesus Christ, who as God experienced your existence, suffered in your humanity in order to bring you to God. Second, it should lead you to worship. I tell my students, when you understand something about theology, don't go out congratulating yourself that you have such wisdom, because then theology has not done to you what it ought to do. If you understand something about God, it leads you to fall prostrate on your knees and to worship and magnify God himself. If you rightly understand the Trinity, that God became one of us in order to lift us to himself, then you fall before him and you worship him, Father, Son and Holy Spirit.

And then third, I think it should lead you to action, and the kind of action that I want you to think about is what I want to call intellectual evangelism. It was the understanding of the Trinity that broke through paganism, that broke through that classical culture and laid the groundwork for the conversion of the Roman Empire. And I tell you, we need again to rediscover the Trinity and the implications of the Trinity for the world in which we live, and if we radically apply that notion to the secular humanism of today, I believe that it has the capacity to break through our humanism and to bring us once again face to face with the fact that the immaterial spiritual God has lived in the material world. He has become one of us in order that he might lift us to himself.

I say to you, live with courage and boldness in that hope, and let that hope rule your life, for if God the Father, God the Son, and God the Holy Spirit be for you, who in hell, and who of all the principalities and powers that rule this universe, can be against you? Let us pray. We worship and magnify and praise thy holy name, O God, Father, Son, Holy Spirit. Amen.

4

A Critique of Popular Evangelical Christianity[1]

I AM AN EVANGELICAL. After all, I grew up in Africa where my parents served under the Africa Inland Mission. I was educated in four Evangelical institutions. I have taught in an Evangelical seminary and two Evangelical colleges. My books are published by Evangelical publishing houses. And even my best friends are Evangelicals. So, I am an Evangelical by birth, by culture, by education, and by choice. That makes me a fourfold Evangelical.

Yet, I come to you not so much as a defender of Evangelicalism but as a critic. It was back in my college days when I began to develop a critical attitude toward my background. I saw it and myself with it as somewhat superficial, exclusivistic, and pharisaic. This discovery sent me in search of something more. I began to look into the past. I asked questions such as: Where did this phenomenon come from? What people and events in history have shaped it? How does it compare with other expressions of the Christian faith? My trek took me into the study of church history, but it wasn't until I discovered the Fathers of the early church that I began to get a grip on what concerned me about Evangelical Christianity.

My comments are not equally applicable to all Evangelical groups. The fact is that there are more than a dozen different Evangelical subcultures. Moreover, the Evangelical movement is so diverse that even a particular subculture does not stand still long enough to assure me that what I say today by way of criticism will be true tomorrow. To illustrate this,

---

1. Originally published in *The New Oxford Review*, October 1979. Used with permission.

let me describe three distinct phases through which Evangelicalism has gone in this century. The first is the fundamentalist phase. It can be dated from 1910 to 1950. This was the period of birth and growth. The second phase began after the Second World War and may be dated through the 1960s. It has been called the neo-Evangelical era.

Because the neo-Evangelical period represents an emergence from fundamentalism it has similar characteristics. Yet, because it is dynamic it is dissimilar. It is not separatistic, yet it is not enthusiastic about ecumenical relations. It's not an extreme biblicism, yet it is cautious about the use of biblical criticism. It is not exclusively personalistic, yet it moves slowly toward social involvement. Its big names are Billy Graham, Harold Lindsell, Carl F. H. Henry, and Harold Ockenga. Its major colleges are Wheaton, Gordon, and Westmont; its best known seminaries are Gordon-Conwell, Fuller, and Trinity Evangelical Divinity School; its outstanding publications are *Christianity Today* and *Eternity*;[2] its most highly recognized publishing houses are Eerdmans, Zondervan, Baker, and Tyndale. In addition it has numerous organizations such as missions, youth ministries, radio and television, social agencies, and others which reach around the world. This group alone, which radiates from Wheaton, Illinois (now fondly known as the Vatican City of Evangelicalism), engages many thousands of people in ministry and touches every country of the world with its influence,

The third phase began in the early 1970s and is variously characterized by radical social involvement, a new openness to biblical criticism, an emphasis on communication theory and practice, a concern for grass-roots ecumenism, and the quest for historical and theological roots. In the 1970s Evangelicalism can be likened to Fourth of July fireworks. Little rockets are being launched everywhere. They light up the sky and scatter. Most of them are still up there and the confusion and mixture are overwhelming. The fact is that nobody can really get a handle on the third phase. So we are all going crazy trying to find a name for it. Richard Quebedeaux called us the "young Evangelicals" in 1973 and now he says we are the "worldly Evangelicals."[3]

---

2. *Eternity* was a monthly magazine published from 1950 to 1988 by The Alliance of Confessing Evangelicals which maintains an online archive at https://www.alliancenet.org/eternity.

3. See Quebedeaux, "Rise of the Left-Wing Evangelicals."

The fact is that all three phases are part of contemporary Evangelicalism, and we Evangelicals are the Heinz 57 variety—nobody can speak for the whole shebang anymore.

I represent only a small minority within Evangelicalism as a whole (as well as within its third phase). We like to think we are "orthodox Evangelicals." What we mean by this is that we are enamored with the Church Fathers and feel that their insights provide some valuable correctives to what we think is a pale shadow of historic Christianity within popular Evangelicalism. But given the complicated and diverse nature of Evangelicalism I want to be the first to recognize that what I have to say simply is not equally applicable to all. So I'm going to shoot my rocket up in the sky. If somebody likes my colors . . . fine. If not . . . well, we'll just keep on being brothers and sisters.

The central problem of popular Evangelical Christianity is *its failure to comprehend the full implications of the incarnation.* It fails to see all things in the light of the mystery of the incarnation. I believe the mystery of Jesus Christ—who was both fully human and fully divine—to be the central paradox of human history. While the incarnation is a unique event in history—not to be repeated again and not to be found elsewhere than God in Christ—my concern is to understand the way in which the incarnation provides us with a way of reflecting on reality. It affirms the coinherence of the divine in the human and assures us of the basic goodness of creation. It speaks a decisive "yes" to the visible, the tangible, the earthly. Consequently, it speaks a decisive "no" to all Gnostic and Docetic denials of materiality.

There are six areas in which popular Evangelical Christianity fails to comprehend the implications of the incarnation. It is in these areas that our greatest weaknesses are found and where attention must be focused in the future if we are to grow into maturity and offer significant leadership to the church. These six areas include our view of history, the church, the Scriptures, theology, worship, and spirituality.

First, the matter of history. An incarnational way of reflecting on history is to recognize the presence of the human and the divine in the process of history. It affirms that the transcendent God is immanent within the created order, that he initiates history through his creation, that he is ever present within history, that he redeems history by taking history into himself in the incarnation, death, and resurrection, and that he is moving history toward its final culmination in the eschaton.

The problem in popular Evangelicalism is that we have not integrated a theology of the incarnation with the theology of creation and redemption, and with eschatology. We have treated creation as a static occurrence—arguing whether or not God has created it in seven days, thus missing the point of the religious meaning of creation and the ongoing activity of God in history. We have made redemption into an individualistic issue debating whether or not the Atonement is limited or offered to all, thus missing the whole notion of the recapitulation of all things in Christ. We have made eschatology into a mere doctrine of millennialism debating over postmillennialism, amillennialism, or premillennialism, thus missing the point that the whole creation "waits eagerly" with "anxious longing" to be "set free from its slavery to corruption."[4]

The result is a near-Gnostic view of history. It would appear that God only touches history here and there, now and then. And at that, God's interest in history is only for souls. Redemption becomes an act through which souls may be released from their imprisonment. Eschatology becomes the final event when the material world will be destroyed forever and that which is spiritual will endure.

A practical evidence of this attitude toward history is shown among those who resist social involvement. This resistance betrays a privatistic and individualistic ethic that spurns the body for the soul, the public for the private, the tangible for the intangible. God, it says, is not interested in the material, the physical, the world of the senses. Furthermore, the repudiation of history is seen in the ahistorical character of Evangelicalism. Our historical consciousness goes back to Dwight L. Moody, or as far back as the Reformation. But few of us count ourselves as part of the flow of church history since AD 100. The notion of continuousness through historical events that would place us in the context of the church's history as a whole is foreign to our minds. We think of ourselves as only standing in continuity with the occasional bursts of evangelical fervor that dot the history of the church.

Second is the matter of the church. From a divine point of view the church is described in such images as the people of God, the new creation, the fellowship in faith, the body. In this sense the church is called to act as the extension of the incarnation. It is the existence of Christ in the world through the ministry, the Scripture, and the sacraments—passed

---

4. See Romans 8:19, 21, NASB.

down through the apostles, protected and cared for by the presence of the Holy Spirit.

On the other hand, the church is thoroughly human. It is a visible and tangible network of people who circle the globe. It is characterized by everything that is human—rivalry, jealousy, misunderstandings, political maneuvering, and competition. It is expressed in as many cultural forms as there are in the world. Here it is against culture, there it is wed to it, and in another place it has converted it. It is dead and alive, weak and strong, yet it is the church—no matter where it is or what it looks like, it is the church.

A problem in popular Evangelical Christianity is that we have failed to recognize this mysterious dual nature of the visible church. We separate the human from the divine and fail to see the coinherence of the divine in the human. The result is a kind of "ecclesiastical Docetism." Like the Docetists who refused to accept the humanity of Christ, we refuse to understand the humanity of the church. The church in the world, therefore, becomes a very nebulous and uncertain entity.

On the practical level this Docetic tendency shows up in our misunderstanding of the human side of the church. First, it results in a crisis of identity. What is the church after all? Since little attention is paid to the nature of the church as the presence of Christ in the world, the church becomes whatever strong persons make it. It becomes a lecture room, a psychiatric couch, an evangelistic tent, or a fellowship hall.

Furthermore, our Docetic tendency results in a crisis of authority. We fail to grasp the way in which Christ's authority is expressed in the church as a ministry of servanthood passed down from the apostles. Instead, we model our structure of authority along the line of human domination. The church becomes an institution through which power may be expressed. Some pastors become tyrants, some use the church as an occasion to build their own kingdom, and others play on the cult of personality.

Third is the matter of Scripture. In the divine sense, Scripture is "breathed of God." It comes from God by way of revelation through inspiration to the prophets and apostles. Scripture is the living voice of God to his people and through them to the world. It is of divine origin and therefore authoritative. It must be handled with respect and reverence. It must be heard in faith.

On the other hand, the Scripture is thoroughly human. It was not written in the sky by the hand of God. It has come to us through the life experience of men and women who have wrestled with the meaning of life. It records the struggles of a people, of persons, of communities.

The Evangelical error toward Scripture has been to overemphasize the divine side of Scriptures. In many of our churches no attention is paid to the historical setting, the cultural background, or the philosophical presuppositions from which Scripture emerged. The text is often wrenched from its context, interpreted through the grid of the reader, and organized into a series of heavenly propositions that can be analyzed and systematized into a handbook of truths.

The result has been disastrous. It has practically closed the door to an intelligent discussion of the origin of Scriptures. Some tend to write off as apostate those who dare to ask the hard questions. Others have locked themselves into interpreting everything including poetry, story, myth, and parable into a literal sense, thus often missing the intended meaning.

Furthermore, some of us have capitulated to the rationalistic and empirical methodologies of Western man. We assert that Christianity can be rationally defended and thus set ourselves up for a Christianity in which the mystery is gone. We have replaced the testimony of the Holy Spirit with the power and persuasion of the intellect and thus have paved the way for the ultimate rejection of the power and authority of Scripture.

Fourth is the matter of theology. From a divine standpoint, theology draws on the common faith of the church—that faith which has always been in the bosom of the church—given as a gift of understanding to the church by the Holy Spirit. This is the undefined, nontheoretical, nonsystematized truth of the Christian perception of reality. It is found here and there in brief creedal statements of the Scriptures, summarized in the early rules of faith, and passed down in the liturgy of the church.

On the other hand, theology is little more than human thinking about truth. It is an exacting effort to understand and to translate into meaningful language the meaning of the church's doctrine. Consequently, there are numerous theologies, each of which takes seriously the content of the biblical framework of reality. But these theologies themselves are not the truth, but only earthen vessels which at best contain truth and at worst hide the truth.

The problem in popular Evangelicalism is that we have failed to make this distinction between faith and formulation. Consequently, we have elevated our human theological systems into positions of truth. We act as though truth is not a person, but a system. This system, then, becomes the means by which we make our judgments against one another. Those who do not agree with our system are at best in error or at worst apostate.

This approach is the practical result of propositionalism, the problem with which is that it is an end in itself. It tends to exhaust truth—to define, clarify, systematize, and analyze the life out of it. It puts truth under the microscope and expects it to hold still. It is cold, dead, mechanical, and shallow. It has no depth, no mystery, no paradox.

Fifth is the matter of worship. The historic church has always recognized that form and mystery in worship are of a single piece. From a divine perspective, we stand in the presence of God. For example, in the St. John Chrysostom liturgy, the worshiper recognizes a communion with the "thousands of archangels, and ten thousands of angels, the cherubim and [six-winged] seraphim."[5] With these blessed powers the worshiper also cries aloud and says, "Holy art thou and all-holy." Furthermore, God in Christ is made present to the worshiper in the blessed sacrament of his body and blood.

On the other hand the human aspect of worship confirms the material as a worthy vehicle through which the spiritual is communicated. The principle of the incarnation affirms forever the significance of form—of the tangible and material—as a means through which the divine is made present.

Popular Evangelicalism has for the most part lost the sense as the mystery of the coinherence of the divine with human form. We have taken a near-Gnostic view of the use of form in worship. This shows up in our antipathy to written prayers, our rejection of the use of the body, our neglect of the senses, the stripping of real presence from the Eucharist, the rejection of the Christian perspective on time as expressed in the church year and liturgy of the hours, and in our failure to understand the relationship between liturgy and architecture, liturgy and art, liturgy and music.

The result of this is a humanization of worship. Worship has become man-centered and as such is geared toward improving the mind, making us feel good, or providing a formula for success. Proclamation has been replaced by explanation; form by spontaneity; Eucharist by invitation; praise by entertainment; presence by personality; the Holy Spirit by subtle forms of manipulation; the liturgical perception of space

---

5. *Orthodox Liturgy.*

by pulpit-centered auditoriums; the Christian perception of time by national holidays; the sacred dance by pulpiteering antics; the chancel by a stage; the procession by loud and bothersome personal greetings; and vestments by flashy, even sexually suggestive clothes.

What we fail to understand is that our denial of form is not so much a denial as a replacement. We are creatures of form, and cannot escape form even in our most spontaneous moments. So the real issue is not form, but art. The fact is that our denial of form is the denial of good art. And what we put in its place is poor art—cheap, baudy, trashy.

Sixth is the matter of spirituality. The two-sidedness of an incarnational perspective on spirituality recognizes both the mystical and practical, or what we may aptly term the human and divine sides of spirituality. These two sides of spirituality, rooted in St. Matthew and St. Paul, are not mutually exclusive but complementary. Matthew stresses the need for a spirituality that takes shape in the mundane structures of life, that expresses itself in the humdrum events of our daily activities. It is an earthly spirituality. St. Paul, on the other hand, without denying the significance of creation or the earthly, definitely leans toward a more mystical spirituality. He calls for abandonment, experience, an "otherworldly" identification.

The problem with popular Evangelical spirituality is that it has become the creation of a particular subculture. Our spirituality begins with an experience. It is not always the experience of "'putting off the old" and "putting on the new" in the sense that we turn our backs on the ideologies that rule the life of the world and embrace the simple and straightforward example of Jesus. Rather it is too often the experience of being born into a subculture whose difference with the world is almost exclusively moral and personal. For example, we stress abstention from drinking, smoking, dancing, lewd conduct, and immorality. But at the same time we blithely wed our religion with capitalism and Americana (and in some cases with socialism). Without blinking an eye some of us support war, American imperialistic policies around the world, and institutions in our world that suppress the poor and impede the development of a more just society. In other words our major problem is that we have a personal and privatistic ethic, but not a public and corporate ethical consciousness.

The task for an Evangelical spirituality is really quite complicated. We do have a human and divine approach to spirituality, but it is incorrectly mixed. The human side is too closely aligned with Americana, with national goals and middle-class values. What we really need is a human form of spirituality which, drawing on biblical values, stands over against the values that rule the middle-class dream.

If my analysis is correct, how is popular Evangelicalism to be viewed? I see popular Evangelicalism as a movement that has emerged to protect the divine side of the Christian experience. Twentieth-century modernist theology overemphasized the human. It produced a cold, dead, sterile, and lifeless form which Evangelicalism is in the process of replacing with a zeal that experiences the presence and power of God.

If it is true that Evangelicalism is a corrective to an overhumanized Christianity, should we bother to bring a corrective to an overhumanized Christianity, should we bother to bring a corrective into Evangelicalism? My answer is a resounding yes! Twentieth-century American Christianity is marked by two extremes: the modernist humanization of Christianity and the Evangelical divinization of Christianity. What we need is balance. Both must stand under the judgment of apostolic Christianity.

What of the future of Evangelical Christianity? I am hopeful. I see many signs of openness. Around the world a grassroots ecumenism is bringing Evangelicals, ecumenicals, Orthodox, and Catholics into touch with each other. Barriers are being broken down and a sense of our belonging to each other as people of God is emerging. My hope is that this spirit will continue to invade the church so that those of us who are called Evangelicals will grow because of our relationship with other Christians and that others will grow because of their relationship with us. Perhaps someday, we will all be able to sit at the banquet of our Lord and praise him for his acceptance of us in spite of our theological errors, spiritual deficiencies, and ethical blunders.

5

Is Our Worship Adequately Triune?[1]

THE CONFUSION OVER WORSHIP today runs so deep that some have lost the sense of the relationship between worship and truth. For example, I attended a conference where we sang the chorus, "Father I adore you," and then the second verse, "Jesus, I adore you." Our singing ended without the third verse, "Spirit, I adore you." When the leaders of the conference were asked, "Why didn't you sing the third verse?" the answer was straightforward and without apology. "We don't worship the Holy Spirit." Unfortunately this example of the failure to comprehend basic Christian truth and how it corresponds with worship is altogether too pervasive in the Evangelical community.

A phrase in the early church speaks of this concern—*lex orandi, lex credendi, est* (the rule of prayer is the rule of faith). How we pray or how we worship forms how we believe. If our worship is not Trinitarian, we will not pass down a Trinitarian faith, and eventually this fundamental doctrine of the Christian faith will be altered or lost. Therefore, I raise the question, "Is our worship adequately triune?"

It is well to remember how worship from its very beginning was rooted in the confession of God as Father, Son, and Holy Spirit. One has only to study the liturgical sources found in the New Testament and the worship literature of the early church. Consider, for example, the Trinitarian nature of the doxologies, benedictions, hymns, creedal statements, baptismal form, the early church literature of the rule of faith, the Apostles' Creed, the Nicene Creed, and the structure of the eucharistic

---

1. Originally published in *The Reformation and Revival Journal*, Summer 2000. Used with permission.

prayers. These Trinitarian confessions regarding God were formed in the worship of the church and handed down as the living tradition of faith in the liturgies of the church. Triune worship has been attested to by time, by the confessions of the Reformation, and still stands as an essential confession of the faith. It is not that our worship should include statements of the Trinity, but that the very structure and substantive essence of our worship is triune.

This Trinitarian essence of worship relates to the biblical teaching that God is both transcendent and immanent. The transcendence is the unknown essence of God that relates to God the Father as the source of the Godhead. The immanence of God is related to the knowledge we have of God revealed in history and incarnate in Jesus Christ and to the immediate experience of God by the power of the Holy Spirit. My article is therefore limited to a brief excursion into the interrelationship between the very essence of worship and the structure of worship. I suggest that while the whole of our worship is Trinitarian, the gathering is oriented toward the Father (praise), the Word toward the Son (proclamation), and Communion toward the Spirit (symbol).

Father Worship: The Language of Praise

The Arians who were the major opponents of the Trinity in the fourth century were characterized by the saying, "I know God as he is known to himself." St. John Chrysostom, the fourth-century bishop of Constantinople wrote that it "is an impertinence to say that he who is beyond the apprehension of even the higher powers can be comprehended by us earthworms or compassed and comprised by the weak forces of our understanding."[2] In his five discourses on the incomprehensibility of God (*De Incomprehensibili*) Chrysostom, asserts that "he insults God who seeks to apprehend his essential being."[3] When God, he argued, is incomprehensible in his works, how much more is he incomprehensible in his essential nature? And if God is unknown in his transcendent majesty, even to the cherubim and seraphim, how much more unknown is God to humanity?[4]

---

2. Otto, *Idea of the Holy*, appendixes.
3. Otto, *Idea of the Holy*, 180.
4. Otto, *Idea of the Holy*, 180.

The notion of God's incomprehensibility is certainly attested to in Scripture. The visions of God like that of Isaiah,[5] Daniel,[6] and John[7] speak in the language of poetry and metaphor, not in propositions that can be dissected and understood. Paul speaks of God as unapproachable light[8] and, in the great doxological cry to the Romans, Paul cries, "O the depth of the riches both of the wisdom and knowledge of God! How unsearchable are his judgements, and his ways past finding out."[9] God's transcendence and otherness is worshiped not in propositions that we understand, but in the doxological language of praise, which is beyond our full grasp.

Throughout history this sense of the incomprehensibility of God is clearly expressed in worship. We find it in the great words of the *Gloria in Excelsis Deo*, the *Te Deum*, the *Kyrie*, and the *Sanctus*. We also find it in the great prayers of the church. Consider, for example, the opening words of the anaphora of the liturgy of St. Basil that dates back to the fourth century:

> O truly existing one, Master, Lord, God almighty and adorable Father, how right it is, and befitting the majesty of your holiness, to praise you, to sing to you, to bless you, to worship you, and to glorify you. You alone are truly God. . . . You are without beginning, invisible, incomprehensible, indescribable, changeless. You are praised by the angels, the arch angels, the thrones, the dominions, the principalities, the authorities, the powers and the many-eyed cherubim, singing, proclaiming, shouting the hymn of victory. Holy! Holy! Holy! Lord of hosts! Heaven and earth are filled with your glory.[10]

Father worship, I contend, evokes the sense of God's mystery and our response of awe, wonder, and reverence. In this language of the numinous we admit "before God becomes for us a rationality, absolute reason, a personality, a moral will, he is the wholly nonrational and 'other'; the being of sheer mystery and marvel."[11] While the mystery of God's otherness may be expressed throughout the text of a worship service,

---

5. See Isaiah 6:1–6.
6. See Daniel 10:5–8.
7. See Revelation 4–5.
8. See 1 Timothy 6:6.
9. Romans 11:33, New International Version.
10. *Orthodox Liturgy*.
11. Otto, *Idea of the Holy*, 193.

a primary place where this aspect of worship may be expressed in the structure or order of worship is in the gathering. The processional hymn symbolizes our journey into the presence of the ineffable God whom we address in an act of praise and a confession of our sin. Our appropriate response to these acts of worship done in the presence of the Holy One who has called us to gather can only be described in terms like that of the *Mystertum Tremendum*, for we stand in the presence of the Father, the source of all being. In his awesome wholly otherness the only possible response is to fall before him and offer the only response we can make, a language of praise.

Son Worship: The Language of Proclamation

While we confess we worship one God, we recognize God in three persons. For this reason, we are able to distinguish the revelatory work of God in history culminating in the incarnation, the Word made flesh.[12] Unlike the mystery of God's otherness, the work of God in history is knowable. While we don't confess to know everything about God's revelatory presence in history, we do acknowledge that our worship of God in this instance lies in the realm of intelligibility.

The Eastern Church Fathers summarized God's work in history with the three words—"creation-incarnation-recreation"—whereas the Western church has used the words—"creation-fall-redemption." While there are different slants to these theologies, what is common to them is the biblical record of creation and the fall. Also, in common to them is the account of how Cod initiated a relationship with Abraham, called a people into being in Israel, became incarnate in Jesus, was crucified, buried, and resurrected to forgive sin and overcome death. He ascended into heaven and established the church by the gift of the Spirit to witness to the dethroning of the powers and principalities. He now sits at the right hand of God to intercede for us continually, and will return to restore the created order where his shalom will rule forever and ever in the new heavens and the new earth.

In current language this litany is called the Christian metanarrative (*meta*-with; *narrative*-story). Christians are characterized by a particular story that we confess to be not just our story, but even in the face of a pluralistic world, *the* story for all people.

---

12. See John 1:14.

This story is the good news (*evangelion*). In worship we signify it (*leiturgia*); in evangelism we proclaim it (*kerygma*); in fellowship we experience it (*koinonia*); in our ministry to each other and in our service to others we live it (*diaconia*). It is the very spiritual heartbeat of who we are.

In worship (*leiturgia*) the work of the church is to proclaim God's work in history, to be transformed by it in the present, and because of it to have hope in the coming of the new heavens and the new earth. This story forms us as a community, gives shape to our ethics, and makes us an eschatological people (not just a people who have an eschatology).

Common images of the narrative of God's activity in history and the creation of a community called to proclaim God's action, to be shaped by it, and to live in it are found in the New Testament descriptions of the worshiping communities such as Acts 2:42–47 and 1 Corinthians 12–14. We are admonished not to forsake worship, but to gather to exhort each other to good works.[13] This worship is for the edification of the saints.[14] It has to do with the information of God's revelation, which is not mere knowledge for the sake of knowledge, but the record of God's truth for guidance, wisdom, and a life that pleases God and brings glory to his name. This metanarrative, which is the stuff of public worship, shapes our personal worship so that all of life is a "living sacrifice, holy and acceptable to God."[15]

History attests to the significant role given to the worship of the Son in public worship. Sermons, hymns, choruses, prayers, litanies, eucharistic prayers, anthems, and the like, sing, proclaim, enact, and extol God's work of creating the world, God's involvement in history to save the world, and God's promise to complete his work. This is the *missio Dei* that worship signifies to the glory of God. While it is found everywhere in worship, it primarily dominates the service of the Word.

Spirit Worship: The Language of Symbol

While Father worship evokes mystery and Son worship proclaims a knowable narrative, Spirit worship is apprehended primarily through the concept of presence. We encounter the very essence of God in the experience of the Spirit through the language of symbol. We confess, of

---

13. See Hebrews 10:25.
14. Ephesians 4:12, King James Version.
15. Romans 12:1, New King James Version.

course, that God is present everywhere by virtue of creation. But we also acknowledge that the presence of God is made available in greater intensity through visible and tangible sign. In the Old Testament God was present on the mountain, then in the Tabernacle, especially in the Holy of Holies, at the ark, between the cherubim.

In the New Testament God becomes present in the Word made flesh. Jesus is the image of God.[16] What is invisible has been made flesh. God has been "earthed" and concretized into our historical reality. The God who cannot be contained in all the universe is voluntarily confined in the womb of woman, was born of her, and participated in our earthly life constricted by time, space, and history. This incarnational theology affirms that the God who is immaterial communicates to us through materiality. Thus the enfleshed God continues to be present to us by the power of the Spirit in visible and tangible signs.

This God, we confess, dwells within the church. God's people are the temple of the Holy Spirit. Consequently the primary focus of God's presence in worship is in the symbol of the assembled body. When we gather to worship we become the actualized church, the body of Christ, mystically united with the head of the church, Christ. And in this assembly, the priesthood of all believers, there are distinct visible signs of God's presence—tangible ways that Spirit worship happens.

Historically the church has acknowledged the communication of the Spirit in the visible signs of Word, ministry, and sacraments. The Spirit attends the reading and preaching of the Word, the Spirit empowers the minister, the Spirit communicates through water, bread, wine, and oil (to name the chief visible signs). For this reason the act of gathering, the presence and work of the ordained pastor, the reading and preaching of the Word, the rite of baptism, the celebration of the Eucharist, the anointing of oil, and the hands raised in benediction are not empty symbols. They are performative symbols that communicate the reality they represent. While these signs of Spirit communication are present in all of worship, they are primarily present in the concrete, tactile signs of bread and wine.

---

16. Colossians 1:15.

Conclusion

In this brief article I have not been able to fully develop the concept that the very essence and structure of worship is triune. But I have attempted to provide enough information to point in a direction that deserves further reflection. The historic structure of worship is the simple fourfold pattern of gathering in the presence of God, hearing God speak to us through the Word, offering praise and thanksgiving at the table of the Lord, and going forth into the world to love and serve the Lord.

Historically this fourfold pattern is replete with references to the Trinity. Triune worship is found in the doxological praise of the *gloria in excelsis deo*, the Psalms, and with triune praise; the sermon begins "in the name of the Father, Son, and Holy Spirit," the creed is triune, and the prayers invoke the name of the Trinity. The structure of the prayer of thanksgiving at the table of the Lord praises the Father, thankfully remembers the work of the Son, and invokes the presence of the Holy Spirit. And finally, the people are sent forth to love and serve the Lord with the promise that it is God—Father, Son, and Holy Spirit—that goes before them.

My point is that while the triune God is praised throughout all our worship, the very structure of the fourfold pattern is essentially triune and offers worship to God in three languages of worship. We approach the mystery of the transcendent Father as we gather in God's presence in language of praise, we proclaim the story of God's saving action in history culminating in the work of Christ in the service of the Word through the language of intelligence; and in the service of Communion we are encountered by the Holy Spirit through the language of symbol.

I suggest that in this time when pastors and people are influenced by the dumbing down of worship to reach outward to the unchurched, that we be reminded that worship is upward. All our worship is directed toward the triune God who created and redeemed the fallen in the *missio Dei* and gave us the Spirit through whom a relationship with the triune God is established. This relationship, initiated and sustained by God, is expressed in the language of praise (Father), the language of proclamation (Son) and the language of symbol (Spirit). So, as I began, I end with the question: "Is our worship adequately triune?"

6

Church Buildings: Shapes of Worship[1]

WINSTON CHURCHILL ONCE SAID, "We shape our buildings, and afterwards our buildings shape us."

Consider that statement in the context of your home. If someone walked into it and declared, "This is exactly the kind of house I pictured you living in!" how would you respond? Is your personal space sometimes a prison because it improperly serves your interests and needs, or is it a haven with room for your growth, development, and comfort?

If someone offered to build you a house that would reflect as clearly as possible the essence of who you are, what would you specify? Would it be closed in with small rooms and few windows, suggesting a withdrawn person? Or would it be open and spacious with many windows, high ceilings, and lots of color, reflecting a gregarious personality? Would it be simple, plain, neat, and pragmatic, expressing commitment to a simple lifestyle?

Churchill made an important point. There is a definite correlation between a given space and what happens within that space. And within the Christian framework, the outward shape of a structure ought to be (in fact, *is*, for good or ill) determined by the inward spirit at work in it.

To apply this thinking to church architecture, one foundational question must precede all discussion of particulars: What is worship? Only when the purpose, nature, and action of worship are grasped can the next question be entertained: How can the interior use of space reflect and enhance what we do within our church buildings?

---

1. Originally published in *Christianity Today*, August 7, 1981. Used with permission.

The Purpose of Worship

The purpose of worship is to glorify God for who he is and what he has done. The *Gloria in Excelsis Deo* proclaims him "God in the highest . . . heavenly King . . . almighty God . . . *alone* the Holy One, the Lord, the Most High." We thus proclaim his transcendence, his ineffable mystery, *the mysterium tremendum* before which the whole of creation bows in adoration.

But we also worship God for what he has done: for creation, for our redemption, and for the church, his covenant community. For these reasons the Apostle John in his vision on Patmos declares God worthy to receive glory and honor and power, because he created all things,[2] and because he was slain and by his blood ransomed men for God and made them a kingdom and priests to God.[3]

Indeed, the church is to be a worshiping community *par excellence*, called to join the heavenly throng. In worship, the earthly church is lifted into the heavens and joins the eternal chorus in praise of God's character and loving action toward his creatures.

To reflect properly this spiritual reality, it is important first to ask whether our church building is conducive to God-oriented worship. Does the architecture say what we are there to do? Is it consonant with the use it is to receive? We come together to this place to offer God our worship—to hymn and glorify him. Is not the sanctuary in which that worship is offered itself an offering of our perception of what the church as a worshiping community is all about?

Certainly we can worship without a building. If necessary, we can worship in a field, a barn, a house, a storefront, or a garage. But that is no excuse for indifference to space when a congregation is called to build a place in which to gather for worship. What is involved is a recognition of the sanctification of space: the physical context of our corporate worship has everything to do with our witness to who God is and what he is doing in our midst (see, for example, the Israelites' ecclesiastical trappings in the Old Testament).

Church architecture throughout the ages has been a sign and a symbol of the presence of God in the world, reflecting in its diversity the various aspects of human interpretation of that presence. The great upward sweep of the Gothic arch as well as Byzantine icons of Jesus, Mary, the

2. Revelation 4:11.
3. Revelation 5:9–10.

disciples, the prophets, and the saints both shadow and illuminate the heavenly realities that give meaning and purpose to our life. This suggests a profound truth: the use of space ought to be harmonized with our pattern of God-oriented worship and become its servant.

Because of such considerations, a congregation must face the implications of its choices. Many questions will surface. How, for example, does a building capture the tension between the awe and mystery of the transcendent God as well as express the warmth of an intimate and personal incarnation? Is transcendence only demonstrated in high ceilings, stained glass, and stark, wooden pews? Can lighting, the use of color, cushions, and carpeting be thoughtfully brought together to express the relationship between awe and intimacy?

In other words, the goal of church architecture is to incarnate the meaning of worship in space, and to demonstrate through space the ultimate transformation of creation. In this way, space proclaims the redemption and ultimate transfiguration of creation.

The Method of Worship

There is a second clue to the relationship of worship to architecture in the method of worship. Here we act out what God has done for us, and present this dramatization of God *for* us *to* him as a reenactment of praise and thanksgiving. Our active participation in the worship experience not only glorifies God but revives within us the spirit of God in response to our efforts. We accomplish this in worship through recitation and drama.

The Pulpit—Ark of the Word

The focal point of recitation is the Word—read, preached, responded to. The custom in both synagogue and church to recite the great deeds of God through Scripture readings makes the worshiping community contemporaneous with God's actions in history. Reading, done in the power of the Holy Spirit, actualizes God's Word and paints a vivid picture of a portion of history, making it live with fresh and renewing power. In preaching, God speaks to his people through the preacher, communicating his will to and for them.

Thought must be given to the location of the pulpit. Should it be in front, to the side, on the same level, above? Each location symbolizes a relationship between Word and people. The pulpit is the symbol of God speaking, and should be where it can be seen, where the reader or preacher can be heard. Some churches have two lecterns, one on each side of the sanctuary—an epistle and a gospel side—with the gospel side emphasized as the place of preaching.

Other churches have ceremonial customs around the reading of the gospel, processing into the congregation to illustrate the truth that God became one of us in the incarnation. Whatever the church custom, care must be taken to locate the pulpit at a place and in a way that provides ample room for the aspect of worship it represents.

The Lord's Supper—Food for the Body

The church also acts out the gospel through drama, with the most important dramatic event being the reenactment of the Lord's Supper. In it the sign of Christ's death is the focus of communication between God and the congregation. As the Jews have acted out the Passover, so Christians have enacted the new Passover of Jesus Christ, the Lamb of God who takes away the sin of the world. From the beginning of Christian worship, the table has been the place where bread and wine, the symbols of Christ's death and our communion with him, have been placed. In recent years, increased attention has been paid to Communion as a vital, if not necessary, part of worship, and many congregations are celebrating it more often.

The Communion table's significance calls for consideration of its placement and of the space around it. Obviously it should be located where it may be easily observed so as to facilitate worship by sight. Many Protestant churches have abandoned the practice of placing a small, inconspicuous table below the pulpit on the same level as the people. Instead, more artistic, even modern, table designs are being placed on the raised chancel along with the pulpit or pulpits. In some churches the table is placed in the center, with the pulpit to the side; others place both table and pulpit off-center to suggest equal importance of Word and sacrament.

Wherever the table is placed, thought must be given to its use in the drama of enacting Christ's death, and of the congregation's communion with him and with each other. The space around it must be designed to allow for clergy and others who minister to perform their functions freely.

The manner in which Communion is served is likewise important. If the congregation walks forward to receive the elements, enough space must be allowed for their movement toward the table and return to their seats without chaos. It is another matter when the elders or the deacons serve Communion.

The Baptismal Font—Waters of Life

A third essential and dramatic element of worship is the baptismal font or pool, for baptism represents the entrance rite into the church, the body of Christ. It is the drama of dying, being buried, and rising again to new life in Jesus Christ. Its location is also significant.

Some churches place the baptismal font at the church entrance as a symbolic reminder that the people have come into the body of Christ through baptism (accompanied by faith). Others place the font or pool toward the front of the sanctuary, enabling the worshiping congregation to see together the major symbols of worship—font, pulpit, and table.

In fact, if these symbols, these facilitators of our experience of God, were not of central importance we could deliberate about bricks and mortar in strictly economic terms and in almost capricious notions of taste. (In churches where these central avenues to God are ignored, the architecture reflects the fact.) However, church architecture from the beginning has established the centrality of these various modes of communion with God. God himself, in the Old Testament, gave detailed instructions about what went where in his tabernacle. He is concerned that our worship extend incarnationally into our places of worship.

The Action of Worship

Worship is something we do, not something we watch. Public worship is congregational, something to be engaged in by all, and not merely a function of clergy and choir. There have been times in history when worship was something accomplished by the minister and choir while the people passively viewed the proceedings.

In the medieval period, worship was regarded as an "epiphany," a great show to be observed. A similar deficiency in understanding has developed again among some Protestants. In an increasing number of instances, worship is not even an epiphany of Christ's life, death, and resurrection. It is no more than a religious talent show.

This modern perversion debases worship at its very center. The only remedy is to recover worship as an action in which all God's people are equally engaged; a corporate drama in which each must play his or her part. The recovery of worship as a recitation and dramatization of the Christ event is central to congregational worship.

It is important, therefore, to work through the arrangement of the congregation and ministers to facilitate congregational action. For example, an elongated building with a raised platform at one end and rows of pews in a straight line, separated from the platform by height and space, gives the illusion that it is only what takes place on the platform that is important. It results in a "them" and "us" sense: *we* are the audience and *they* are the actors or players.

If worship is to be truly congregational, no such false dichotomy should be built into the church structure. A building in the round (or three-quarter round) is significantly more conducive to congregational worship. Here all the people, the members of the body, can see and sense each other's presence. The worship leaders and the worship symbols are closer to the congregation, giving a sense of congregational action and participation.

Space must also be allocated for special worship events—Christmas, Palm Sunday, Easter, Pentecost, and other significant days—in the life of God's people. Adequate space must be allowed for processions, creative dance, plays, and activities that call for the active movement of the congregation or other members of the worshiping community.

Planning for Building

I have attempted to describe how the use of space must be determined by the activity that takes place within that space. It is thus essential for a congregation to come to grips with the purpose, method, and action of worship.

While this article could not address the economics of the issue, it is obvious that in this day of environmental concern and sensitivity to the poor, any building plan undertaken should be born out of a responsible perspective on simplicity, flexibility, and stewardship of money.

Not everyone has the opportunity to start from scratch to accomplish a church building that reflects the current congregation's understanding of worship. Edward A. Sovik, in *Architecture for Worship* (Augsburg, 1973), demonstrates how these matters, along with the theology of worship, can be taken into consideration not only in building a new building, but also in refurbishing an existing sanctuary. In brief, his suggestion involves the development of an all-purpose sanctuary with movable chairs, tables, pulpit, and font, which would allow the same space to be used for multiple purposes and to be arranged in a variety of ways to accommodate the space required by a particular worship event, the season of the year, or to provide variety as needed to encourage congregational participation.

Just as you would design your home to best serve your needs and style of life, so should the house of God be constructed in a way most conducive to his worship. Dealing with the issues of style of worship as well as stewardship is necessary whether you build from the ground up or merely adjust to a preexisting situation. And the endeavor contributes greatly to the spiritual health and vitality of the congregation. Selecting an architect with a grasp of the meaning of Christian worship will greatly enhance the prospects of a satisfactory outcome. Whatever the outcome in each individual congregation, the process of sanctifying space for the corporate worship of God can itself be a profound worship experience.

"Unless the Lord builds the house, they labor in vain who build it."[4]

---

4. Psalm 127:1, NKJV.

7

Behind the Scenes: A Personal Account[1]

THE GATHERING OF EVANGELICALS in May of 1977 to draft the Chicago Call was a climactic point in the spiritual journey of many of us. In the past ten years or so, a number of Evangelicals have been growing beyond the borders of what has, until now, been regarded as the limits of Evangelicalism. In the same way that our current Evangelical fathers, Billy Graham, Harold Ockenga, Harold Lindsell, Carl F. H. Henry, and others grew beyond the borders of fundamentalism, so we, following their example, have continued to look beyond present limitations toward a more inclusive and ultimately more historic Christianity.

In this sense we take very little, if any, issue with the doctrines of our current fathers. We can affirm that we, as twentieth-century Evangelicals, stand in continuity not only with the Evangelicalism of the seventies, the sixties, the fifties, and the forties, but also with the fundamentalism of the thirties and the twenties.

What is happening to us is analogous to the growth process. The adult still has the same identity as when a child, but the child has grown outside of himself. So we are still Evangelicals, but Evangelicals in the process of growing out of our previous narrow strictures. The Chicago Call and the people who framed it represent this process of change. The underlying essence of the Call and the firm commitment of its writers is to Evangelical Christianity. But the writers of the Call recognize the theological weaknesses of Evangelicalism and thus appeal to Evangelicals to enlarge the borders of their faith. This enlargement will be accomplished

---

1. Originally chapter 2 of *The Orthodox Evangelicals: Who They Are and What They Are Saying* (Nelson, 1978). Used by permission.

by a more expansive reach into the witness of the church in history and a more inclusive attitude toward the various forms of the church in today's world.

Because this process of expansion characterizes the framers of the Chicago Call as well as the content of the Call itself, let me give a brief personal account of my own pilgrimage (as an example of what others may have gone through) as well as some personal insights into the way the Chicago Call actually took shape.

In 1965 I was a graduate student in New Testament studies at Concordia Theological Seminary in St. Louis. At that time graduate students were required to have two minors. I chose systematic theology as my first minor and historical theology as my second.

My first course in historical theology was on the "Apostolic Fathers." I didn't know what to expect since my own previous seminary education had been very weak in church history, and about the only contact I had had with patristics was in the area of Scripture and canon.

To my surprise the study of these Fathers revolutionized my thinking. To begin with it challenged the opinion I had held that a knowledge of the New Testament was sufficient, and that the study of the church and her theologians was at best an exercise in academic antiquity. I began to see for the first time that it was as foolish to skip over the life of the church in the world as it would be to ignore the history of Israel in the Old Testament. God was God in history, not only in biblical times, but also in the ongoing life of the church.

Furthermore, the study of the early Fathers raised the question of continuity. I had blindly assumed that my own brand of Christianity was clearly apostolic. But when I saw what the Apostolic Fathers thought, I began to realize that my own faith and practice were not exactly in tune with that of the second century. Could it be, I asked, that the early Fathers had actually strayed that quickly from the New Testament? In some ways, perhaps, I had to answer yes. But what about other areas where my practice was lacking and not quite as full as what I was seeing in the early church? Could it be, I wondered, that my faith suffered from a kind of reductionism?

My second course was "Bibliography and Methodology of Historical Theology" under Carl S. Meyer, then dean of the graduate school and chairman of the department of historical theology. My fascination with the material must have become obvious to Dr. Meyer. At the end of the course he took me aside and said, "You're in the wrong major, Bob. You should be doing your doctorate in historical theology."

"Give me a good reason to switch majors?" I asked.

"I'll give you one good reason that I want you to think about seriously," Dr. Meyer said. "Evangelicals have numerous good scholars in the area of New Testament but almost none in the area of historical theology. If Evangelicalism is to mature she is going to have to develop an interest in history, and this will come from trained historical theologians teaching in Evangelical institutions. I simply think you can do much more for Evangelicals in the area of history than you can by going on with your studies in New Testament."

Three months later I was a major in historical theology.

My own interest in historical theology centered on the Reformation and beyond, and it was in this area that I finished my degree. However, during my last ten years of teaching at Wheaton College, I have become progressively more interested in the Fathers of the church and in the strong theological foundations they laid. In the first place I came to realize that the Reformation was firmly rooted in the insights of the Fathers. My doctoral thesis on William Perkins was as much a study of Perkins's love of the Fathers as it was a study of Perkins himself. It gradually dawned on me that I could not really understand the Reformers until I had a firm grasp of the classical theology of the early church.

My interest in the Fathers was also heightened by my students. I noticed the immense interest they took in the Fathers when I spoke about them in class. It was significantly more than a casual interest. It was as though they had found some really significant roots—roots that did more than confirm their faith. They were challenged and stretched by the insights of the Fathers and felt that in these earliest thinkers of the church were leaders who could offer them positive insights and a faith that clearly articulated their gut-level feelings and concerns.

Organizing the Planning Committee

Gradually, I became aware of the fact that I was not the only one with these concerns. I heard of the interest being expressed at other evangelical schools, institutions, and organizations. One day in November of 1976, Peter Gillquist (editor at Thomas Nelson Publishers), who also shares concern for a more significant return to historic Christianity by

Evangelicals, called me to talk about our mutual interests. We both mentioned many others who shared our interest and for the first time I realized that a grassroots movement toward a more traditional shape of the faith was actually emerging.

In the course of the conversation I said to Pete, "I think a conference of these people should be gathered for the purpose of giving a unified voice to these issues."

Pete replied, "If one is called, count me in."

Immediately after hanging up the phone, something inside of me said, "Why not, it's now or never . . . do it." I sat down immediately and penned the following words to Donald Bloesch, Peter Gillquist, and Thomas Howard:

> I think you agree with me that the time has come for evangelicals who are concerned for historic Christianity to meet together for prayer, discussion and action. For that reason I'm asking you to join with me to constitute a planning committee for a National Conference of Evangelicals for Historic Christianity to meet in the fall of 1977. The purpose of the conference is to bring together Evangelical leaders to hammer out a brief declaration calling Evangelicals to return to the historic faith and to discuss further ways and means of making an impact on the Evangelical sub-culture to move it toward an affirmation of a truly catholic faith. As I see it, our responsibility on the steering committee would be to (1) determine when and where to meet, (2) set forth an agenda and (3) decide who should be invited. To give you some idea of what I have in mind I've enclosed a proposed agenda for the conference. My own feeling is that our purpose should revolve around a summary statement, a call, you might say, to historic Christianity. It should be inclusive of our major concerns, but brief. Also, I think only those persons who are both committed to the historic faith and are in positions of leadership and influence should be involved. It would probably be desirable to draw from all regions of the U.S. as well as from a number of different denominations.

It soon became apparent that it would be impossible to put the conference together with three other committee members who lived such a long distance from each other and whose schedules were too full to permit frequent meetings and brainstorming. The realization that we needed an executive committee forced me to look within my own church where there was a small cadre of young men and women who were exceptionally aware of the issues and were eminently qualified to provide leadership in calling such a conference. These persons were Lane Dennis, a doctoral student at Northwestern University; his brother Jan Dennis of Lithocolor Press; Gerald Erickson, professor of English at Trinity College in Deerfield; Isabel Erickson, book editor at Tyndale House; Victor Oliver, then editor in chief of Tyndale House; and Richard Holt, a dentist in Wheaton.

Organizing the Call

This little group of people (along with Donald Bloesch, who frequently came for Saturday meetings from Dubuque, Iowa) began to meet on a regular basis to discuss, pray, and wait on the leading of God's Spirit. As I think again about these meetings I cannot recall a spirit of negative criticism or cynicism dominating these meetings in any way. We were all united in the conviction that Evangelical Christianity was suffering from a reduction of the historic faith and practice. But our concern was always to offer something positive rather than to be mere critics of the Evangelical movement. Furthermore, most of us by our vocations were firmly committed to Evangelical institutions. We felt that we were speaking from inside the movement rather than from outside.

Our first major project was to discuss what we felt were the problems or weaknesses in Evangelical Christianity. We brainstormed over such areas as church, ministry, and sacraments; Scripture, tradition, authority, and hermeneutics; worship, preaching, and music; theology; evangelism, education, and cross-cultural communication; ecumenism; social issues; spirituality; and seminary education.

In general we concluded that Evangelicalism was suffering from two basic failures. First, an insufficient recognition of the implications of the incarnation. Specifically, we felt that Evangelicals were suffering from a kind of gnostic rejection of creation. We concluded that this failure to affirm the visible as "good" and as a "means through which God communicates himself in saving grace to mankind" is evident in the low view Evangelicals have of the church, worship, sacraments, and ministry. The corrective, we felt, would be found in a return to an incarnational view of theology. Second, we agreed that Evangelicals were failing to recognize their continuity with the church in history. This is evident in the fact that many Evangelicals pay little or no attention to church history or to the traditions of the church. And even those who do have a concern for church history usually trace their roots back only as far as the Reformation with a near disregard for everything that happened in the church up to that time (except perhaps for consideration of the Nicene Creed and a few of the Fathers).

A major concern that emerged in these discussions was to what extent our emphasis on the early church (the Fathers and catholicity) could be inclusive of the Reformers. Our small committee was somewhat divided on this issue. Some felt that the Reformation represented a departure from the early church in the areas of church, ministry, and sacraments. Others felt that the true spirit of the Reformation was catholic and that the departure from a true catholicity was more the result of the Enlightenment. In the midst of this discussion a crucial letter came from Jim Hedstrom (a doctoral student at Vanderbilt University and a participant in the conference) in which he effectively argued that "to recover catholicity we do not have to jettison our Protestant heritage, but exactly *recover it in its finest models*."[2] After a brief discussion of Calvin's catholicity, Jim went on to argue:

> Many other examples could be drawn from our Protestant forebearers to support this contention, which to working historians should be no contention at all, but the simple truth. It was one of the tragedies of modern ecclesiastical history that the Oxford Movement felt it necessary to despise the Reformation, to achieve catholicity. Subsequent scholarship has shown that the view of the Protestant movement held by leading Tractarians was very defective, and has suggested that if Oxford men had lived a bit later, in the light of a rediscovered Luther and Calvin interest, their position might have been much modified in favor of the Protestant tradition. For those of us who *do* stand this side of modern Reformation study, it is altogether impossible to build a platform of catholic concern which ignores the genuine catholicity of Protestantism. This is a simple matter of scholarship and truth. But further, no emphasis upon catholicity among Evangelicals especially is going to get anywhere by denying Evangelical and Reformed traditions, as these have had a genuinely catholic aspect. A movement which did this would be doomed from the outset to play the role of, not a reforming influence, but only a cult of private (I guess Anglo-Catholic) interest.

---

2. This letter and all other materials pertaining to the Call are housed in the Wheaton College Archives and Special Collections.

In this very discerning and spirited letter, Hedstrom went on to advocate caution against mere external changes that would adopt the trappings of catholicity:

> Now I believe, of course, that an emphasis on catholicity can accord with the deepest aspirations of our own Protestant heritage. But we have to be very discerning in the way we approach, and voice, these concerns and intended reforms. We in no wise want to suggest that imposing certain externalisms is going to produce that *catholicity in spirit* which is the essence of our concern. Doing what culturally accommodated liberal or Neo-orthodox congregations have done, in taking in catholic trappings, can be a kind of death rite for declining Evangelical churches. We're not advocating this! What we are advocating is the rediscovery of a catholic *comprehension*, which *may* or *may not* express itself today in some of the catholic forms of the past, *may* or *may not* find useful some of the historic modes of Christian worship and churchmanship. We must *be* catholic, in the inward man, before we can *act* catholic in formulating intelligently a program for our (Reformed) Evangelical communities. As you have mentioned in your letter, *prayer* is involved in this effort. This is a spiritual exercise of profound dimensions, and not a mechanical programmatics, where one can say "do this, and that will happen." We have here to do with meeting the Lord of the church, and his will for our collective future as Evangelicals amid the currents of a greater Christian tradition and community. We need room for the Holy Spirit to lead us, and need to guard against assuming that we know *now* everything that needs to be done. The Lord leads a genuine reform one step at a time. My personal perception of this was behind my caution to you regarding perhaps waiting for a reaction to the book, before laying out a too formal program for all of your concerns. Let the Spirit have a chance to work, and perhaps bring some real participation into this. After all, if reform is to come, it will take a great host of people committed to the task, and this is not going to happen overnight.

The letter managed to put our divergent opinions into perspective and set us on a course that determined to bring together the Catholic, Reformed, and Evangelical perspectives.

Our next step was to outline the shape of the Call. Having spelled out the weaknesses we began next to set forth the correctives that we believed, if followed, would lead Evangelicals back to a more historic faith. More than anything else this was a matter of organizing our concerns, finding proper headings, and arranging them in order of an inner dynamic. This matter of an inner sequential dynamic was crucial to us. We were all concerned with what we believed to be a "point theology" among Evangelicals. By this I refer to a mere listing of doctrines, such as the inspiration of Scripture, the deity of Christ, and the substitutionary atonement as though they were "points" of theology that could stand or fall alone.

The organization of the Call therefore represents what we believe to be a sequential unfolding according to an inner dynamic. We placed "A Call to Historic Roots and Continuity" first because we felt that nothing else could change among Evangelicals until there was a recovery of the past. As long as we exist in a narrow, isolated, and sectarian vacuum, there is no hope that we can be open to the broader and more inclusive scope of God's church in history.

This is true, for example, in the area of Scripture. The contemporary debate over inerrancy operates from a single model of Scripture and fails to take into account the significance of the authority of the Scripture in the church. Thus an appreciation of history provides us with a more adequate way to deal with the issue of authority and the problem of hermeneutics. We are to stand in a tradition and not in some isolated modern argument. This interconnectedness reaches, then, from the call to the past all the way to a call to the future, namely, "A Call to Church Unity." Our concern was to bring Evangelicals back into the mainstream of the church: past, present, and future.

An outline with suggested emphases was the fruit of our discussion. It was sent to all the conferees *prior* to the conferences so that they could see the direction we felt the conference should take. The outline read as follows:

A suggested working outline for The Chicago Call: An Appeal to Evangelicals

In the planning committee's discussions, we have developed the following suggested structure and general content of the call. We recognize, however, that the final form of the call will be a product of the dynamics of the conference, and will not exactly replicate this structure.

As shown on the suggested docket there will be both sectional and plenary sessions. To help us organize the conference, we need to have you indicate three areas of most interest to you. Please do so on the enclosed preregistration form.

Prologue

Suggested emphasis:

—a general statement of the need for the call

1. A Call to Historic Roots and Continuity

Suggested emphases:

—return to apostolicity and catholicity

—recover pre-Reformation roots

—affirm the true insights of the historic reform movements

2. A Call to Biblical Fidelity

Suggested emphases:

—affirm a high view of Scripture (without error in all that it affirms)

—recognize the biblical witness, illumined by the Spirit in the church, as the basis of authority, and the crucial role of church traditions in the proclamation of this witness

—replace subjective hermeneutics with one that respects the objectivity of the unique revelation given in biblical history and conveyed through church traditions

3. A Call to Creedal Identity

Suggested emphases:

—affirm the normative value of the ecumenical creeds

—affirm the contextual value of confessional statements

—affirm the need for contemporary confessional witness

4. A Call to Holistic Salvation

Suggested emphases:

—affirm that the atonement has as its object both the spiritual and the material creation and thus has implications for all of life

—recognize the corporate as well as the individual implications of salvation

5. A Call to Church Order

Suggested emphases:

—affirm the priesthood of all believers while recognizing also the diversity of callings

—recognize the community of faith as the continuing visible presence of Christ in the world

—affirm the necessity of biblical discipline and authority

6. A Call to Sacramental Integrity

Suggested emphases:

—recognize that creation and the incarnation affirm the material world as both the object of and the vehicle for the creative activity of God's grace

—recognize the church as the primary environment in which the visible signs and means of grace operate through faith

—recognize the necessity of sacramental living

7. A Call to Spirituality

Suggested emphases:

—recognize the essentiality of and complementary relationship between contemplative and active spirituality

—rediscover genuine prayer, discipline, and worship

—restore the social and moral imperatives of the faith to their proper place within the church

8. A Call to Church Unity

Suggested emphases:

- —reaffirm the basis of unity in fidelity to biblical and apostolic proclamation, worship, and doctrine
- —reject both mere spiritualization and the confederational concept of church unity
- —work toward the visible witness and unity of the church in light of the kingdom, present and future

Our next order of business was to determine who should be invited. Since we had already decided to try to achieve a statement that was catholic, Reformed, and Evangelical, there was little debate that those invited to the conference should reflect these traditions. Our modus operandi was to make a list of all Evangelical schools and institutions and draw representative conferees from them. We purposefully invited people from the various traditions, such as Lutheran, Reformed, Anabaptist, and free church as well as Roman Catholic and Orthodox (no Orthodox representatives came). We wanted to see whether or not theologians and church leaders from these traditions could actually agree sufficiently enough to produce a call that was essentially catholic in spirit. In this sense we knew we were taking a risk. As a matter of fact, several members of the committee were certain that no consensus could be reached and that no statement would be forthcoming from such a divergent group.

The Conference Proceedings

When the conference convened, I think all members of the planning committee were a little nervous about what would happen. We had decided not to assume a strong role in the conference itself. We felt we had brought these people together to see whether or not a consensus could be reached, and that it would not be honest to attempt to manipulate the conferees into our agenda. The first challenge came when Don Tinder, associate editor of *Christianity Today*, questioned the proposed subtitle, "An Appeal To Evangelicals." He thought the word *Christians* should replace the word *Evangelicals*. We had actually spent hours discussing this very issue in our committee and concluded that the Call must be directed to a specific group to have an impact. An appeal to Christians in general, we felt, would simply be too nebulous. We were appealing to a specific group of Christians and not to *all* Christians. At first there seemed to be some support for Tinder's view. Actually, my heart sank for fear that the title might be changed. It would, in my opinion, have destroyed the whole appeal of the Call. After some discussion, the title the committee had chosen was accepted unanimously.

The second hurdle came with the discussion of the outline itself. A few questions were raised about the order, and "A Call to Church Order" was changed to "A Call to Church Authority." But other than these items, the conferees seemed satisfied with the proposed structure of the Call and approved the outline unanimously.

Following this the conferees gathered in the groups they had selected prior to the conference and began working on the statements for their sections. The initial conference document, a compilation of each group's work, was put together by early evening. It was reviewed in a plenary session after supper and the conferees agreed that it was particularly weak stylistically. Consequently, the planning committee suggested the final format of two paragraphs for each section, the first paragraph stating the problem and the second offering an answer—or at least a redirection in which an answer might be found. All the conferees returned to their small groups to rewrite the statements. Late that night the planning committee went through the entire rough draft, ironing out particular difficulties and developing stylistic unity.

The next day in plenary session the entire assembly went through the draft word by word. The main contention throughout the day was between those who desired a more Catholic expression and those who wanted to retain a language more common to the Reformers. This issue became particularly evident in "A Call To Sacramental Integrity," which was sent back for rewriting before gaining approval. The conferees were in good spirits throughout the day, evidencing a real sincerity in seeking to understand other points of view. The statement was completed late in the day and signed by all but three of the conferees.

Reaction to the Call

A response to the Chicago Call occurred immediately in some of the major publications in the United States. *Newsweek* magazine took a strong interest in the Call and regarded it as pointing to a "significant drift" among Evangelicals "toward more traditional forms of Christianity." They saw the Call as "an unprecedented appeal" urging Evangelicals to achieve "full maturity" as Christians by abandoning their narrow "sectarian mentality." And the writers correctly recognized that the Call represented the fact that some Evangelicals were dissatisfied with their inherited identities as Christians, and that "they hope to recover what their forefathers rejected."

An editorial in *Christian Century* compared the writing of the Call to the beginnings of the Oxford Movement in England in the nineteenth century. Mentioning the fact that numerous calls and manifestos are coming forth today, and that most of them get dumped into the wastebasket, the writer went on to say "this 'Chicago Call,' however, we've lingered over and savored, for in it is a serious call to a devout and more ordered church life." The author concluded that "if the 'Call' draws response, it is possible that what people now call 'mainline' religion will be strengthened . . . at the very least, this kind of call will help conservative Protestants and some Catholics look into overlooked dimensions of faith and life, and that is all to the good."

Christianity Today compared the Call with the Chicago Declaration and the Lausanne Covenant. "The Chicago Declaration challenged Evangelicals to greater concern about the ills of society; the Lausanne Covenant focused on world evangelization. The Chicago Call supplements, rather than differs from, the others with an appeal to greater concern for more traditional 'churchmanship.'" The writer went on to "endorse heartily" the giving of "careful theological consideration" to the issues set forth in the Call, and suggested that "where present practice is found to be out of keeping with biblical precept, let us 'be doers of the word, and not hearers only.'"

Not everyone, however, greeted the Call with such favorable response. In a letter to *Christianity Today*, one concerned person warned against the Call's statement that Scripture must be interpreted "with respect for the historic understanding of the church." "Such folly," he argued, "will only serve the cause of scriptural disobedience under the guise of interpretation with respect for tradition, and will sow the seeds of a new battle for the Bible some decades hence." Another respondent wondered, "Why there was not a more representative body which drafted the call," observing that "a group so unrepresentative of the church can be unrealistic if they are not careful."

How to Read this Book

In a personal conversation with Harold Lindsell—then editor of *Christianity Today*—I asked him what he thought of the Call.

"It's good, it's really good," he said, "but it was put together by such a mixed bag."

Evangelical Christianity, properly understood, *is* a mixed bag. By bringing together the "mixed bag" the Chicago Call succeeded in drawing up a platform for a "maturing evangelicalism." We need to come to the place where we stop building walls, even within our own camp. Instead we need to search for the common basis from which we can not only work together, but begin to reach outside of ourselves toward Christendom in general. This, I believe, may be accomplished by regaining our past without in any way affecting our firm conviction that the Scriptures are the final source of our authority.

Nevertheless, we have not yet achieved that unity, even among those who drafted the Call. The contributions to this book evidence the fact that we have only begun our pilgrimage toward a more appreciative understanding of each other. Because the Call is a "consensus statement," it should be noted that the authors of each chapter write from their own particular background, whether that be Catholic, Reformed, or more generally Evangelical. For that reason it must be remembered that only the Call itself is representative of the entire group that met to call Evangelicals to maturity. Each writer, therefore, represents his own point of view, and the reader must judge each writer individually and not treat the writing as representative of a "movement." In this way, both that which is "uniformly agreed upon," namely the Call, and the individual's approach to the corporate statement retain the integrity that belongs to each.

Of the forty-five scholars, pastors, theologians, and students who attended the Chicago Call meeting, only three found they were unable to sign the Call statement. One of them declined for reasons of prior commitment to a fraternal order whereby signing would tend to commit the whole order to the Chicago Call statement. Another feared that signing the statement would draw unpleasant reprisals from the institution he served. The third person declined to sign because he differed from the consensus of the other forty-three participants in the Call. His reasons for abstaining were as follows:

(1) He saw the Call as leaning toward Roman theology in certain of its statements. I personally differ with him on this. The Call is catholic

in that it seeks to revive the historic theology of the church—namely that which the church agreed upon in the centuries before it became distinctly Roman. The Reformers rebelled against the Roman takeover of the church in the fourteenth and fifteenth centuries, and sought to restore the insights of the Fathers. You might say that the framers of the Call were concerned about restoring those insights into the church that are both ancient and Reformational.

(2) He also felt that certain aspects of the Call, in particular the section on a "Call to Sacramental Integrity," leaned toward Eastern church orthodoxy. My own feeling is that the Eastern Orthodox Church has developed some valid insights into spirituality, and they need not be rejected simply because they are Orthodox. However, I rather doubt that anyone consciously drew from Orthodoxy. The emphasis was drawn more from the current recognition on the part of biblical scholars that the Christian faith is holistic, having to do with the whole man. Thus, being and action are emphasized as central to spiritual growth.

(3) He felt that the Call tended to be soft on Scripture. It is true that we chose not to deal with the "inerrancy" issue. However, the reason this was done had nothing to do with a low view of Scripture. The concern was that the point of the Call be a return to historical appreciation. What we wanted to emphasize was the need to interpret Scripture in the context of the church's tradition as a means of showing that the authority of Scripture does not rest on inerrancy alone. The Scripture traditionally has been regarded as the supreme authority in the church. (This did not break down until the fourteenth and fifteenth century, and then, not universally.) The point is that there is a measure of strength in the recognition that the church has always held a high view of the Scripture. To go against that conviction is to go against the tradition of history. That cannot be taken lightly. And that was the point we wanted to make. In short, the framers' concern was to put together a statement that, drawing on the history of the church, was truly catholic, orthodox, Reformed, and Evangelical.

What We Hope the Call Will Do

It is a very difficult thing to state exactly what we hope the Chicago Call will effect in the church. But I can dream for a moment and state what I would like to see happen as a result of the Call. These points are not listed in any order of priority, but more as they come to mind.

First, I hope the Call will help to restore a sense of historical awareness among Evangelical Christians. We are, for the most part, a people without roots. Some of us can only trace the beginnings of our denomination or church to some time in this century—arising out of a split over this or that doctrine, or maybe even a personality clash between two strong leaders. Most of us have no sense of the past, no understanding of where we came from or what our original concerns even were. A true sense of the whole church in history, and our "belongingness" to it, should result in a more inclusive spirit on our part. It will help to break down our divisive and somewhat judgmental temperament and make us more charitable, open, and loving toward others whose traditions we may not now understand. Furthermore, a renewed historical awareness will help us become more ecumenical in the true sense of the word. By understanding the historical occasion that stands behind every denomination including our own, we will become, hopefully, more concerned for unity and oneness as the goal of the church. I don't mean a mere organizational unity, but one in spirit and in anticipation of the ultimate unity of the body of Christ.

Second, I hope the Call will help restore the content of Christianity to Evangelicals. We tend toward a superficiality, a pop-evangelicalism that markets Christ in the mass media. He's the cure for all ills—mental, physical, and social. I do not intend to demean the healing power of Christ; what is offensive is the rather simplistic and instant-cure formula that he has become. This is demeaning to Christ's person. It overlooks the complexity of man's problems and it bypasses the more in-depth, far-reaching implications of the Christian faith. For example, the healing that Christ brings into our broken lives is generally accomplished in the nurturing and healing context of the church and the sacraments. If we deny, both in doctrine and then in action, what the church is and what God can do and does in the church and by the sacraments, then we have cut ourselves off from the channels through which God continues to work in the world. By recovering the content of Christ, we will open ourselves to new ways to grow as well as discover new ways to serve. The specific content we want Evangelicals to grapple with is outlined in the eight points of the Call. These are the areas of our greatest weakness.

Third, I hope the Call will eventuate in a sense of community among Evangelicals. We are really a very fragmented group—all of us going our own way. We have too heavy a dose of individualism in our midst. We tend to build our own empires and dogmatically rule our own little spheres. What we need is not only a common base, but the sense that we are moving toward the fulfillment of the base. I do not mean to deny the Trinitarian character of the church, i.e., unity within diversity. What I am hoping is that we can affirm and fulfill the Trinitarian character of the church. We have the diversity but lack the unity. Perhaps the Call can serve as an expression at least of our common concerns, and therefore provide us with the sense of community we so desperately need.

How Can These Changes Come About?

Now the question is how, by what means can this be accomplished? Naturally, we have no chain of command, so to speak, through which this can be channeled. What we need are people who will capture this vision and effect it in their places of influence. There are specifically three institutions through which this can be accomplished.

First, I would look to the schools—particularly our seminaries, Christian liberal arts colleges, and Bible colleges. What we need in these schools is a good dose of church history and historical theology. In the past our curriculums have paid scant attention to these disciplines, but in recent years, they have begun to come into their own. Students are hungry for the knowledge of the past, particularly the past of the church. We need young men and women to train in these areas, to catch the vision, and to enter these schools to inspire and train others.

Second, I look to our Evangelical publishing houses. It's safe to say that much of the popular material published by Evangelicals is lacking in solid content. The argument is that you have to publish what will sell. The point I want to make is that it is a matter of responsibility. People can only read what is published. We need to take more seriously the task of publishing good, solid reading material—literature that bears truthful content and makes us think. I am not against writing clearly and interestingly. What I am against is the blatant superficiality of our best sellers. Many of these books are offensive to the Christian gospel, and yet they bear the stamp of approval by virtue of their publication. We need a few fearless editors and publishers, along with a few writers who have some understanding of the problems we face and the direction given to these problems by the application of solid biblical principles. There is too much sugar-coated secular psychology passed off as gospel truth. And in too many of our books on the church we suffer from the desperate attempt to model a divine institution along the lines of a successful corporation. Somebody is going to have to stop this trend. Maybe the Call will help.

Finally, some people on the local level will have to catch the vision. If we really believe the principle of the priesthood of all believers, then the lay people of our churches must be allowed to speak and lead. What we need are some lay people who will refuse to allow their Christian sensibilities to be dulled by the reductionism of pop-Evangelicalism. There are many intelligent lay people, elders, deacons, and ministers in the Evangelical movement who know that the faith is deeper than the superficial image we give it. They are the ones who will have to stop buying the cheap books. They are the ones who will have to turn their backs to closed-mindedness, judgmentalness, and divisiveness. They will have to learn to stand up for a faith with content, and demand change. Perhaps the Call will provide them with the basis and be the means to strengthen their convictions.

My hope is that this book will help you understand the content of the Call better and provide you with a new vision of what it means to belong to Christ and his church.

8

Are Evangelicals Becoming Sacramental?[1]

OVER THE PAST DECADE, an increasing number of Christians who can be identified as twentieth-century Evangelicals are espousing a sacramental view of life. While these people represent a minority within the Evangelical fold, they are nevertheless in positions of significant influence. My purpose in writing this article is to probe the cause of this phenomenon, identify the signs of sacramental life, and make some predictions about the future of a sacramental consciousness within Evangelicalism.

To begin, it is necessary to identify the particular group of Evangelicals I have in mind. Although the word *Evangelical* is often used as a label for the fundamentalism represented by Jerry Falwell and company, I do not have them in mind. Nor am I referring to the Evangelicals within the Reformed, Lutheran, Anabaptist, holiness and charismatic communities. Rather, I am speaking specifically to the coalition of Evangelicals put together by Billy Graham, Carl F. H. Henry, Harold Lindsell, and others of that generation.

After World War II the men mentioned above and others broke from fundamentalism and established a school of thought dubbed "Neo-Evangelicalism." Their platform differed from fundamentalism in three areas specifically: they disdained ecclesiastical separatism; insisted on a more intellectually credible expression of the faith; and called for greater social involvement and responsibility. This movement spawned Fuller Theological Seminary and influenced seminaries such as Gordon-Conwell and Trinity Divinity School. It also controlled colleges such as

1. Originally published in *Ecumenical Trends*, March 1985. Used with permission.

Wheaton, Gordon, and Westmont, and infiltrated publishing houses like Zondervan, Revell, and Baker Book House.

In addition, numerous Christian agencies, small conservative denominations, and independent local churches were counted as part of the Neo-Evangelical movement. It is within this group—in the very heart of it—in their educational institutions and publishing companies, where an advocacy for a sacramental consciousness has recently emerged.

Before proceeding it is important to define how the word *sacrament* is being used in this article. I have two specific uses in mind. The one refers to a sacramental view of life in which all things are seen as sacred in the sense in which Teilhard de Chardin wrote "because of creation, and even more because of the Incarnation, there is nothing profane for those who know how to see." The other use is the more ecclesiastical concept of God working through the sacraments as mediums of salvation, healing, reconciliation, and growth in Christ as expressed in Eastern Orthodoxy, the ancient Catholic view, and more recently in the documents of Vatican II.

What are the reasons for the emergence of a sacramental consciousness among Evangelicals? A detailed examination of this question would point to factors such as the contemporary cultural concern over secularism, the intellectual longing to go beyond rationalism, and sociological studies that demonstrate the upward mobility of Evangelicalism. More obvious reasons, however, for the rise of a sacramental consciousness may be found in the wide readership of C. S. Lewis, the growing interest in the early Church Fathers and the pursuit after Catholic spirituality. These three movements in the order delineated have had decisive influence toward a recovery of the sacramental. A comment about each is in order.

First, the Anglican writer C. S. Lewis is a household word among Evangelicals. His books, which have sold in the millions, are read widely among Evangelical Christians. More importantly, within Evangelical colleges, courses are taught that probe the thought of Lewis as well as G. K. Chesterton, Owen Barfield, Charles Williams, J. R. R. Tolkien, Dorothy L. Sayers, and George MacDonald. The primary source works, letters, and memorabilia of these "Oxford Christians" are housed in the Marion Wade collection at Wheaton College due to the vision of Dr. Clyde Kilby, professor emeritus of literature at Wheaton. Students from around the world come to Wheaton to study the sources and to research masters and doctoral theses. The impact these sources have made on the emergence of a sacramental sense of life has been immeasurable.

The second source is the rediscovery of the ancient church and especially the writings of the early Church Fathers. My book, *Common Roots: A Call to Evangelical Maturity*, suggests that insights of the early Church Fathers, including their sacramental view of worship and spirituality, offers a corrective to the twin problems of emotional subjectivism and barren intellectualism. More importantly, The Chicago Call of 1977, which brought together Evangelicals from a variety of schools and positions of institutional leadership, called for an end to the ahistorical mentality of Evangelicalism coupled with a return to its Catholic roots in Western history.

More recently Evangelicals have sought spiritual direction by going back to ancient and medieval spiritual traditions. Books such as Augustine's *Confessions*, Bernard of Clairvaux's *The Steps of Humility*, the anonymous *The Cloud of Unknowing*, and *The Imitation of Christ* by Thomas à Kempis are being read by Evangelicals. Further, modern Catholic writers on spirituality like Thomas Merton and Orthodox writers like Anthony Bloom and Alexander Schmemann are widely known and read among Evangelical intellectuals as well. ∂Richard Foster's books *Celebration of Discipline* and *The Freedom of Simplicity*, which are widely acclaimed by Evangelicals, have exposed thousands to the rich heritage of the Catholic spiritual tradition.

But what evidence is there that these three movements have actually created a return to sacramental practice among Evangelicals? Obviously hard cold statistics are hard to come by. But there are three signs which seem to suggest that the impact of C. S. Lewis, the early Church Fathers, and Catholic spirituality are expressed in tangible and concrete ways that relate to the emergence of a sacramental consciousness.

First, one of the most interesting phenomena is the influence of Evangelicals into the Episcopal Church. On every Evangelical college campus there is a small, but highly visible, element of faculty and students who have become confirmed Episcopalians. One can identify Evangelicals turned Episcopal in major evangelical centers such as Fuller Seminary, *Christianity Today*, Intervarsity, Zondervan Publishing House, and numerous other such institutions. At Wheaton College, for example, there are more than a dozen faculty members who have recently become Episcopal, one literature professor who has been ordained a priest, and several dozen recent graduates who have entered Episcopal seminaries, some of whom are now ordained and serving in Episcopal parishes. I have written about this movement in a book titled *Evangelicals on the Canterbury Trail*, to be published by Word Books in the fall of 1985.

A second very interesting movement is the creation of the Evangelical Orthodox Church. This sacramentally-oriented church was begun by six former workers of Campus Crusade. Longing for more depth, these men began to study church history and the ancient Church Fathers. Enamored by the Greek Fathers, they set about creating a denomination that brought together the best of the Evangelical world with the best of Orthodoxy. The Church, officially formed in 1979, has an aggressive outreach in Orthodox jurisdictions, and looks toward the day when it will become an official arm of the Orthodox Church, with nearly every city in the US in dialogue.

Although these two examples of some Evangelicals who have become Episcopal and others who have moved in the direction of Orthodoxy may appear to be moves to break away from Evangelicalism, it is a mistake to interpret them that way. What is unique about both of the above named movements is that many of the people who have become Episcopal or Orthodox remain in leadership positions within Evangelical institutions. The impact of these teachers on their students and the influence of the writers on their readers who remain in their Evangelical churches ought not to be underestimated.

One example of this influence may be found in the current interest in worship among Evangelicals. During the twentieth century fundamentalist Evangelical publishing houses produced no works on worship and the sacraments. However, since 1980 a stream of books by Evangelical authors have called for a renewal of worship. Some of these, notably Ralph Martin, *The Worship of God*, Thomas Howard, *Evangelical is Not Enough*, Robert Shaper, *In His Presence* and Robert Webber, *Worship Old and New*, and *Worship is a Verb* call for a more sacramental approach to worship. Consequently it is not uncommon to find Evangelical churches that are increasing the frequency of the Eucharist, thinking in terms of real presence, and desiring to restore a more sacramental sense to the whole life of the church. Also, the interest in restoring the church year as a spiritual discipline for personal, family, and corporate worship is beginning to emerge. Evangelical churches that formerly shunned the church year and the use of the lectionary are now restoring both, especially during Advent and Lent.

In conclusion we must ask whether Evangelicals are becoming sacramental or not. With regard to the sacramental consciousness of life, the question can be answered in the affirmative. But, in terms of ecclesiastical sacramental practice, the question has to be answered with some qualifications. When it comes to the ecclesiastical sacraments there are *persons* who are becoming sacramental, but Evangelicalism as a *movement* remains non-sacramental. However, the presence of the sacramental viewpoint within Evangelicalism, particularly its educational institutions and publishing houses, may eventually make a distinct impact on the Evangelical movement as such. After all, the interest in returning to a sacramental Christianity among Evangelicals is less than ten years old, and growing steadily.

9

Ecumenical Influences on Evangelical Worship[1]

THE JANUARY 15, 1990, issue of *U. S. News and World Report* carried an article entitled "From Evangelicalism to Orthodoxy." The author, Jeffrey Sheler, an evangelical member of the Nazarene Church, wrote the article because of his own fascination with historic worship and an interest in what is happening among Evangelicals.

The article featured the recent move of a group of Evangelical churches into the Antiochene Orthodox Church. The leadership of this group, all former workers in evangelical Bill Bright's worldwide organization Campus Crusade, became disenchanted with an evangelical worship lacking historical roots and substantial ritual content. About twenty years ago they founded their own denomination, the Evangelical Orthodox Church, and more recently became incorporated into the historic Antiochene Orthodox Church.

On February 10, 1990, *The New York Times* contained a small article entitled "Against the Current" that featured a Pentecostal congregation in Valdosta, Georgia that became an Episcopal church. Four years ago the pastor, Rev. Stan White, began to use the Book of Common Prayer in his own personal devotions and introduced Episcopal rituals and services in his Assemblies of God congregation. The church split, and Pastor White founded the independent church, the Church of the King, with 250 people who came to him.

In a comment to *The New York Times*, Reverend White said, "I began to realize that there are a lot of things in the historic church—sacraments,

1. Originally published in *Ecumenical Trends*, May 1990. Used with permission.

creeds, liturgy—that we had thrown out and need to claim again." In January 1990, Bishop Harry N. Shipps received the now 315-member church into the Episcopal Church.

These two illustrations point to a change taking place here and there among Evangelical Christians. There seems to be a growing desire to relate to the whole church, and particularly to the traditions of the early church. While this concern is probably not widespread enough to call a movement, it has certainly grown considerably in the past few years and seems to be growing, not shrinking. I say this, not on the basis of statistical research, but from my travels among Evangelicals and my contact with a number of Evangelical churches. Wherever I travel I find Evangelicals who are interested in the early church and particularly in its worship. I have, through these contacts, been able to identify four trends: 1) a new focus on Sunday morning worship; 2) a concern to integrate the arts in worship; 3) a new interest in the Christian year; and 4) a recovery of the sacraments. All of these interests draw on the common liturgical studies of ecumenical scholarship.

A New Focus on Sunday Morning Worship

There seems to be a strong interest in the recovery of a Christocentric focus of morning worship. Liturgical studies have demonstrated how worship is a celebration of the saving deeds of God in Jesus Christ, how the work of the people (*leiturgia*) is to tell and enact the story of God's redeeming actions in Jesus Christ. Because Evangelicals are very Christ-centered in their approach to the Christian faith, they naturally gravitate toward this perspective on worship when they hear it.

However, I have found "when they hear it" to be a key issue, because the most popular notion of worship in evangelical circles is rooted in the English word "worship," which is translated to mean "worth." Consequently, the most widespread approach to worship renewal among Evangelicals is that of "praising God for God's worth." The let's-tell-God-of-God's-worth approach to worship has resulted in many new choruses praising God for God's character and thematic services that do the same thing. But after a while this style of worship grows thin and Evangelicals search for "something more."

Consequently, it is my experience that "when they hear it," that is, when Evangelicals are exposed to the rich implications of a worship that celebrates God's saving deeds in Christ, they gravitate toward it readily. For example, Rev. Henry Jauhiainen, an Evangelical influenced by the Christocentric approach worship, recently wrote in his denominational publication, *Fellowship Today*:

> Recent worship renewal has brought a fortunate and refreshing emphasis upon the majesty of God. . . . However, this worship pattern is often left truncated or incomplete. For its completion we need a strong renewal focus upon God's saving acts down here in our human history.

The inevitable result of a Christocentric approach to worship is the adoption of the order of worship in four acts: Entrance, Word, Table, Dismissal. I have presented this order of worship in my writings and workshops and find a ready response. Evangelicals are searching, not only for an adequate biblical focus, but also an order that is faithful to the focus of worship and historical tradition. The emphasis of coming before God, hearing God speak, celebrating at God's Table, and being dismissed to love and serve God in life tells and acts out the Christ event in such a way that a person's relationship to God through Jesus Christ is rehearsed in a meaningful way. Because Evangelicals are committed to an experienced faith, experience of an encounter with Christ through the historical shape of worship is seen as a significant way for the worshiping community to establish, maintain, and repair a relationship with God.

I have no idea how many Evangelical churches have been influenced by the biblical and historical model of worship made available to us through liturgical studies. But I do sense from my own networking that there is a growing trend in this direction.

The Arts in Worship

Perhaps the most significant movement within Evangelical worship is the recovery of the arts—environmental art, drama, and even dance, although of the three, liturgical dance is traveling an uphill road.

I recently worshiped at the Crescent Hill Baptist Church, a Southern Baptist church located near the Southern Baptist Theological Seminary in Louisville, Kentucky. What I found here was an astonishing oasis of the arts.

As I was making my way up the back steps to the sanctuary, I was greeted by an attractively appointed banner that welcomed me with the word REJOICE! I needed to see that word because I had been traveling for a succession of weekends, was worn out physically and wondering whether or not this trip was going to be worth it.

I thanked God for that word of welcome and made my way into the spacious southern sanctuary complete with a balcony on both sides. Even before I sat I was struck with the "Passion Collage" on the large communion table located in front of the pulpit. I sat closely enough so I could see the objects prayerfully set on the table covered with a purple cloth (the color of Lent) with another cloth overlay, a rose colored runner that crossed the middle of the Table (symbol of hope).

I began to study the stunning display on the Table prepared by artist Dwight Cobb and soon found I had entered into prayer. Here were all the signs and symbols of the events surrounding the death and resurrection of our Lord, the event for which we prepare during the season of Lent.

On the left side of the Table, perched against an earth-toned first-century water pot, was a striking crown of thorns with its visible ugly and cruel thorns. In full view in front of the crown of thorns were several large cruel-looking nail spikes, and to the right a money bag to hold the thirty pieces of silver awarded to Judas. To the right of these symbols of the passion stood a striking bowl of fresh green and red grapes, slightly to the right but a little behind them was a chalice and bread on a paten with a small pitcher for the wine standing nearby. To the far right was a basin for washing feet. Behind the basin was a large earthen pot for water with a towel draped around the handle. And to left of the water vessel, behind the other sacred objects described above, were stalks of wheat, palm branches, and a long stick with a hyssop on the end of it.

Here I was on the Second Sunday of Lent, a long way away from home again, and among a thousand people I did not know—but there before me were all the visual symbols that unite black and white, male and female, children and retirees, liturgical and non-liturgical people. Through my eyes the entire passion was brought to me and I encountered Jesus. There was the Jesus who washed the feet of the disciples, instituted the Lord's Supper, was betrayed for thirty pieces of silver, nailed to the cross, and offered vinegar to drink when he was thirsty. This was the Jesus who died for me and took my place on the cross. Here I was simultaneously present to all of these saving events because artists cared to minister to me visually through the gifts God had given to them to communicate the most important event in human history. I was not only ready for worship, but I was actually worshiping and anxious to offer my God my praise and thanksgiving with this community of people I did not know.

Many evangelical churches like Crescent Hill Baptist Church are discovering the gifts God has given to the artists and are releasing their gifts for ministry in the church.

The Christian Year

Another trend which has been growing rapidly over the last several years, moreso than I would have expected, is the recovery of the church year. In part the restoration of the church year is rooted in the recognition that the services of the Christian year are great festivals of God's saving deeds. This gospel orientation of the Christian year is naturally attractive to the Evangelical who desires at nearly every opportunity possible to proclaim the gospel.

I have found that the great majority of Evangelical churches do something to celebrate Advent. I think the recovery of Advent at first is not rooted in a biblical concern as much as a concern to counter the secularization of Christmas into a materialistic hoopla. Evangelicals are finding Advent to be a necessary corrective that helps people focus on the real meaning of the season.

In my workshops on worship with Evangelicals I introduce them to the evangelical nature of the church year. I argue, using modern liturgical scholarship, that the source of the Christian year is the Paschal Event—the dying and rising of Christ, and that every season of the church year must be connected with the Paschal Event: Advent celebrates the one who will come to liberate us and the world from the bondage of the powers; Christmas celebrates the incarnation, which is inextricably linked with the Atonement; Epiphany manifests Christ as savior of all people and of the entire cosmos; Lent is a time for us to identify with Christ, to prepare to bring to death in his death the powers of evil that tempt us to be in rebellion against God; Holy Week is no mere historical memory of Jesus' death, but a real, actual experience of going to death with him, of putting our own sins on the cross and letting them be buried with Jesus, not to be raised; Pascha is not only the resurrection of Jesus from the overthrow of the powers, but the overthrow of spiritual wickedness in our own lives and thus a personal resurrection to newness of life; and Pentecost is not only a memory but an actualization of the Spirit coming to us now in this time and place to empower us in faith and Christian ministry.

As Evangelicals hear this message of the Christian year and its eschatological implications for hope in the God who brings us into the future, they see how gospel-oriented the Christian year is, and how significant it is for the ordering of congregational spirituality. I have met many Evangelical pastors who now use the common lectionary and are gradually bringing their people through worship and preaching into a fuller experience of God's saving deeds as celebrated in the Christian year.

The Sacraments

Evangelicals have been influenced by the so-called Zwinglian idea of the sacraments known as the memorial view. In my workshops I call this a belief in the doctrine of the real absence. This term seems to cut right to the heart of the issue and get the "cards on the table." What interests me is that this statement, instead of producing anger and defensiveness, is usually met with an embarrassed laughter followed by an intense interest and discussion in the early church's experience of Real Presence.

Pastor Doug Mills of Gatlinburg, Tennessee provides an example of an Evangelical who has rediscovered the central place of the Eucharist in worship. He once wrote to me that when he first came to his pastorate "Communion has never been served at a Sunday morning service." In describing the change his congregation went through, he writes:

> As to actually making changes in our worship service, we did this in several ways. One of the first things we did was to include the Lord's Supper on a regular basis. We did not want the people to be frightened by sudden change, so we began with quarterly communion. . . . From quarterly we went to monthly, from monthly to 1st and 3rd Sunday of each month. This is where we are presently, but at the last elder's meeting, it was decided that we were going to weekly communion.

This is not an isolated case. I regularly meet pastors in my workshops who tell me of their newfound persuasion of the meaning of the Eucharist and of their deep concern to find a way to increase the celebration of the Lord's Table. I tell them to do what one pastor told me he did. He offered the Eucharist every Sunday after the service. At first only a few people came, then more. Eventually nearly the entire congregation stayed to receive the Eucharist. It was a small step to take for the congregation when the Eucharist became a regular part of worship.

Conclusion

Finally I have noticed how significant these trends have been to bring Evangelicals into a more ecumenical outlook. Those individuals interested in understanding and practicing worship, in a way that is more consistent with the historic practice of worship, are themselves becoming more open and inclusive in their ecclesiology. This seems to suggest that the true identity of the Christian faith is not found in this or that theological system but in the worship of the church.

10

Bring Them In: Three Models for Evangelism Through Worship[1]

THERE IS A STORY in the *Russian Primary Chronicle* that tells how Christianity came to Russia. According to this true story Vladimir, prince of Kiev, sent several of his followers in search of "true religion."

First they went to the Moslem Bulgars of the Volga but returned with the report that they found "no joy" but only "a mournfulness and a great smell."

Next they went to Germany and Rome, where they found the worship more satisfactory but still lacking in power.

Finally they made a trip to Constantinople, where they visited the Church of the Holy Wisdom, and here they found what they were looking for.

They went home and reported to Vladimir,

> We knew not whether we were in heaven or on earth, for surely there is no such splendor or beauty anywhere upon earth. We cannot describe it to you: only this we know, that God dwells there among men, and that their service surpasses the worship of all other places. For we cannot forget that beauty.[2]

EVANGELISM THROUGH WORSHIP

What these seekers experienced in Constantinople was *evangelism through worship*. In other words, the worship service they took part in allowed them to truly encounter, experience, and believe in God.

1. Originally published in *Reformed Worship*, March 1992. Used with permission.
2. Ware, *Orthodox Church*, 269.

Many of us expect such evangelism to occur through our worship services. But does it? Do visitors to our worship services "know that God dwells there among" us? As we prepare for worship, we should keep before us four characteristics of worship that will evangelize those who gather with us.

First, we should recognize that *worship itself arises out of the gospel.* Worship is not primarily a classroom in which the Scripture is taught, an evangelistic service that preaches for decision, or a psychiatric couch that reaches to the needy. While true worship may accomplish all of this, real, authentic biblical worship is at its fundamental core a celebration of the living, dying, and rising of Christ in recognition that through this historical action the powers of evil have been dethroned and will ultimately be destroyed.

Second, we should understand that *worship that would evangelize must grow out of community.* The public celebration of the Christ event was never meant to be individualistic. God, through Christ, brought into being an *ekklesia*, a fellowship of people who are the "people of the event." As people of the event, we now share a common experience that results in a new fabric of social relations. We embody the reality of the new creation as we live our lives out in authentic relationships of love, compassion, friendship, giving, and the like. Such a community has the magnetic power to draw people into faith in a subliminal way.

Third, we should know *worship that evangelizes needs to be aware that evangelism is a process.* Instant conversions do occur. But more often, conversion and subsequent growth in Christ is a journey that includes various stages of development and growth. Worship that truly celebrates God's saving deed in Jesus Christ in authentic community provides both the impetus and context in which the whole community is continually evangelized.

Finally, we should understand that *worship that brings people to Jesus recognizes the complexity of evangelism.* Because the gospel speaks to us as whole people, evangelism touches different aspects of the person. Ultimately, evangelism has to do with faith in Jesus as Lord, but people may need to come to that faith in different ways. Some may need their morals or values evangelized; others may need to experience the church as a Christian community; still others may need to encounter the reality of God. All these needs are addressed in a worship that celebrates the Christ event and applies the meaning of that event to the lives of the people.

Fortunately for those of us who wish to evangelize through worship, there are models worth examining. I will refer to three, and develop the third one in particular.

Manifest Presence Evangelism

Manifest presence, our first model, may be described as the experience of being grasped by the overpowering presence of God in worship. Karen Howe writes of her experience of manifest presence in an Episcopal church:

> I became a Christian sitting in a pew, experiencing worship. It wasn't the sermon that did it. No one presented me with the plan of salvation or led me in a prayer of commitment (though that did come later). I simply basked in the presence of God as the worship service progressed around me, and when I left the church, I knew that God had entered my life. He was alive. I had encountered him. That day I was born again in my spirit.

Being "grasped by God" in worship may occur in many different ways. It may "happen" through the hospitality of the community, through the proclamation of the Word, through singing (God inhabiting the praises of the people), or through the presence of Christ in the bread and wine.

Seeker-Service Evangelism

A second model of evangelism through worship (or a kind of worship) is the seeker service.[3] This approach, pioneered by Willow Creek Community Church in South Barrington, Illinois (the second largest church in the US), separates the seeker service (designed for non-Christians) from believers' worship (designed for Christians). The seeker service is held on Saturday night and Sunday morning, while believers' worship takes place midweek.

The seeker service fits into an overall sevenfold strategy of mission at Willow Creek Church. In summary, the steps are as follows:

Every member should

---

3. See Vander Hart, "Seeker Service."

1. take part in evangelism.
2. be able to give a verbal witness.
3. bring the person he/she is witnessing to to the seeker service.
4. bring converts (after their conversion and baptism) to believers' worship. Converts will then
5. attend a small group in which they can be discipled,
6. discover their personal gifts and put them to work in the church,
7. learn stewardship of money and life.

The seeker service is designed as a non-threatening service for secular people who, because a member of the church has entered into relationship with them, wish to be exposed more fully to the faith. It is not like a church-service, although it contains elements of Christian worship.

The Willow Creek Church auditorium, where seeker services are held, is more like a theater than a church. It contains no Christian symbols and provides a neutral context in which an unchurched person can feel comfortable and unassailed. Also, both the music and the message at seeker services are subtle and deal generally rather than specifically with spiritual themes.

In a seeker service I attended recently, for example, the theme was parenting: How do you raise children in a world full of turmoil and temptation? One of four points was, "Don't neglect the spiritual side of the child," but nothing specific was said about Jesus Christ. Witnessing about Christ and his work is rather the responsibility of the friend who brought the "seeker."

Liturgical Evangelism

The third model of evangelism through worship is a third-century model that has been resurrected by the Roman Catholic Church. Among Catholics it is called the Rites for the Christian Initiation of Adults (RCIA). I like to call it liturgical evangelism.

This kind of evangelism may be defined as follows: Liturgical evangelism calls a person into Christ and the church through a conversion regulated and ordered by worship. Services that span the church year order the inner experience of repentance from sin, faith in Christ, conversion of life, and entrance into the Christian community.

In the third-century church, evangelism was based on seven progressive steps that took place over a period of three years:

1. Inquiry
2. The Rite of Welcome
3. The Catechumenate
4. The Rite of Election
5. The Period of Purification and Enlightenment
6. The Rite of Initiation
7. Mystogogue

Note that of the seven steps, four are periods or times for growth and development (Inquiry, the Catechumenate, The Period of Purification and Enlightenment, Mystogogue) while three are rites of passage (the Rite of Welcome, the Rite of Election, the Rite of Initiation). Each of these steps can be tied to a place in the church year in a very meaningful way by Protestants as well as Catholics.

Inquiry

The point of beginning is Pentecost Sunday. On that day you may celebrate a special commissioning service for those in your community of faith who are called to the work of evangelism. These persons will now seek to fulfill their calling in a special way in the months of the season after Pentecost. They will invite friends and neighbors to church and will engage with them and possibly other members of the church or elders in discussions about the gospel and its meaning for their lives. During these months, some of these people will consider a deeper commitment. We can speak of them as "converting persons."

The Rite of Welcome

The next step, the first passage rite, is the rite of welcome, a ritual that is celebrated today on the first Sunday of Advent.

As part of this rite in the early church, the converting person renounced false gods, received the sign of the cross on the forehead, and was received into the church as a catechumen.

Similar symbols may be used today. Each church may develop symbols that express a renunciation of the old way of life and the embracing of the new life in Christ.

The Catechumenate

The catechumenate is the longest stage. In the early church it spanned two or three years, depending on how certain the church leaders were of the spiritual formation of the converting person.

During this stage the converting person is instructed in the Scripture, in prayer, and in holy living. Today this period of learning stretches from the first Sunday of Advent through the Epiphany season. Some churches extend it for another full year, but that is not typical.

The Rite of Election

Once the instruction of the catechetical period is complete, the converting persons gather in public worship for the second passage rite, the rite of election. This ritual takes place on the first Sunday of Lent.

In the ancient church and again today the primary symbol of this ritual is the dramatic moment in which the converting person, in response to a question such as "Do you choose the one who has chosen you?" will step forward, say "yes," and then write his or her name in a book placed in front of the pulpit.

The Period of Purification and Enlightenment

This fifth stage, which occurs during Lent, is a time for intense spiritual preparation for baptism. It is a time to wrestle with the "principalities and powers" that seek to control life.

In the ancient church the converting person came to the church for daily exorcisms during this stage. Today, a church may instead lay hands on the catechumens and pray for them in the struggles they have with the powers of evil that continue to knock on their door and bring temptation into their lives. In this way catechumens may learn that the Christian life is a life of struggle, a life that demands constant attention to the ways in which the church offers God's help in times of temptation or distress.

The Rite of Initiation

The sixth state is then the act of baptism itself. In the early church and again today, converting persons are baptized on Easter Sunday morning in the context of the great Paschal vigil.

As part of the early church rite, those to be baptized renounced the powers of evil, received the baptism of water in the name of the triune God, were washed with oil, exchanged the kiss of peace, and for the first time celebrated the Lord's Supper with the faithful. Today the adaptation of these rites for the converting persons places special emphasis on the completion of one phase of the journey of faith and the beginning of another.

Mystagogue

The continuation of the converting person's lifelong experience of faith is expressed in the final stage, the period of *mystagogue*, an old term that means "learning the mysteries." Today, as in the early church, the stage of mystagogue occurs during the fifty days of the Easter season.

In the early church's mystagogue, new converts were instructed in the meaning of the Eucharist and were incorporated into the full life of the church. Today, churches use this time to discern the new convert's gifts and to enroll the fully converted person into an active membership wherein his or her gifts are used in the life of the church.

While you may not have heard of liturgical evangelism, let me assure you that it is a form of evangelism used quite effectively by renewing Catholic churches around the world and by an increasing number of Protestant liturgical churches (especially the Episcopal Church).

But a congregation does not have to be strictly liturgical to use this form of evangelism. Any church that celebrates the pilgrimage of the Christian year can use this form of evangelism effectively both for converting persons and for bringing new life into the present congregation. In this approach the whole church is aware of the process and can even be involved in a continual process of conversion ordered by the meaning of Advent, Christmas, Epiphany, Lent, Holy Week, Easter, and Pentecost.

Three Steps to Change

These three approaches to evangelism through worship demonstrate that there is no one way to do evangelism through worship. If your congregation is not engaged in any form of evangelism through worship, I suggest you take three steps.

First, discuss these three approaches to evangelism and decide which one is most suitable for your congregation.

Second, having chosen one or the other, study it. Read books. Attend a conference. Bring someone in who can present the approach to the entire congregation.

Finally, do it. You may find yourself faltering at first, but as you continue to experiment and perhaps fail, pick yourself up and try again. The approach will take shape in your congregation and will stimulate you to be an evangelizing community of worship.

11

Evangelism and Christian Formation in the Early Church[1]

RECENTLY I SAT WITH a longtime friend in a local coffee shop discussing matters related to theology. We have both enjoyed the benefits of Reformed thinking so our discussion turned to the impact of Reformed theology on our lives. "I'm not willing to call myself Reformed anymore," my friend said. "Why not?" I asked. "It's too shaped by the Enlightenment."

This conversation raised a brief but lively discussion on the nature of Reformed theology. Is Reformed theology, particularly the theology of the Reformers—Luther, Calvin, Menno Simons—an attempt to recover the ancient theology and practices of the church or is Reformed theology what it became in the modern world?

It seems clear to me that the Reformers were concerned to *return* to a pre-Medieval, patristic approach to the faith. The Anabaptists wanted to situate faith in the practices of the pre-Constantinian church, while Luther and Calvin were concerned to locate their theological tradition in Scripture as interpreted by the Apostles' Creed, the Nicene Creed, and the Chalcedonian Creed. While there are differences between the Reformers, they were all concerned to restore the ancient faith and practice which they felt had been corrupted by the late Medieval church. The Reformers did not have an inkling of the Enlightenment to come and how that would reshape their recovery of the past.

We now live in a time in which the awareness of post-Reformation developments have resulted in a new criticism of culturally-shaped

[1]. Originally published in *The Reformation and Revival Journal*, Fall 2004. Used with permission.

Christianity. Reformed thought filtered through reason and science has distanced us not only from the early church, but also from the Reformers who called us to return to the early church. This is, of course, a return to Scripture as well, seeing that the formation of the canon was intertwined with the formation of the creeds and many of the practices of the early church. This relation between Scripture and tradition can be maintained even as the final authority of Scripture in all matters of faith and practice are embraced.

I have stated this brief *prolegomenon* above as a way of legitimizing a return to the ancient practice of evangelism and Christian formation.[2] I needed to develop this apologia because what I'm about to present is not found in any developed form in the writings of the Reformers. The failure of the Reformers to refer to the ancient practice of Christian formation is not due to their rejection of it. Rather, because the particular documents that yield an understanding of the ancient practice of Christian formation had not been recovered by the sixteenth century, the Reformers knew nothing of it. I would like to think that if they knew the material, they would have translated it for their day.

I speak here of the ancient catechumenate, which was revived by Vatican II. It has been revised by the Catholic Church and incorporated into the universal mission of the Roman Churches. Other denominations and fellowships are following the Roman Church in adapting the ancient catechumenate to their mission and ministry. What follows here is my attempt to translate this material for the Reformed church and for the Evangelical community in general. One important preliminary comment must be made. What I present is drawn from the third century and is most applicable to the mission of the church in bringing new converts into Christian formation. The process is therefore oriented around *adult* baptism and immersion. I advocate, but do not develop in this article that a church in the Reformed tradition may practice both adult and infant baptism. Those adults who are converted as a result of the mission of the church would obviously be baptized as adults. However children, baptized under the covenant, would be formed in a process of Christian formation in keeping with that church's tradition. One process of Christian formation would be directed toward adults, the other toward children.

---

2. This article is an adaptation of Webber, "What Is Liturgical Evangelism?" in *Celebrating Our Faith*. Also see Webber, *Journey to Jesus* and *Ancient-Future Evangelism*.

Evangelism and Spiritual Formation in the Early Church

A chief source for our knowledge of evangelism and Christian formation in the early church is *The Apostolic Tradition* written around AD 215 by Hippolytus, a bishop in Rome.[3] In this document Hippolytus reveals the method and content of evangelism in the early church. The method was a process, not a one-time decision made under emotional pressure without a support community. This process brought a person into Christ and full communion with the Christian community through the periods of development and growth related to baptism. For example, the following stages of formation can be discerned in *The Apostolic Tradition*: (1) a period of inquiry, (2) a time of instruction, (3) an intense spiritual preparation for baptism, and (4) continued nurture in the church. Further, each of these periods is set off by a passage rite that marks the transition to the next period of growth. These passage rites include (1) the rite of entrance into the time of instruction, (2) the rite of election into the intense period of spiritual preparation, and (3) the rites that surround baptism. Consequently, we may discern four periods of growth and development framed by three rites of passage. These seven parts constitute the framework of ancient evangelism and Christian formation.

Within this sevenfold process, four basic principles of this process can be discerned: (1) Christ as victor over the powers of evil, (2) the church as a nurturing and mothering community, (3) the power of external rites to order inner experience, and (4) the principle of growth into Christ and the church through various stages of development. This article comments on each of these principles and thus clarifies the meaning of liturgical evangelism more fully.

Christ as Victor Over the Powers of Evil

According to Gustaf Aulen, the fundamental view of Christ's work held by the early church is *Christus Victor*.[4] This theme, which may be traced back to the Pauline writings, perceives the world in terms of a conflict between light and darkness, Christ and Satan, the kingdom of God and the kingdom of evil. This biblical story begins with creation and the fall and extends into the future to the end of history. The scope of the story

---

3. See Dix and Chadwick, eds., *Treatise on the Apostolic Tradition of St. Hippolytus of Rome*.

4. Aulen, *Christus Victor*.

is cosmic and includes everything from creation to re-creation. The elements of the story, such as the fall, the covenants, the incarnation, the death, burial, and resurrection, the ascension and Pentecost, as well as the history of church and its anticipation of the future, tell of Christ's conquest over evil.

The Christian makes the confession of faith that Christ is victor over sin, death, and the dominion of the devil. He has "disarmed the principalities and powers and made a public example of them, triumphing over them" (Colossians 2:15). Yet the victory of Christ over the powers of evil is no mere intellectual proposition. It is essentially a doxological affirmation, a proclamation of praise, a liturgical affirmation. Thus, in worship the church experiences this victory and cries "Jesus is Lord,"[5] "Hallelujah! For the Lord our God the Almighty reigns."[6] The church joins heavenly worship in its hymn to Christ the victor, "To Him who sits upon the throne and to the Lamb be blessing and honor and glory and might forever and ever!"[7, 8]

Through evangelism and Christian formation a person is brought into an experience of Christ as victor. In this process the converting person is turned away from following the "prince of the power of the air" and is made "alive together with Christ."[9] In the early church, this process of conversion was ordered around the rites that culminated in baptism and entrance into the Christian community. Through these rites the new Christian experienced Christ as Lord over the powers of evil.

This emphasis on the experience of Christ's present lordship over the powers of evil is clearly evident in the rite of initiation. It is expressed, for example, in the exorcisms, the renunciation of evil by the baptismal candidate, the anointing with the oil of thanksgiving, and the eucharistic prayer. The words of the eucharistic prayer represent a climax in the process of conversion and coalesce the entire experience of turning away from sin toward Christ, the victor over the powers of evil.

A unique feature of the baptismal journey and the culminating eucharistic experience is that *my* story and *his* story converge. The Christ

---

5. Romans 10:9.

6. Revelation 19:6, Revised Standard Version. Hereafter cited as RSV.

7. Revelation 5:13, RSV.

8. See Berkhof, *Christ and the Powers*; Morrison, *Powers That Be*; Caird, *Principalities and Powers*; Schlier, *Principalities and Powers in the New Testament*; Yoder, *Politics of Jesus*.

9. See Ephesians 2:1–10.

story is the overarching story that gives meaning to my story through the incorporation of my story into his. This one story is captured in the biblical image of Christ as the second Adam, who, because of his sin, brought us under the dominion of death and condemnation. Were it not for the second Adam, Christ, we would all be left in the state of condemnation and alienation from God. The second Adam is the one who brings righteousness, life, and justification. Only through Christ can the human condition and that of the entire universe be restored and renewed. Consequently, the baptismal journey makes one a participant in the story set forth in the eucharistic prayer. This story, for which we give thanks, locates Christ in a cosmic setting. He who is one with the Father became incarnate in the womb of the Virgin Mary, destroyed death by his death, trod down hell by his resurrection, and gained for himself a holy people, the church.

The liturgy of the church celebrates this true story through re-enactment. Through baptism one makes the journey to union with Christ who, by his destruction of the powers of evil, makes fellowship with God in the earthly life of the church possible. The Eucharist repeatedly celebrates the victory of Christ over the powers of evil, a celebration that brings the healing effect of the Christ event to the worshiping community again and again.

This supernatural conception of Christ as victor over the powers of evil and thus Lord of the cosmos and Lord and Savior of my life lies at the heart of liturgical evangelism and Christian formation. The evangelism of the early church did not seek to evangelize people into a cosmic idea, myth, or a mere window to the Father. For the early church, Jesus was the incarnate Son of God, victor over sin, Savior of those who repented and put their faith and trust in him as Lord.

The Church as a Nurturing and Mothering Community

A second principle of liturgical evangelism in the early church asserts that conversion into Christ takes place through the church. The church, far from being a mere aggregate of human persons, is, from the standpoint of Christian formation, the mother in whose womb God's children are born, the mother who offers her breast for nurture and sustenance.

The theme of *Ecclesia Mater* originates in both the Old and New Testament and is rooted in the fusion of the symbols of bride and groom.[10] For example, the relationship between God and Israel is depicted in Isaiah[11] and Jeremiah[12] as that between a bride and bridegroom. This marriage relationship between God and Israel is expressed in the mystical union between Christ and the church in the New Testament.[13] Consequently, at the end of history, the holy city, the new Jerusalem that is understood as the church, is proclaimed to be the bride of the Lamb.[14]

The early Church Fathers drew on the image of the bride to develop the feminine and mothering qualities of the church. Perceiving a mystical union between Christ and the church, they stressed the need to be converted to Christ in and through the church. Cyprian declared that "he can no longer have God for his father who has not the church for his mother."[15]

Descriptions of the church as mother abound among the early Church Fathers. Tertullian speaks of "Our Lady Mother the Church" who nourishes us "from her bountiful breasts."[16] Clement of Alexandria extols the church as "Virgin and Mother—pure as a virgin, loving as a mother."[17] Cyprian, whose writings on the church are replete with female imagery, proclaims the church to be "the one mother copious in the results of her fruitfulness... [B]y her womb we are born, by her milk we are nourished, by her spirit we are animated."[18]

But how does the church fulfill its mothering role? First, according to the early Church Fathers, the church is the womb in which God's children are born. This image of gestation appears as early as the second century in the *First Apology* of Justin Martyr, a work written to the Emperor Titus that draws an analogy between the water of baptism and the "moist seed" of conception. In the water of the church, the candidate is washed "in the name of God the Father and the Lord of the universe, and of our Savior Jesus Christ, and of the Holy Spirit. For Christ said, 'Except ye be born again ye shall not enter into the Kingdom of Heaven.'"[19] In the

---

10. See Minear, *Images of the Church in the New Testament*.
11. See Isaiah 61–62.
12. See Jeremiah 25 and 33.
13. See Ephesians 5:21–33.
14. See Revelation 21:9.
15. Cyprian, *On the Unity of the Catholic Church*, 6.
16. Tertullian, *On Martyrdom*, I.
17. Clement, *Instructor*, Book I, 6.
18. Cyprian, *On the Unity of the Catholic Church*, 5.
19. Justin Martyr, *First Apology*, 61.

womb of the church, conversion to Christ is conceived. And the water of baptism, which is the unique possession of the church, symbolically represents the creation of new life.[20]

Second, the church is mother because of the quality of the nurture it provides. Augustine is so assured of the loving nurture of the church that he can say, "You are safe who have God for your Father and His Church for your Mother."[21] In his treatise on baptism, Augustine stressed both the birthing and nurturing aspects of the church. The church "gives birth to all . . . within her pale, of her own womb."[22] The church brings to birth, nurses, cares for, and even agonizes over her children. In spite of these statements, Augustine acknowledges that not all who are in the church are of God. Some may stray from the naming that was done over the waters. These repudiate their birthright and disclaim God's ownership of their lives. Those "who are born within the family, of the womb of the mother herself, and then neglect the grace they have received, are like Isaac's son Esau, who was rejected, God Himself bearing witness to it, and saying, 'I loved Jacob, and I hated Esau; and that though they were twin-brethren, the offspring of the same womb.'"[23]

Evangelism and Christian formation, then, is evangelism in and through the church. It is not mass evangelism, parachurch evangelism, or even one-on-one evangelism. While each of these models may feed into Christian formation, ancient formation takes place in the context of the local church, of the mystery of faith that is experienced and modeled by a local spiritual family born and nurtured by its mother, the church.[24]

The Power of External Rites to Order Inner Experience

Another principle of Christian formation in the early church recognizes that external rites have the power to order an inner experience. This principle, which unites external action and internal reality, is rooted in the Christian doctrine of incarnation. The confession that the human and divine are united in the person of Christ affirms that God can and does work through material and physical creation. The rites of initiation make

---

20. See Tertullian, *On Baptism*.
21. Augustine, *Against Petilian*.
22. Augustine, *Against Donatists*.
23. Augustine, *Against Donatists*.
24. See Dujarier, "Survey of the History of the Catechumenate."

God and his saving presence a reality through physical signs. In order to clarify this principle, I have set forth eight statements that will illuminate more clearly the idea that external rites order inner experiences.[25]

First, the rites of initiation must be seen as commemorating an historical event. The historical reference point for Christian formation is the life, death, and resurrection of Jesus Christ. In the Christian vision of reality, this story rises above all other stories of life. We may be enchanted by the stories of Abraham or the life of Moses, the glorious account of a David or a Paul, but these stories, important as they may be in the Christian family, cannot compare with the story of Christ set forth in the Gospels. As Christians our ultimate identity is found not with Moses, David, or Paul, but with Jesus Christ. Christian formation, then, particularly in the rites of initiation, connects our story, our life, and our journey with the one story, the one person from whom and through whom our life gains ultimate meaning. By this means our inner experience of living, dying, and being resurrected with Christ is ordered and accomplished.

Second, the external process of Christian formation symbolically represents the original Christ event. Liturgy, like art, seeks to bring us into the truth. For example, the very form of the rite of initiation—its design, its symbols, its sequence, its content—illuminates the original event of Christ. It represents what is fundamental, what is enduring and essential, what is central to the gospel in its action of representing the truth. Consequently, this evocative form lifts the original event from its historical roots and brings it down through the corridors of time into the present moment.

Third, the sevenfold process of Christian formation is the external agency through which the belief of the Christian community is handed down to the new believer. All forms of formation require an external agent that will break in upon the recipient, distress that recipient with a sense of sin, and arouse that person to faith. Faith results from the work of the Holy Spirit, which sometimes acts through the agency of personal witness and at other times acts through proclamation. However, in the case of evangelism, the Holy Spirit incites contrition and faith by the entire process of initiation. These stages of conversion and passage rites symbolically organize, assist, and carry along the inner experience of the soul. Thus, the process itself—what is symbolized—and the sequence

---

25. See Nichols, *Art of God Incarnate*; Johnson, *Rites of Christian Initiation*; Harmless, *Augustine and the Catechumenate*.

through which it proceeds represent the faith of the community and present God's call to faith, awaiting the soul's desire.

Fourth, Christian formation may next be seen as a way of ordering and giving shape to Christian experience. It is not a series of events that the participant judges. One does not set oneself against the periods of formation, for that would be presumptuous. Rather, the person places himself or herself under the process of initiation and freely allows it to name the experience of conversion. When the recipient feels the process speaking in his or her heart and realizes an inner correspondence to the meaning that the outer forms symbolize, that person is truly named as Christ's own and led into a deeper relationship with God.

Fifth, the symbolic forms employed in Christian formation cannot be exhausted intellectually. The rites, such as the inquiry, the catechetical period, the exorcisms, the washing with water, anointing with oil, and so on, are all pre-logical forms of expression. These ritual forms of communication cannot be exhausted by logical inquiry or empirical investigation. These symbols communicate through the senses to a level of consciousness that lies deeper than our thoughts. The point of contact in human personality that builds the bridge between this world and the next is not the mind, but the heart.

Sixth, formation, to function in the ways described previously, has a sacramental character and ought not to be regarded as merely illustrative. If the process of initiation only illustrates and informs, we cannot speak of the rites as embodying the original event they represent. Unlike illustration, sacrament is participatory. It is incarnational, commingling the physical and the spiritual. Thus, through the rites the conversion that is represented may actually take place. The rites must be seen as a necessary element of the process, for they not only represent the Christ event, but they also embody the event, so that the participant actually enters into the Christ event and its saving reality through the participatory experience of the rites observed.

Seventh, because Christian formation is sacramental, it requires faith. Faith, of course, is not in the thing itself but in that which it embodies, namely, Jesus Christ. In this process of formation the person also carries a responsibility to discern truth, to exercise his or her will to affirm and intend what is represented.

Finally, then, the response of faith to the event represented in the rite creates participation in the reality the rite represents. Participation in Christ and his church is the goal of formation. Christian formation that only brings a person to a detached intellectual acquiescence is not a spiritual formation at all. It is a mental affirmation of God who exists as the other alongside of the self. Spiritual formation strives to accomplish not a mere recognition of God, not a mere acknowledgment of his existence, but a participation in the life of Christ through the life of the church in which he dwells. This inwardness is achieved not by the rejection of the external rites and orders of the church, but by the recognition that these rites, attended by the desire of the soul, actually bring us into participation, into a relationship with Christ and the salvation he brings.

The actual ordering of the rite of initiation, together with the symbolic gestures that signify the meaning of the action taking place, give shape to and order the inner experience of spiritual formation—but not without the faith and intention of the convert.

Growth in Christ Through Various Periods of Development

A final principle of Christian formation in the early church recognizes that growth into Christ and the church is subject to process and development. This assertion does not preclude the possibility of instant conversion. Certainly, there have been and will always be conversions "on the road to Damascus." But even these conversions require development and nurture that may be represented by stages of maturation and growth. For example, St. Paul went away to Arabia, then, after three years, went to Jerusalem for fifteen days to confer with Cephas. Next, he went off to the regions of Syria and Cilicia. And finally, fourteen years after his conversion, he went to Jerusalem and on to his famous missionary work.[26] Exegetes agree that these fourteen years were a time of growth and development for Paul. Like Jesus, who "increased in wisdom and in stature, and in favor with God and man,"[27] Paul underwent periods of growth and maturation. Consequently, formation looks upon conversion into Christ and the church as a process that, even if preceded by a dramatic conversion, still requires a person to develop over time a responsible and dynamic relationship with Christ and the church.

The notion of process and development was not foreign to the early Church Fathers. Irenaeus, for example, refers to growth this way: "Man has first to come into being, then to progress, and by progressing come to

26. See Galatians 1:15—2:1.
27. Luke 2:52.

manhood, and having reached manhood to increase, and thus increasing to persevere, and by persevering be glorified, and thus see his Lord."[28] Even more interesting, Irenaeus argues that Christ himself sanctified the various stages of human life. "He came to save all through his own person; all, that is, who through him are re-born to God; infants, children, boys, young men and old. Therefore he passed through every stage of life."[29] Today, the insights of Jean Piaget's cognitive developmental structuralism, Erik Erikson's psycho-social theory, and James Fowler's stages of spiritual growth provide a fertile contemporary basis for the restoration of a Christian formation that takes into account various periods of development.[30]

The process of formation consists of a series of readily identifiable stages of development. The period of *inquiry* presupposes a certain degree of commitment; the period of *intense spiritual preparation* before baptism assumes a resolute determination and an inner resolve to identify with Christ; the rite of initiation (baptism) is a turning point, a crisis moment in which one plunges fully into a relationship with Christ; this results in the final period, that of *incorporation into the church*, participation in the body of Christ, and an acceptance of responsibilities implied by belonging to the family of faith.

Conclusion

Allow me to return to where I started this article. My contention is that when Calvin is read as a return to the early church and not as a forerunner of the Enlightenment, he will be read in full support of the ancient form of evangelism and spiritual formation. A few quotes from the *Institutes of the Christian Religion* will point in this direction.

First, while Calvin did not expand *Christus Victor*, he did acknowledge it. He writes, "Nor are we to understand that by the curse which he endured he was himself overwhelmed, but rather that by enduring it, he repressed, broke, annihilated all its force." Quoting Colossians 2:15, he comments that "Paul magnificently celebrates the triumph which Christ

---

28. Irenaeus, *Against Heresies*, Book 4:38, 2–3.
29. Irenaeus, *Against Heresies*, Book 2:22, 4.
30. See Piaget, *Structuralism*; Erikson, *Childhood and Society*; Fowler, *Stages of Faith*.

obtained on the cross, as if the cross, the symbol of ignominy, had been converted into a triumphal Chariot."[31]

Second, Calvin was very clear on his view of the church as the womb in which we are conceived and the school in which we are to continue in all of our life. Calvin writes.

> It is now our purpose to discourse of the visible Church, let us learn, from her single title of Mother, how useful, nay, how necessary the knowledge of her is, since there is no other means of entering into life unless she conceive us in the womb and give us birth, unless she nourish us at her breasts, and, in short, keep us under her charge and government, until, divested of mortal flesh, we become like the angels (Matth xxii. 30). For our weakness does not permit us to leave the school until we have spent our whole lives as scholars. Moreover, beyond the pale of the Church no forgiveness of sins, no salvation, can be hoped for, as Isaiah and Joel testify (Isaiah 37:32; Joel 2:32).[32]

And then, third, what about the power of external rites to order internal experience? Calvin was certainly against the notion of a sacramental *ex opere operatum*—and rightly so. But he would not have found himself in sync with the later Enlightenment approach that viewed sign as mere illustration either. He repeatedly uses the phrase that sacraments are "visible signs of invisible grace."[33] While early Church Fathers do not use this term, they recognize the same principle. For them, as for Calvin, spiritual realities are not separated from the material. Both Calvin and the ancient Fathers reject a form of dualism that sets the spiritual against the material. So ritual, properly understood, is the physical side of a spiritual action.

Finally, the notion of stages of growth in the spiritual life is also not foreign to Calvin. He does not present specific stages marked by passage rites as in the early church. However, he acknowledges progress and growth in the Christian life. He writes of the first inkling of faith as a point "we begin to behold the face of God placid, serene, and propitious; far off, indeed, it." He then refers to the "progress made" in the Christian life as a "nearer and surer view, the very continuance making it but still so distinctly as to assure us that there is no delusion in more familiar to us." We move, he suggests, from a "knowledge of God" which "is at first

---

31. Calvin, *Institutes*, Book 2, chapter 16:7, 440.
32. Calvin, *Institutes*, Book 4, chapter 1:4, 283.
33. Calvin, *Institutes*, Book 4, chapter 19:1, 623.

involved with much ignorance—ignorance, however, which is gradually removed."[34]

Today we live in a tumultuous time. A time when the methods of ministry that have been used to evangelize people are in question. I have suggested in this brief article that we look again to the ancient church, to the biblical and early Christian sources of evangelism and Christian formation. Our vision for the future will be better served, I suggest, by going *behind* the Reformers whom we admire and embrace. For the roots to which they returned are more biblical than the adaptation of their writings made by their Enlightenment successors.

---

34. Calvin, *Institutes*, Book 3, chapter 2:19, 486.

12

Narrating the World Once Again: A Case for an Ancient-Future Faith[1]

Introduction

THE PHILOSOPHER HANS GEORGE Gadamer says that we always speak out of our prejudices and we should let our hearers know what they are. He is not using the word *prejudices* in a negative way, as we so often do, but in the way of acknowledging those influences that have made us who we are. In keeping with Gadamer's advice I confess that I write out of four important prejudices: 1) an education in a fundamentalist university and in three conservative seminaries—Episcopal, Presbyterian, and Lutheran, 2) graduate education in historical theology, 3) a doctoral thesis on William Perkins, one of the founders of Puritanism, and 4) teaching at Wheaton College for thirty-two years.

These four prejudices have led me to the following convictions: 1) no one denomination has the corner on the truth; 2) the cultural context of ministry must be subject to critical evaluation by Scripture principles; 3) all reforms seek to restore the original faith; and 4) Evangelicals need to return to the essentials articulated in Scripture and its earliest interpreters. I bring these prejudices to my current assessment of the Emerging Church and to the task it faces in ministry. Evangelicals, including the Emerging Church leaders, do indeed hold to the essentials—to the authority of Scripture and to its basic structure of Trinity, creation, fall, incarnation, death, resurrection and to the church, its worship and the new

---

1. Originally published in *The Criswell Theological Review*, Spring 2006. Used by permission.

heavens and the new earth. *But these essentials have been so thoroughly defined by the Enlightenment philosophy and culture, by the scientific theological method of the Enlightenment, and by current trends in business, psychology, communications and other areas that at the moment demands a critical appraisal of ministries conditioned by culture and a rediscovery of ministry situated in the divine narrative.* The most appropriate image of our problem can be illustrated by looking at an artichoke. In order to get to the heart of this fruit, one must strip off the leaves. Evangelical Christianity is like that artichoke. Deep down, hidden within the leaves, is the heart of the faith. But to get there the leaves of cultural baggage must be stripped away, so that we can minister out of the essentials uncluttered by all the additions of modernity and the culture of the last fifty years.

The people who most clearly see the culturally conditioned nature of contemporary Evangelicalism are those who have been called the "Emerging Church." They are reacting against an Evangelicalism that has become corrupted by its alliance with modern and contemporary American culture. The Emerging Church is a movement of reform, renewal, and restitution. But, like the culture, the Emerging Church is pluralistic and moving in a number of directions at the same time. For that reason I want to articulate three very specific paths for the Emerging Church to follow in order to restore the ancient biblical and historical narrative from which to minister in a post-Christian world: 1) deconstruct the current accommodation of ministry to the cultural narrative, 2) recover the story-formed nature of the good news, and 3) resituate ministry in the divine narrative.

II. Three Paths of Restoration

Deconstruct the Current Accommodation of Ministry to the Cultural Narrative

In recent years Evangelical Christianity has become increasingly informed and shaped by culture: the culture of narcissism, the business models of the church, the leadership approaches of the powerful, the marketing of the faith to a consumer audience, worship as presentation, a spirituality of the self (based on psychology), and preaching that is therapeutic. What has emerged in the last fifty years seems to be a cultural phenomenon, a constant chasing after culture to make the church and its message more relevant. But the result is a faith that is more and more disconnected from the divine narrative. Three cultural narratives that have especially influenced the Evangelical mindset are the anti-historical outlook, reason and science, and pragmatism.

First, evangelicals are *anti-historical*. It is the nature of Evangelicals to disregard historical connection to the past in favor of starting over again. A few evangelicals want to go back to Wesley, to Stone and Campbell, to the Reformation or to the origins of their particular movement, but rarely do you find a traditional Evangelical who wants to go back to the ancient church and affirm continuity with the whole church through the centuries. This attitude was painfully driven home to me by a colleague not in favor of my early church interest who said, "Webber you act like there never was a Reformation" to which I responded "And you act as if there was no history prior to the Reformation."

Christopher Lasch in *The Culture of Narcissism* speaks to the problem of being anti-historical: "Our culture's indifference to the past . . . furnishes that culture's bankruptcy . . . a denial of the past . . . proves on closer analysis to embody the deep despair of a society that cannot face the future."[2] This denial of the past, which evangelicals share with the rest of the culture, has resulted in a faith influenced by a narcissistic emphasis on the self, a resurgence of the Gnostic separation between matter and spirit, the embrace of business models of the church, the philosophy of material and numerical success and the commitment to repeated innovation, a starting over again of the church. This redefining of Christian faith and practice through an alignment with the cultural narrative must be deconstructed as a biblical case for the future is reclaimed.

Evangelicalism's indebtedness to the current culture is also expressed by bringing reason and science to the aid of Scripture authority. This modern approach to Christian foundationalism was developed in the aftermath of the sixteenth-century Reformation. The Reformers all claimed the Scriptures, not the church, to be the foundation of truth. But many theological systems emerged, all equally claiming to have the right interpretation of Scripture. Who was right? Calvinists? Lutherans? Anabaptists? René Descartes, John Locke, and others who were Christians disturbed by the many claims to truth, sought a basis outside of Scripture to be the foundation of truth and they found that first in reason and science. This new foundationalism is illustrated in John Toland['s] (1696) *Christianity Not Mysterious*. He argued "There is nothing in the Gospel contrary to Reason, nor above it; and that no Christian Doctrine can be properly call'd a mystery."

2. Lasch, *Culture of Narcissism*, xviii.

For Toland and a whole host of others, reason verified truth. Soon science, because it delivered "Facts," was also used to verify the Bible. The liberals embracing reason and science committed themselves to a rational and scientific foundationalism and reinterpreted the Bible as myth. But conservatives, who were equally committed to reason and science, continued to use reason and science to "prove" the Bible right. In this way Evangelical theology has allowed itself to become defined by the rational method of foundationalism. The Gospel does not "stand on its own." It is not true simply because it is true. It is true because reason and science verifies it to be true. This is a culturally formed argument that must be deconstructed so that the Bible can once again stand on its own as the vision of God for the world without the need of reason and science to make it true.

The third way modern Evangelicals work out of the cultural narrative is in their commitment to pragmatism. The approach to ministry—to the church, worship, evangelism, preaching, spirituality, and counseling—has been divorced from the divine narrative. Wrenched from the context from which they should emerge, the practices of the Christian faith have been informed and shaped more by culture than theology. We minister out of "whatever works." So the church is shaped by the models of successful corporation. The pastor, once the shepherd, is now the CEO. Worship, which is to tell and enact God's story, is now shaped by broadcast communication and has become oriented toward entertainment. Spirituality, shaped by psychology, has shifted from a journey into God to a journey into self. Preaching, which historically opened the Word of God and called God's people into holy living, is now influenced by the triumph of the therapeutic.

Obviously the entire church has not become captive to the culture. But the three trends I have mentioned seem to be uncritically embraced by many. In our attempt to be relevant and meet the needs of society, we have unwittingly accommodated ourselves to the anti-historical spirit, to the privileging of science and reason, and to pragmatic ministries that are divorced from God's narrative, thus allowing the culture to shape the church. This evaluation of the state of evangelical Christianity at the beginning of the twenty-first century is not unique to the younger evangelicals of the Emerging Church; it is equally the observation of sociologist Alan Wolfe. In his work *The Transformation of American Religion* he writes, "Evangelicalism's popularity is due as much to its populist and democratic urges [and] its determination to find out exactly what believers want and to offer it to them as the certainties of the faith . . . The biggest challenge posed to American society by the popularity of the megachurches and other growth-forms of Protestantism is not bigotry but bathos." I was sitting on the couch next to my wife when I read these words. Not sure of the meaning of *bathos* I asked her, "What does *bathos* mean?" To which she replied, "The sudden appearance of the commonplace." I thought for a moment about how true that word was to my own experience of Evangelical Christianity. It seemed so commonplace, so trivial, so much like the culture. Then I returned to the text and read on. Wolfe concludes this paragraph with these words: "Television, publishing, political campaigning, education, self-help advice all increasingly tell Americans what they want to hear. Religion, it would seem, should now be added to that list." In these words a sociologist, a man who admits to being an unbeliever, puts his finger on the problem. Evangelicalism is so thoroughly conditioned by the culture in which it seeks to minister, that it has the appearance of the commonplace. It has become what people want to hear, not what it is that God wants to say and do. This indictment of Evangelical Christianity that it is culturally conditioned is only the surface problem. The deeper problem is that by allowing itself to become conditioned by the "surface culture," it misses the point of the deeper cultural crisis. This crisis is that our world has become storyless. There is no unified story that gives meaning to life and history. Everything has been reduced to "my" story. But there is no universal story in which my story is situated.

Recover the Story-Formed Nature of the Good News

The Christian faith is a story not just about a private personal relationship with God, but a story about the world—its origins, its meaning, its destiny. God's story once shaped the world. It shaped culture, nations, and civilization. It was told and enacted in the liturgy. It shaped architectural space, inspired artists, shaped literature, gave rise to philosophy, was expressed in poetry, dance, and music. It shaped personal self-understanding, spirituality, personal and national ethics, the understanding of history, the goal and destiny of the world.

But this public face of the Christian faith, this world-encompassing understanding of reality, was *attacked by the process of secularization*. Secularization eroded historic religious sensibilities and undermined the narrative that gave rise to the Western world. A new worldview shaped by reason and science eventually emerged, forming the world by the narrative of autonomy and progress, a narrative that promised to usher in a new golden era of peace and prosperity for the world. But the secular narrative has failed, and the world now lives without a defining narrative. Postmodernity has been described by Francis Lyotard as the time of the "incredulity of the meta-narrative." The world without a story has become the empty wasteland of the narcissistic self. It is Samuel Beckett's world described in *Waiting for Godot*. We wait for Godot to give us a future, but the future has not yet come and we feel like Sartre, that there is "No Exit."

We live in a world that has no comprehensive defining story. But we also live in a world of competing stories. The Neo-Pagan movements, New Age sects, the Eastern religions of Hinduism, Islam, Buddhism, Confucianism and even newer religions like Scientology have their stories that aim at world domination. Even the story of democracy and freedom aims to narrate the world. In spite of all these competing stories, our Western world is currently in a state of "narrative collapse." But eventually a story will emerge that will narrate the world. Whose story will it be? Islam? Paganism? New Age? Eastern Religion? Democracy? Christianity?

It is in this world, as a people without a defining story, that the church cannot afford to be defined by culture. It can no longer be "the sudden appearance of the commonplace." The task of the next generation of leaders is to disassociate themselves from the culturally conditioned practices of the Evangelical church, and recover the divine narrative in which all ministry is situated.

The challenge to narrate the world once again must begin with a *restoration of the original story*. The future will not be narrated by a particular Lutheran, Calvinist, Wesleyan, or Evangelical version of it. We must start again with the story of Israel and Jesus as interpreted by the apostolic and ancient church. This return to the divine narrative is the burden of both post-Evangelical and post-liberal leaders. Stanley Hauerwas comments that we need to recover "the past to help us see what has been lost, in the hope that our imagination will be renewed and begin to see what we must do." Mark Noll asks, "Is the Reformation over?" These voices and many others are telling us that modernity is coming to an end. But I also hear in these words that ministry should not ask, "What is the next innovation?" but "How can we get connected to the past once again?" "The future," it must be said "runs through the past." And the place to start is not in a "previous system," as good as that may be, but with God's story. For God's story truthfully narrates the world.

God's story is the story of the triune God creating a world for union with himself, the story of a world rebelling against God and going its own way, the story of God's involvement in history, incarnation, death, resurrection and coming again to restore the world as the place of his glory and to reign over it forever. This is the story of creation, incarnation, and re-creation. It is the story of recapitulation, the good news that Jesus Christ is Lord of all creation and someday all will be under his reign, reconciled to God by his own two hands—the incarnate Word and the Spirit. What we must recover is not this or that piece of the story, but the story as a whole.

In order to recover this story we must go back. I mean start the story where it started. This engagement and involvement of God in creation and history is handed down in history on the following form:

> The Triune God (being in community) acts in history (creation, incarnation, re-creation).
>
> God's acts create a story.
>
> God's story is embodied in a people (Israel, church).
>
> God's story is preserved in the sacred texts (Scripture).
>
> God's story is told and enacted in the cult (worship).
>
> God's story tells us how to live (ethics).
>
> Creedal statements preserve the original story against those who would change it.

Theological systems explain the story within different cultures.

This unfolding of the story shows the vital connection between the story and the *people*, the story and its *authoritative texts*, the story and its *worship*, and the story and its *ethics*. *Ministry is always connected to the story. Ministry does God's story, actualizing it in a people, in their worship and living.*

The fundamental issue in Evangelicalism is that God's story has been changed from a narrative that describes God's vision for the world into a scientific theology that focuses on this or that part of the story. For example, after a lecture on the story of God in an Evangelical college, I was asked a very telling question by an astute student. "Are there no propositions in the Christian faith from your perspective?" "Yes," I answered, "all the elements of the story can be broken down into propositions. You could treat 'God is' or 'God created' or 'God revealed' or 'God became incarnate' or 'God was in Christ reconciling the world to himself' as propositions. You could take each one out of the story and subject it to reason and scientific inquiry. You could do this because the story is not a myth. It has to do with reality, with the stuff of creation, with history, with the destiny of humanity and of the world. But when you treat the story as a series of propositional statements, you lose the story, and that is exactly what we have done in modern Evangelicalism. The current reaction against Enlightenment evangelicalism is not against the story, but against the compartmentalization of the story and the defense of its parts through the method of reason and science, a method that makes the story indebted to something outside of itself. The story needs to be put back together again, seen as a whole and told as the story that interprets the world and the meaning of human existence."

The point is this: when God's story is recovered, all ministry will flow from the story.

In sum, 1) the ancient divine narrative has been subjected to rational defense and scientific analysis; 2) the compartmentalization of scientific theology has resulted in a separation between the story of God and ministry; 3) ministry, which in the ancient church was situated in the divine narrative, now, no longer proceeding from God's story, has become subject to pragmatic innovation. The church and its ministry now draws from secular disciplines not informed by God's story, and has become subject especially to corporate business models of the church, worship that is a programmatic presentation, and spirituality informed by a narcissistic emphasis on self. This is why ministry must be resituated in the divine narrative.

Resituate Ministry in the Divine Narrative

I will illustrate the need to resituate ministry in the divine narrative by commenting briefly on the crisis of the church, its worship and spirituality.

The crisis of the Church.

In brief, the current crisis of the church is that we do not envision the church flowing out of God's story.

The source of the problem is that the church is defined out of the world's narrative such as business, economics, marketing, and advertising. Before this problem occurred I stood on the campus of Wheaton College and conversed with a person who was to become the architect of the market-model of the church. He spoke of his graduate training in marketing and said, "We need to apply principles of successful business to the church. I have seen these principles work in business; I know they can work in the church as well."

The architects of the business model of the church meant well. I do not fault them. The problem goes much deeper. It reaches into the anti-historical mentality, the bias against tradition as valueless, and the enterprising spirit of the American entrepreneur. The leaders of the CEO model of the church are visionaries with a heart for God and a longing to see people come to Christ. They did not foresee how the business model of the church would be shaped by consumerism. They envisioned "big," "successful," "relevant," "effective." This has always been the Evangelical way and while it has resulted in numbers, it struggles to form depth.

Not all pastors and Christian leaders are upset by the business model of the church. Many leaders of these successful churches are "on top of the world" and feel that all churches should "go this route." And to be fair, many lives have been changed through the ministry of the business model church. These churches do reach out to numerous people with shipwrecked lives. So why not jump on the bandwagon and go the CEO way? My concern is not that the church has drawn from the business model, but that the church has been so thoroughly redefined by big business that its servant nature is being lost in the clamor for power, people, buildings, programs, and recognition. One pastor writes, "It doesn't seem to matter if one speaks of a congregation (of whatever size) or a presbytery, the concern is always numbers, power, and control." He compares being in the church "like being in any other club or secular organization" and tells of a colleague, a second-career minister who "touts his 'management experience' as qualifying him to make judgments about campus ministry." He concludes that "vulnerable, authentic leaders who model the struggle" will be eaten alive by the "predators in the church" who "consider them weak."

When the church is "put back into the story of God," it is seen, not through business, but through the Trinitarian activity of God in the world as God moves the world toward its final destination in the new heavens and the new earth. The church is the continuation of the presence of Jesus in the world, witnessing to the overthrow of the powers of evil, establishing a way of life, serving the world as it forms a worldwide network of people who embody the new humanity revealed in the life, death and resurrection of Jesus Christ. The challenge for the Emerging Church is to reconnect the church to God's story.

The crisis of worship.

It is my contention that worship has also been wrenched from the story of God. In its free-floating state, it has become shaped by program, presentation, and entertainment. Worship leaders must be able to plan a program down to the minute, and influenced by broadcast communication, they must think of how this program presents and whether or not it entertains (engages) particularly the senses. I do think that most worship leaders have a heart for Jesus, they want to present "Jesus died for your sins" and "'you need to come to Jesus." But, in my experience of current worship, its music, and to a large extent, its sermons, the story of God appears to be truncated.

The problem of current worship lies not in its concern to be contemporary, but in its failure to proceed from the story of God. Worship should do God's story in its fullness. Worship is not about me, as if worship proceeds from me. It is about God. Worship tells and enacts the story of God creating, of God becoming involved in the history of the world, in Israel, and in Jesus Christ who became one of us to restore our union with God through his incarnation, death, and resurrection. Worship tells and enacts the story of God who is bringing history to its culmination, working now in the nations of the world and in the lives of people.

Worship is therefore not a program *about* God, but an organic unfolding of God's story in Word and Sacrament. There is a pattern of worship—gathering the people to tell the story (Word) and enact the story (Eucharist), to send them forth to live the story (embodiment). The challenge for the Emerging Church is to reconnect worship with the story of God.

The crisis of spirituality.

The crisis of spirituality is that having been separated from the theological reflection on God's story, it has become subject to the culture's narcissistic emphasis on the self.

Spirituality, rooted in God's story, first affirms that our spiritual relationship to God is a *gift*. Our *union* with God does not derive from self, but from God himself who chooses to become incarnate with humanity. In the incarnation God becomes one of us that we might be united to him. In union with us God enters our suffering, overcomes sin and death and in his resurrection begins the new creation. The spiritual life is not a contemplation of the self, but a contemplation of the mysteries of the God who creates, becomes incarnate, and re-creates. The spiritual life is also a baptism into Jesus, so that in union with him we live in the pattern of his death and resurrection. In this pattern of life we continually "put off" the old person fashioned after the first Adam and continually "put on" the new person fashioned after the second Adam, Jesus Christ, who not only restores us by his death and resurrection, but reveals to us what a person fully ablaze with the presence of God looks like. The spiritual life is a participation in the life of God in the life of the world as we surrender our will to the purposes of God revealed in Jesus Christ.

In review, the church and its ministries of worship and spirituality, which have become shaped by business principles, broadcast communication, and narcissism, will only change when we do the hard work of reflecting on God's story and resituate the church as the continuation of the story, worship as the telling and enacting of the story, and spirituality as the contemplation of the story and participation in the life of the story as revealed in Jesus Christ. To situate these and all ministries back into the story of God is a goal of an ancient-future church. Will the Emerging Church travel in that direction? It is possible. The emerging generation of leaders is very different than the Boomers who were given to innovation and change. The emerging generation, having grown up with innovation and perceiving the accommodation of Evangelicalism with contemporary culture, seems to be looking back as a way of looking forward.

III. The Emerging Generation of Leaders

According to Neil Howe and William Strauss the generation of leaders that emerge in a new period of crisis will, if the cycles of history hold true, bring society into a new period of stability. World War II was crisis of worldwide import and the generation that brought us out of that period and into a time of stability was, as Tom Brokaw wrote, *The Greatest Generation*. It is clear that this current generation of leaders is very different than the Boomers or Gen X generation. They have been born since

1982 in the period of the unraveling and final dissolution of the Christian narrative that once defined the world. They are now being trained for leadership and will soon become the leaders of America, of the West and of the world. Strauss and Howe describe them as follows:

As a group, Millennials are unlike any other youth generation in living memory. They are more numerous, more affluent, better educated, and more ethnically diverse. More important they are beginning to manifest a wide array of positive social habits that other Americans no longer associate with youth, including a new focus on teamwork, achievement, modesty and good conduct. Only a few years from now, this can-do youth revolution will overwhelm the cynics and pessimists. Over the next decade, the Millennial generation will entirely recast the image of youth from downbeat and alienated to upbeat and engaged with potentially seismic consequences for America.

Other studies on the Millennial youth point to religion and spirituality as the most important issues of the next generation. If this is so, and statistics seem to point in this direction, then the following convictions should motivate our ministry:

1. The world is no longer narrated by the Christian story.
2. In the period of secularization the Christian story was co-opted by reason and science. The Christian faith took on the characteristics of the culture and became anti-historical, pragmatic, and narcissistic.
3. The postmodern culture represents the collapse of all metanarratives.
4. New ways to narrate the world have emerged in Islam, New Age and Eastern religions.
5. The next generation of leaders, having been born and raised in the collapse of Western culture, seeks a new religious and spiritual base to narrate their personal lives and the life of the world.
6. The time has come for the church to restore the ancient story-formed faith of Christianity and narrate the world from God's story, once again.

IV. Conclusion

So, I ask, will the Emergent Church, the newest trend in the Evangelical era, allow itself to be formed by a postmodern culture? Or, will it, because of its disdain for the current culturally formed pragmatic faith of late twentieth-century Evangelicalism, return to the roots of the faith in the ancient church? Will it recover the original questions of faith in a culture that bears a striking similarity to the ancient Roman culture, or will it become one more commentary, one more system or non-system of faith, one more culturally-formed expression of the faith to be overturned by the next generation of leaders cheerfully following the culture? The time has come to stop thinking that history moves in a straight line, and to return to the beginning. It is not an easy road to travel and it will not be popular. But it is necessary, even critical for the survival of an Evangelical faith that has a biblical and historical identity. By a call to return to the ancient church, I subscribe to a post-Evangelical, post-liberal, recovery of roots. Post-liberal Yale professor George Lindbeck describes his own journey back to the origins of the Christian faith. He acknowledges "the horizon of a crumbling modernity that brings Christians closer to pre-modernity than they've been in perhaps 300 years, and closer to the situation of the first centuries than they've been in more than a millennium and a half." For this reason, he argues, "We are now better placed than perhaps ever before to retrieve, critically and repentantly, the heritage in the Hebrew scriptures, apostolic writings and early tradition. This retrieval is also more urgent than ever if the churches are to become the kind of global and ecumenical community the new age needs."

Considering the current dead-end journey of Evangelicalism with its culturally-conditioned faith, the *challenge* that lies before the Emerging Church is not to adapt the faith to a postmodern culture, but to recover God's story, and resituate all ministry in the divine narrative.

13

Ethics and Evangelism: Learning from the Third-Century Church[1]

A NUMBER OF YEARS ago, I enrolled in a "preacher-boys" class at a fundamentalist university in the South. The only requirement of the course was to witness to seven people every week and write a brief report on each contact. The teacher of the course—and the founder of the university—was an old-time Southern evangelist who wanted his preacher-boys to be evangelists.

The teacher's method of evangelism had three steps: tell people they are sinners, tell them about Christ, and lead them to salvation. This approach may have converted some people, but statistics would probably show that many of those conversions didn't stick—which is one of the reasons mainline churches are not attracted to hit-and-run evangelism. Mainline churches are, however, becoming increasingly interested in practicing evangelism. The recurring question for such churches is, What kind of evangelism? In response, I would recommend a liturgical approach to evangelism, one that is based on the evangelical practices of the church in the third century. Liturgical evangelism, which is being revived in the Catholic Church, is also an evangelism that emphasizes the ethical side of the gospel. It is this kind of evangelism that will, I believe, take hold in many mainline Protestant churches.

Third-century liturgical evangelism consisted of seven steps—four stages and three rites of passage. This process was designed to bring the converting person to Christ and into the church through a series of seven

1. Originally published in *The Christian Century*, September 24, 1986. Used by permission.

successively deeper commitments. These stages can be described under the headings of inquiry; rite of entrance; catechumenate; rite of election; purification and enlightenment; rites of initiation; and mystagogy. The ethical content of evangelism appeared in all seven stages.

Here is how it worked: A person who evidenced interest in the gospel was brought to the pastor and elders of the church. An inquiry into or a formal presentation of the gospel took place that emphasized not so much belief in this or that doctrine but the converting person's willingness to adopt the Christian lifestyle—to take up the cross of Jesus and to follow him. If this kind of commitment was made, the converting person went through the rite of welcome, a rite that brought the person into the fellowship of the church as a catechumen.

During the catechumenate, which could last up to three years, the converting person was given time not only to learn the faith, but to live it. When the converting person was able to demonstrate clearly a commitment to the ethical demands of the gospel, he or she entered the period of purification and enlightenment via the rite of election. During the period of purification and enlightenment, which corresponded with Lent, the converting person underwent a time of intense spiritual preparation for baptism. The focus of the preparation was on being purged of the power of sin and on preparing for the rites of initiation into the church. A final renunciation of the power of evil was made in baptism as the converting person stood in the waters. Finally, during the mystagogic period, the convert received teaching regarding the Christian life and the doing of good works, as he or she was integrated into the church.

This form of evangelism in the early church must be viewed in its cultural context, the paganism of the Roman Empire. The people of the Roman world were steeped in an amoral way of life: accustomed to belief in many gods, reliance on magic, and faith in the stars. Consequently, evangelism had to confront people both in the sphere of belief and the realm of lifestyle. Because converts were steeped in paganism, the church needed time to wean them away from their former lifestyle and to teach them the Christian lifestyle.

Inquiry was the initial stage of this process. In inquiry, the good news of salvation was presented and the qualities of life demanded by the gospel made clear. Fortunately, the details of the inquiry have been summarized for us by Hippolytus in *The Apostolic Tradition*, a document written in Rome about 215.

The central issue of inquiry was making the commitment to a new lifestyle, even if that meant changing vocations. Vocations that were related in any way to the powers of evil—such as making idols, being a heathen priest, a user of magic verses, an enchanter, astrologer, diviner, soothsayer, juggler, mountebank, or amulet-maker—had to be abandoned, and any lifestyle that led one into immorality was to be rejected. Also, anyone in a job that led to killing—such as that of a charioteer, gladiator, soldier, military commander or civil magistrate with power over people's lives—was required to give it up.

In brief, the period of inquiry was a weeding-out process. Those who came to the church for the wrong reason would not remain. And those who had begun a genuine conversion had to commit themselves to the next phase of the journey. The emphasis was on saying No to the kingdom of evil, which has been overcome by the power of Christ exhibited in his death and resurrection. Those who are to be baptized into his death must learn to "walk in newness of life."[2] One who claims to follow Jesus and becomes baptized, yet lives in darkness according to the course of this world, is no better than Simon Magus,[3] whose soul, according to Cyril of Jerusalem, "was not buried with Christ, nor did it share in his resurrection."

It was not enough in the third century to have a subjective experience of faith. Faith was to result in works, for "faith apart from works is dead."[4] Far from assuming a position of works righteousness, the inquiry recognized that commitment to a Christian lifestyle has the effect of producing faith. Behavioral modification produces an inner experience of the external habit. But this transformation does not occur without intention; the convert must intend to adopt the new lifestyle. This act is not an instant accomplishment, taking place in the secret chambers of the heart, but, as the inquiry suggests, a lifelong public commitment.

The ethical emphasis of the inquiry continues throughout the six succeeding steps. For example, in the rite of entrance, a formal repudiation of the old lifestyle takes place in a ceremony of renunciation. In the catechumenate, a weekly prayer of exorcism occurs for the candidate following instruction in the Sunday liturgy. In the rite of election, the sponsor of the converting person must testify to her or his conduct as well as faith. In the period of purification and enlightenment, special emphasis

2. Romans 6:4.
3. See Acts 8:9–24.
4. James 2:26, RSV.

is placed on equipping the converting person to wrestle against the principalities and powers of evil. In the rite of baptism, the convert renounces Satan and spits in the direction of the West, a symbol of the repudiation of the old lifestyle. Finally, in mystagogy, the convert is encouraged to continue to do the good works that characterize the Christian.

The emphasis on ethics in evangelism is viable today because, as in the third century, our cultural context is essentially pagan. In Russia, China, and other countries where the government maintains an avowedly atheistic stance, commitment to a Christian worldview and lifestyle clearly separates one from society. There, a price is exacted from those in the church, and that price is higher the more deeply one is involved: it is one thing to attend church, another to be baptized, and still another to commune at the Table of the Lord regularly. Each step distances Christians from an attachment to earthly powers, and each step intensifies their relationship with Christ and the church.

The paganism of American culture is less obvious, for we do not have to contend with a government that suppresses religious freedom or harasses religious leaders. Churches must therefore exert themselves more to distinguish themselves from the pagan values of the surrounding culture—values that often sneak into our churches themselves.

One such value is that of a fervent, messianic Americanism. Much of our recent nationalistic fervor has gone beyond healthy patriotism into the belief that capitalism and democracy are the saviors of the world. Even many religious leaders are adopting the "America saves" slogan. America, many television evangelists are telling us, is God's answer to the problems of the world. They are propagating a secular salvation which the church must oppose. Another Western value is materialism: the goal of life is more money, larger houses, bigger cars, longer vacations, fancier clothes. Come to God, our religious hucksters tell us, and he will bless you with riches beyond your imagination. To this the church must answer, "Nonsense, bunk, heresy!"

Another Western value that has crept into many of our churches and pulpits is the emphasis on success. Climb the ladder, get to the top, be authoritative, aggressive, and commanding. The sign of God's approval is big budgets, huge programs, masses of people.

The ethical emphasis in liturgical evangelism calls these secular values into question. It asks people to see the world as Jesus saw it, from the underside. It calls for a world view and a lifestyle that do not buy into the secular salvations of nationalism, materialism, and success.

What kind of congregation will welcome a liturgical evangelism that emphasizes the ethical side of the gospel?

First, it must be a church that seeks to be the church rather than a mere institution or social club. It must recognize the pagan nature of its surrounding culture, and seek to become God's alternative community. It must be a community of people willing to define itself by God's standards rather than by the prevailing standards of our culture.

Second, it must be a congregation committed to evangelism. Many Christians are not involved in evangelism because their local church neither encourages it nor has an effective program for dealing with the new convert. What is needed is a two-sided thrust in evangelism, one side encouraging Christians to share their story of faith with neighbor and friend, and the other side providing a program of inquiry as a formal way of dealing with people genuinely interested in converting to Christ. Church members will be more likely to take the first steps of evangelism if there is a support group in the church to carry converts through the various stages of conversion. To bring a person who shows an interest in the gospel into a church that has no program for helping the convert to grow, organize, and deepen his or her experience of Christ is self-defeating.

Third, it must be a congregation willing to actualize the mothering role of the church. In general, most Western churches are a collection of individuals who go to church rather than a community of people who are the church. This is a perversion of the meaning of the church as it was experienced by the early communities of faith and advocated by the Reformers. John Calvin, for example, had the mothering instincts of the early church in mind when he said, "There is no other way to enter into life unless this mother conceive us in her womb, give us birth, nourish us at her breast, and lastly, unless she keeps us under her care and guidance."

Finally, a church that emphasizes ethics and evangelism is confident that its leaders are able to model conversion. In the ancient church, each converting person had a sponsor who was a spiritual director and a living example of what it means to be a Christian.

As we have seen, evangelism in the third century began with the hearing of the gospel and the call to a new lifestyle. The converting people were led step by step to reject their former way of life and enter the new life in Christ as shared and experienced by the Christian community.

A revival of third-century evangelism is required at the end of the twentieth century for several reasons. First, the recovery of the relationship between ethics and evangelism is a biblical task. Jesus' message was less about a belief system and more about a lifestyle. He did not say, "Believe the right things about me," but, "Take up your cross and follow after me." While certain doctrines about Jesus and his mission were developed by the early church, the emphasis still remained on Christian lifestyle. This is evident, for example, in the primitive baptismal catechesis we find in the Letter to the Ephesians.

Second, evangelism that stresses the ethical dimension of the Christian faith is most relevant to our culture, which is pagan and amoral. To reject materialism, greed, sensualism, militarism, power, status and the American way of life, and to affirm peace, justice, the unity of all peoples, the sanctity of human life, human rights and equal economic opportunity, is to be radically different in worldview and action from the world around us.

Third, in liturgical-style evangelism, the third-century church transcended individualistic evangelism and stressed the salvation found in the community of the church. This makes it an evangelism particularly suited to the local church. Through its stages of ever-deepening commitment, and its rites of passage that symbolically represent the conversion journey, liturgical evangelism brings the converting person into a supportive community.

The recovery of the type of evangelism practiced in the third century, adapted to twentieth-century circumstances, could meet the evangelistic needs of the mainline church. Here is a model of evangelism that can involve the whole congregation both in calling other people to Christian discipleship and in strengthening the ethical commitment of the faithful.

14

From Jerusalem to Willow Creek: A Brief History of Christian Worship[1]

THE DEATH OF ALEX Haley early this year reminded Americans of his quest for *Roots*, a quest that awakened the desire of many to understand their own past. For Christians, that curiosity extends beyond family history to the history of the church. In a recent poll conducted by *Christian History* magazine, the question asked most often was, "How did people in the early church worship?" The answer to this question is not historical trivia but a window to our worship of the future.

New Testament Worship

In New Testament times, worship was a response to the life, death, and resurrection of Jesus Christ. For 1 Peter 2:9 states, "You are a chosen people, a royal priesthood, a holy nation, a people belonging to God, *that you may declare the praise of him* who called you out of darkness into his wonderful light"[2] (emphasis added).

That last phrase expresses the New Testament principle that *worship is a response to the gospel*. Here are the reasons for worship: the living, dying, and rising of Jesus; the forgiveness of sin that comes from the work of Christ; and the ultimate overthrow of evil that results from the Christ event.

---

1. Originally published in *Leadership Journal* 13, issue 70, 1992. Used by permission.
2. 1 Peter 2:9, NIV.

While Peter addresses the main reason why the church praises God, Luke gives us the earliest description of how the New Testament Church worshiped. In Acts 2:42 Luke describes early Christian worship: "They devoted themselves to the apostles' teaching and to the fellowship, to the break of bread and to prayer."[3] Here, Luke states the focus of primary worship (apostolic teaching and breaking of bread) and the context of the worship (prayer and fellowship). This picture is expanded by other writers to include singing. For example, Paul admonishes believers to "speak to one another with psalms, hymns, and spiritual songs. Sing and make music in your heart to the Lord."[4]

Let's take a look at worship throughout the history of the church, using the New Testament *why* and *how* of worship as the standard.

Early Christian Worship to AD 300

The church in the first three centuries gets very high marks for its faithfulness to the biblical tradition of worship. Its worship was rooted in the historical work of Jesus Christ and the hope of the new heaven and the new earth. Worship, like that in Revelation 4 and 5, was an experience of heaven, a foretaste of heavenly worship, a songfest with the angels and archangels who surround the heavenly throne and sing the new song.

The *spirit* of worship, like that of the New Testament, was rooted in the living, dying, and rising of Christ. In particular it stressed the theme of the overthrow of the powers of evil.

For example, in the great prayer of thanksgiving said over bread and wine the minister prayed, "When He was betrayed to voluntary suffering that He might destroy death, and break the bonds of the devil . . ." Here, in this record left by Hippolytus in *The Apostolic Tradition* (AD 215), we encounter what has been named the *Christus Victor* theme of the work of Christ. Christ is the victor over sin and death. He is the Lord of the universe. In worship, the church praises God for the defeat of Satan and for the freedom from the power of evil he has secured for believers by the death and resurrection of his Son.

To understand *how* Christians worshiped in the early church we turn to Justin Martyr, who described worship in a document written to the Emperor Titus around AD 150:

---

3. Acts 2:42, NIV.
4. Ephesians 5:19, NIV.

And on the day called Sunday there is a meeting in the place of those who live in cities or the country, and the memoirs of the Apostles or the writings of the prophets are read as long as time permits. When the reader has finished, the president in a discourse urges and invites us to the imitation of these noble things. Then we all stand up together and offer prayers. And, as before, when we have finished the prayer, bread is brought, and wine and water, and the president similarly sends up prayers and thanksgiving to the best of his ability, and the congregation assents, saying the Amen; the distribution, and reception of the consecrated [elements] by each one, takes place and they are sent to the Absent.[5]

Here is the basic form of early Christian worship:

- The Gathering
- Scripture readings
- Sermon
- Prayer
- Bread and wine (Communion)
- Prayers and thanksgiving
- The Amen
- Distribution of the elements
- Bread and wine sent to the absent

Worship in the second century, like that of the New Testament, was twofold. It proclaimed the praise of God for the work of his Son through Scripture (apostolic teaching) and through bread and wine. While this account does not mention singing, we know from other descriptions that the believers sang together.

The Ancient Church: 300–600

After the conversion of Constantine in the beginning of the fourth century, the church continued to worship in the spirit of the New Testament—celebrating the death and resurrection of Jesus Christ and the overthrow of evil. It also maintained the form of New Testament worship:

---

5. Justin Martyr, *First Apology*, 67.

the proclamation of Christ through the reading and preaching of the Word and the enactment of the death and resurrection of Christ at the Table. The church continued to sing—even singing in the Spirit was a central part of worship. (Singing in the Spirit was a spontaneous singing of praise by the congregation, normally at the worship leader's bidding.) Nevertheless, worship went through some changes in the Constantinian era.

In the first three hundred years of Christianity, congregations met mostly in homes or in houses converted into churches. Most assemblies involved probably thirty to sixty people. In this context worship was characterized by informality and intimacy. After the conversion of Constantine, small worshiping communities became the exception. It was now popular to be Christian. The government gave huge basilicas to the church, which were converted into places of worship. Large churches were built as well. The megachurch movement was born in the fourth century!

In this new context, informality was replaced by formality and intimacy was placed by theater. Worship became more highly ordered (the term we use to describe this phenomena is *liturgical*) and more clerical. It centered more around what the clergy did than around what the people did. This change laid the foundation for what took place in the medieval era.

Worship in the Medieval Era: 600–1500

The trend toward formality, theater, and the clericalization of worship that began in the fourth and fifth centuries continued to develop during the medieval era. Both the spirit and the form of New Testament worship was lost, especially in the late medieval period.

First, the church took the spirit of worship—the celebration of the death and resurrection of Christ—and turned it into the sacrificial theory of the Eucharist (the conviction that each celebration of the Eucharist is another sacrifice of Christ). Many excesses were associated with this sacrificial theory of the Eucharist, such as the notion that sacrifices could be sold for the dead.

Next, the reading and preaching of the Word of God fell into disuse as the Eucharist became the main event of worship.

Finally, worship was taken away from the people: It was conducted by the priest with no involvement by the congregation. The Mass was said in Latin, which was no longer the common language. Even the singing was done by choirs. The people were merely spectators at a spectacular program.

Worship among the Reformed: 16th Century

The Protestant Reformers rightly rebelled against the worship of the medieval era and sought to return worship to the biblical and early church tradition. The Reformers disdained the sacrificial theory of the Eucharist and regarded the Roman Catholic Mass as, in the words of Luther, an abomination. They also sought to return worship to the people. Consequently, Reformation worship was in the language of the people. It restored the reading of the Word of God and preaching, and it restored the singing of psalms, particularly by the congregation.

The Reformers also argued for a recovery of both the spirit and form of early Christian worship. Worship for them was a celebration of God's mighty deed of salvation in Jesus Christ, which was to be proclaimed in both Word and Table.

But they disagreed on the use of the ancient ceremonies in worship, specifically, the ceremonies developed in the fourth and fifth centuries that brought theater to worship. These ceremonies included vestments, processions, candles, the use of incense, the services of the Christian year, and forms of song such as Gregorian chant. Both Luther and his followers and the Anglicans argued that these ceremonials *could* be used in worship because they were not expressly forbidden in Scripture. Calvin and the Anabaptists argued that only that which God prescribes in the New Testament may be used in worship. Hence, Lutherans and Anglicans, drawing from the ancient church, have been more liturgical while Calvinists and Free Church people have opted for a more simple, nonceremonial worship.

Worship among Free Church Protestants: 1600–1950

The spirit and the form of worship desired by the Reformers was influenced by the rise of the Enlightenment, which was a rational approach to the Christian faith.

The spirit of worship shifted from a celebration of the death and resurrection to teaching about God from Scripture. And the form of worship among Free Church Protestants during the seventeenth and eighteenth centuries focused primarily on the reading and teaching of God's Word, with the celebration of Communion relegated to the background.

However, this pedagogical approach to worship was quite participatory. It involved the people in prayers, the singing of the psalms, and in a regular discussion of the sermon (yes, as part of worship!).

By the end of the eighteenth century this form of worship had grown too intellectual and the people longed for a more feeling-centered experience of worship. The rise of the evangelistic approach to worship swept away the more pedagogical model. The new, evangelistic model, taken from evangelists like Wesley and Finney, emphasized preaching and the invitation to receive Christ. Its order of worship is well known to Evangelicals today: singing, preaching, and invitation.

Worship since 1950

A theologian once struck an image of what has been happening in the last half of the century when he said, "Let's face it, our kids are choosing either artistry or ecstasy." Artistry is the desire for more order—the liturgical church—and ecstasy is the desire for more freedom—the charismatic church.

The Liturgical Renewal movement asks for a return to worship as a celebration of the death and resurrection of Jesus Christ. Evangelicals are discovering the celebrative nature of a worship centered around the Table—Communion—and the form of worship given at the Table is beginning to be recognized as necessary to the fullness of worship.

The Charismatic movement has called both Catholics and Protestants to a very important aspect of worship—the recovery of song and of the immediacy of the Holy Spirit in worship. This has brought a new openness to healing, particularly the healing of emotions and relationships.

Both of these movements have made such an impact on worship around the world that we can make some predictions for the future of Evangelical worship based on them.

The Future of Evangelical Worship

Today, in addition to the contributions of the Charismatic and liturgical movements, there is a trend among Evangelicals that I believe will eventually reshape the way we worship: the conviction that evangelism and worship are two very different ministries of the church (these two ministries were confused by the development of worship between 1600–1950). Consequently, churches are separating evangelism from worship. Many churches, like Willow Creek Community Church in South Barrington, Illinois, have a Seekers' Service with an evangelistic thrust on Saturday night and Sunday morning, and a Believers' Worship in the middle of the week. This gives worship its rightful place as something different than evangelism or teaching.

In the future I see a return to early Christian worship—rooted in the death and resurrection of Jesus Christ; having balance of both Word and Table; seeking both intimacy and theater; and involve the people in a more participatory way. I call this convergence worship. It is worship full of promise because in it God speaks and acts, and the people respond. It is a worship that is not done to the people or for the people, but by the people.

Contemporary Models of Worship

Liturgical Worship

In *The Liturgy Explained*, Thomas Howard defines liturgical worship as "the work of the people." And this work of the people, he adds, is "to offer themselves and their substance and their praises as an oblation (offering) to God, made acceptable by virtue of the One Offering, namely the sacrifice of our Lord Jesus Christ." Liturgical worship is associated with the ancient Orthodox and Catholic church and among Protestants with the Lutherans and the Anglicans.

The order of liturgical worship is entering into God's presence (Acts of Entrance); hearing God speak (Service of the Word); giving thanks for the death and resurrection (Service of Communion); and being sent forth into the world (Acts of the Dismissal). Within these four acts of worship there are various fixed acts that are repeated in every service. For example, the hymns, prayers, acts of praise, Scripture, responsive reading of psalms, creed, eucharistic prayers, acclamation, and the like are always at the same place in the liturgy. However, the content of the songs, prayers, and Scripture changes from week to week.

Liturgical worship orders the spiritual experience of the worshiping community and "rehearses" the believer's relationship with God. This is known as a sacramental experience.

Traditional Protestant Worship

Traditional Protestant worship is derived from the Reformation and from the modern historical developments between 1600 and 1950. The forms that Protestant worship takes vary significantly. One area of consensus is that in worship a divine action occurs as God speaks and acts, and a human response is made as the people respond with song, prayer, and personal dedication. In modern Protestant churches, particularly those of the mainline (Presbyterian, Methodist, Congregational) there is a conscious effort to move worship in the direction the biblical and historical form of the four acts—Entrance, Word, Table, and Dismissal. While this order is similar to liturgical worship, it is different because it does not use a prayer book and because the parts within each of the four acts of worship are more flexible.

Praise and Worship

The praise and worship tradition is primarily associated with the churches of the Pentecostal and Charismatic movement. This approach to worship has also made an impact on Evangelical churches and newly-formed independent church movements such as Calvary Chapel and The Vineyard. In praise and worship communities the emphasis is on profound adoration, giving God the glory due his name, bowing down before God, drawing near to God, ministering to God in song.

Worship is accomplished through song and instruction. The first thirty minutes is usually spent in singing. This singing usually follows the progression of the Tabernacle—Outer Court, Inner Court, Holy of Holies. The people may begin with Outer Court songs, which set up what is to follow, such as "Enter Into His Gates" and move to Inner Court songs, which are about God, such as "To Thee We Ascribe Glory," followed by Entrance to the Holy of Holies where the community sings more intimate songs to God such as "I Love You Lord." After the congregational singing, there is a time of instruction followed by ministry or more singing.

This approach to worship gives the believer an intense personal sense of ministering to God through songs of praise and worship and of receiving from God a sense of healing in mind, body, and spirit.

Creative Worship

Creative worship is not a particular tradition of worship. Rather it is found here and there among Protestant worshiping communities where Evangelicals are seeking to be more innovative in their worship.

Specifically, it is concerned with communication, particularly through the arts—the use of art, drama, storytelling, and creative dance. Creative worship involves the whole person and communicates through the senses.

This worship does not have a specific form. Rather, it seeks to incorporate the creative arts within the worship common to its own tradition. Thus, a procession may be led by dance; a Scripture may be dramatized or told through story; and the environment may express the season or theme of the day through banners and seasonal decorations.

Seekers Service/Believers Worship

The Seekers Service/Believers Worship is found at Willow Creek Community Church in South Barrington, Illinois, and among hundreds of churches around the world that now follow the Willow Creek model.

The distinction of this model is the separation of evangelism from worship. The Seekers Service is not worship; it is evangelism. It draws on the creative arts and presents the Christian message in a nonthreatening way. The service is like a program, presenting the message through song, drama, and sermon.

The mid-week service, which is for believers, is the church's worship service. This service usually follows the praise and worship model of singing and instruction with Communion celebrated once a month.

Convergence Worship

Convergence worship is growing among those churches aware of what is happening in worship around the world. These churches draw from various communities of worship to enrich their own worship.

Worship is understood as telling and acting out the work of Christ in both the proclamation of Scripture and in the enactment of the drama of the death and resurrection of Christ in Communion. In these acts God is glorified and worshiped. Convergence worship also draws on the music and immediacy of the praise and worship tradition and on the communication arts of the creative approach to worship.

This approach to worship rehearses the believer's relationship to God, involves the whole person—body, soul, and spirit—and engages the gifts of all the people in ministry to God and to each other.

What We Can Learn from Catholic and Charismatic Worship

Traditionally, Evangelicals have been wary of both Catholics and Charismatics because of doctrinal differences. In many cases, our concerns are valid. But in spite of these differences, Evangelicals need to ask, "Is there something we can learn from Catholic and Charismatic worship?"

Catholic: Retaining the Majesty

Like the picture of worship in Revelation 4 and 5, Catholics have a sense of beauty and majesty that is missing in many of our Evangelical churches. We can also learn from their order of worship, an order that goes back to the biblical and historical tradition of worship. It organizes the experience of the congregation around entering into the presence of God, hearing God speak, responding to God at the Table, and being sent forth by God into the world to serve and love the Lord.

Catholic worship is dialogic. Worship is not a one-way monologue but a dialogue between the leader and the people—a kind of drama in which God and the congregation are involved in a communication of proclamation and response. God speaks. The people respond. God acts. The people respond.

Catholics also have the rich heritage of music that goes back to the ancient Gregorian chants and includes the hymnody of the ancient and medieval churches. Many of the new hymnbooks contain these chants and hymns. They are not only beautiful to sing, but they contain a rich and empowering content of praise, adoration, and thanksgiving.

Finally, Catholics have maintained the ancient commitment of the church to regular Communion. While Evangelicals have legitimate concern over the Catholic doctrine of transubstantiation, Evangelicals have gone too far in the act of de-supernaturalizing the presence of Christ at bread and wine. While the early church proclaimed an unexplained, mysterious real presence, we Evangelicals have practiced an explained, non-mysterious real absence. Catholic worship asks us to reconsider our sterile and overly-intellectualized view of what happens at bread and wine.

Charismatics: Experiencing God's Presence

Evangelicals can also learn from the Charismatics. Among Charismatic worshipers there is a desire for intimacy—both with God and with each other. Charismatics, like Catholics, believe in the supernatural presence in Christian worship. They speak of how "God inhabits the praises of his people," how in worship it is possible to experience "the manifest presence of God." This view of the supernatural presence of God in worship can help Evangelicals break through the intellectualized and pedagogical practice of worship.

Charismatics offer us a way of experiencing the presence of God through both their choruses and the ministry of healing and other ministries of help. While some of the choruses are trite, many others are words of Scripture set to hauntingly beautiful and expressive music. These songs, though short, are sung to God and recite the worth and glory of God. They are songs that give the people an opportunity to be personal and intimate with God. While Evangelicals are right in not wanting a steady diet of these songs, there are particular places in worship where they are highly appropriate.

Finally, the presence of God in worship leads the Charismatic worshiper to experience the healing presence of God in worship. God through Jesus Christ not only wants to save us, but to heal us as well. This is the healing of emotions, the healing of relationships, the healing of the spirit. It happens through the ministry of the laying on of hands and the anointing of oil. This ministry may occur at a special time in worship or even after worship. God has called into being more than one group of Christians and gifted each group with a special approach to worship. As we open ourselves to these traditions and learn from them, God not only enriches our worship but blesses us in new and special ways.

Best Resources on Worship

Reference

The New Westminster Dictionary of Liturgy and Worship by J. G. Davies. (Westminster Press, 1986.) This book features brief but thorough articles that define terms and present worship in various communities.

Introduction to Christian Worship

Worship Old and New by Robert Webber. The seminary education on worship that you didn't get. Summarizes biblical roots and historical development of worship, and theology and practice of worship, as well as music and the arts (Zondervan, 1985).

Introduction to Christian Worship by James White. This popular seminary textbook deals with the meaning of Christian worship, the service of the Word and Table, baptism, and other issues (Abingdon, 1990, 2nd edition).

Word, Water, Wine and Bread by William Willimon. An excellent historical survey of the development of worship from its Jewish roots to current practice (Judson, 1980).

How-To Books

Worship: Rediscovering the Missing Jewel by Ronald Allen and Gordon Borror. A popular how-to book that presents guidelines for various aspects of worship, such as planning, music, arts, and the moods of worship (Multnomah, 1982).

Mastering Worship by Jack Hayford, John Killinger, and Howard Stevenson. Three practitioners of worship-leading draw on their learning and experience to provide guidelines for those who struggle with the whats and hows of worship (Multnomah, 1990).

People in the Presence of God by Barry Liesch. Addresses worship from a contemporary point of view. Calls for variety in worship, which includes contemporary choruses, drama, dance, and congregational involvement (Zondervan, 1988).

Up with Worship by Anne Ortlund. Seventy brief tidbits on how to improve worship. Articles cover a range of matters that relate to worship, such as bulletins, prayers, sermons, music, ushers, etc. A practical handbook (Regal, 1982).

Worship Is a Verb by Robert Webber. Presents eight principles for a highly participatory worship (Abbott-Martyn, 1992, 2nd edition).

Inspirational Books

How to Worship Jesus Christ by Joseph S. Carroll. This book is about personal worship. Drawing from Scripture, primarily the book of Revelation, the writer sets forth simple, practical concepts essential to true worship (Moody, 1991).

Worship His Majesty by Jack Hayford. Studies biblical characters and their lives of worship. Emphasizes the principle that people discover genuine wholeness only as they recognize the holiness of God (Word, 1987).

Learning to Worship as a Way of Life by Graham Kendrick. Emphasizes the relationship between personal and corporate worship and how it impacts one's personal lifestyle (Bethany House, 1985).

The Ultimate Priority by John MacArthur, Jr. Calls for a radical lifestyle that seeks to worship God continually, according to a biblical pattern (Moody, 1983).

Real Worship by Warren W. Wiersbe. Combines personal and corporate worship and calls for an integration of the two (Thomas Nelson, 1986).

Periodicals

Worship Leader. This new bimonthly magazine features resource reviews, ideas, and information designed to enhance church worship.

15

Let's Put Worship into the Worship Service[1]

*And let's end gospel pep rallies
and Sunday morning variety shows*

FOR THE PAST DECADE I have made it my business to sample various services of worship and to ask pastors, students, and lay people to define worship for me. Occasionally I have come across some people with extraordinary insight into the subject. But more frequently the answers are groping, tenuous, and even muddled. Recently a student who knows of my interest in worship renewal caught the frustration many of us experience by saying, "We are working against 400 years of neglect."

Unfortunately, there is more truth than fiction in that statement. The fact is that we have not continued the interest in worship demonstrated by the Protestant Reformers. Rather, *we have allowed worship to follow the curvature of culture.*

I contend that there are at least four substitutes for worship in our contemporary culture, substitutes shaped more by the culture than by biblical teaching.

The first may be aptly called *the lecture approach* to worship. The cultural source that gave rise to the "classroom" church is the Enlightenment. The emphasis on the mind, learning, and education to the neglect of the senses and the inner spirit has resulted in a worship mentality that views the sermon as the be-all and end-all of worship. All else is lightly dismissed as "preliminaries."

---

1. Originally published in *Christianity Today*, February 17, 1984. Used by permission.

A second substitute for worship is *evangelism*. This approach to worship resulted when evangelistic field preaching replaced worship in some quarters. It turned the church into an evangelistic tent. In churches influenced by such preaching, Sunday morning is seen as the most propitious time to get the unconverted saved. All else is made subject to this overriding theme. The climactic point of the service is the altar call.

A third replacement for worship occurs when the overriding concern is *entertainment and numbers*. Television has given this approach its powerful support. It speaks in terms of the stage, the performers, the package, and the audience. It is a three-ring circus by the roadside. It gets the crowds, but what it feeds them is frequently shallow, hollow, and tasteless.

Last and not least is *the self-help approach* to Sunday morning. It's the Me generation dressed up in church clothes. Those who attend learn how to affirm and fulfill the possibilities of personal greatness, wealth, health, and beauty. The ministers in churches with this emphasis play into the hands of such narcissistic indulgence. "Come to Jesus, and he will make you one of the beautiful people. An expensive home, a big car, popularity, and power are yours for the asking."

At this point you are probably saying, "Webber, you are too hard on these approaches to worship." Worship, however, is one of the most important callings of the Christian church—along with evangelism, education, mission, fellowship, servanthood, and emotional healing. If some biblical, historical, and theological instruction could help us to *do* worship better, what have we lost?

And "do" is an appropriate word. Worship is not something that someone does for us or to us. Rather, it is done by us. It is a verb, not a noun. It requires action. It is not passive—it is not merely watching or observing.

False approaches to worship perturbed the Reformers. The medieval church had taken worship away from the people and located it in the work of the celebrants and choir. Everyone else watched as if they were at a play. A monumental achievement of the Reformers was to give worship back to the people. Now we have come full circle. Worship no longer belongs to the people. It has become something someone does for us. Ministers lecture at us, move us into decisions, entertain us, and tell us how great we are. And we put up with it. We pay our money, go home, complain, and come back for more.

But the Bible understands worship as God-centered. In worship, God's people act out the Christ event and thereby praise, honor, and glorify God. God himself is present in the telling that occurs through Scripture and preaching. And the God who was in Christ reconciling the world to himself is savingly present as we act out his death and resurrection in the Lord's Supper. In and through the telling and acting out of the Christ story we respond to God in prayer, praise, confession, and thanksgiving. Our purpose is to give, not to get. The giving of praise and the offering of thanks is the supreme calling of the church. In those actions we minister to God and do what we were created to do—give him, Creator, Redeemer, and Judge, the glory due to his matchless name.

It is time to turn our backs on substitutes for real worship and to learn what it means to be a people who truly worship God. We are working against centuries of neglect, so we must not expect instant success. Rather, in our local congregation we must commit ourselves to honest evaluation, to study and prayer, and to new directions for Sunday morning that will bring greater glory to God.

16

Praise and Worship Music: From Its Origins to Contemporary Use[1]

WHAT DO "CONTEMPORARY" WORSHIP, "traditional blended" worship, and "liturgical convergence" worship have in common? Answer: They all use the "contemporary praise and worship chorus" in worship. My goal in this article is to offer a brief description of the origins of the contemporary praise chorus, show how it is used in different worship settings, and comment on the value of praise and worship choruses in your worship.

The Origin of Praise and Worship Choruses

Many readers will remember the phenomenon of the Jesus Movement in the early seventies. By that time, the hippie subculture was in its final stages of dissolution, and the local gathering point for remaining hippies was centered in Southern California, where hippies tripping out on drugs and sex roamed the beaches in search of meaning.

Chuck Smith, the young pastor of a small nearby church, took to the beaches to tell the hippies about Jesus and how meaning could be found through faith in him. Gradually a small group confessed Christ, coming to the church barefoot in hippie dress and with their guitars. Pastor and people opened their hearts and doors to them, and an increasing number of young hippies found Jesus in this loving community. As they began to read the Bible, especially the Psalms, they put music to the stirring words

---

[1]. Originally published in *Pastoral Music*, February-March 2003. Used by permission.

and phrases of psalm texts, giving birth in the process to the contemporary genre of "praise choruses."

One of the early converts of the Jesus Movement was Tommy Coombs. Tommy told me that he was looking for God at the time, that he had been looking in various religions and in drugs, sex, and music (he was the leader of a fairly well-known traveling band), but his search only led him to a sense of increasing loneliness. One day a person from the church pastored by Chuck Smith said to Tommy: "I know where God dwells... he dwells in the worship of this church." Tommy went with him to church. According to Tommy's own testimony, "I opened the door to that church. They were singing (psalm choruses), and I knew I was in the presence of God."

Coombs's entire band became Christian. They turned their life to the worship of God, wrote many of the early choruses, and took to the road to do worship chorus concerts throughout the United States. At the same time this small church established a publishing house for these new choruses: Maranatha! Music. Maranatha! put these choruses on tapes that were sent all over the world. The praise and worship movement had been born. Numerous new churches were established using the praise and worship genre. This style of music spread rapidly among Pentecostals and Charismatics, and lately it has been "I know where God dwells, he dwells in the worship and in the Holy of Holies." The imagination is invoked as people gather at the gates and sing loud songs of entering into the outer court, such as "We Bring the Sacrifice of Praise." Once in the outer court, songs are sung about coming to worship such as "We Bow Down." As the songs transition into the inner court, the congregation sings songs *about* God such as "O Lord, You're Beautiful." Finally the congregation moves into the Holy of Holies. Here quiet songs are sung to God. These songs usually express a personal relationship with God, such as "I Love You, Lord." This song can be quite effective in moving the congregation toward a relationship with God and creating an open and vulnerable spirit to hear the words of God that follow in the preaching time. Most of these churches have no eucharistic theology, although that seems to be changing with a renewed interest in the early church among these communities.

Traditional Blended. Traditional Protestant churches that have incorporated praise and worship songs into their order of worship are described as practicing "blended" worship. Generally, traditional musical instruments such as the piano and organ are united with a guitar; in large churches a full orchestra is used. Traditional churches that have embraced blended worship generally keep their established order of worship but will "frame" a hymn or a psalm with a praise and worship chorus. For example, an opening hymn may be framed with "He is Lord" or the refrain of "Our God Reigns." One hymnbook for blended worship provides suggestions on what hymns and choruses may be "strung together" in a coherent medley of songs that would be sung primarily in the gathering. Many blended worship communities will also sing a blend of hymns and praise songs during the reception of communion. This form of blending traditional and contemporary songs has spread rather widely in traditional Evangelical churches and in some mainline Protestant churches.

Liturgical Convergence. The convergence movement in liturgical churches draws on all musical forms and integrates the best of contemporary choruses as well. Instrumentation in these churches usually includes woodwind and stringed instruments as well as the guitar. These instruments help create an atmosphere of prayer and engage the congregation in songs that are sung from memory. The gathering hymn may be followed by several choruses. After the *Gloria in excelsis Deo* and the confession and absolution, the congregation may linger in quiet singing that expresses relationship and vulnerability. It is incorporated into traditional and "liturgical" churches as well.

During the previous thirty years, the praise and worship movement has spawned a number of different kinds of choruses and songs as well as a huge industry known as Christian Contemporary Music (CCM), located in Nashville. At least three kinds of music have been generated by CCM.

First, many of the new songs put Scripture texts to a contemporary sound. These Scripture songs seldom use more than a phrase or an entire verse usually from the psalms—which is sung over and over again, much like the ostinato style of a Taizé chant.

Second, there are also new songs written by "Christian artists." Most Christian artist music does not lend itself to congregational singing, although some does. For example, the artist may sing a verse and engage the congregation in the chorus.

The third type of song is the worship song. These songs are more complex than praise songs. They invite congregational participation, make use of repetition, and are generally of higher quality both in lyric depth and in musical sound than the praise songs and Christian artist songs.

The Use of Contemporary Praise and Worship Music

As I mentioned at the beginning of this article, there are typically three different styles of worship in which praise and worship songs are used: contemporary, traditional, blended, and liturgical.

Contemporary Worship. What distinguishes contemporary worship from traditional blended and liturgical worship is that contemporary worship only sings choruses. Most of these communities are new independent churches that have emerged in the previous thirty years, but some are formerly traditional churches that have abandoned traditional worship to "go contemporary."

The instrumentation in these churches is always a band. The band includes one or more song leaders and instrumentalists: guitars, piano or synthesizer, a drum set, and, if available, a saxophone. The structure of worship follows a twofold pattern: The congregation sings for twenty to thirty minutes and then a sermon of thirty to forty minutes is preached. The singing is seen as a spiritual journey that follows the path suggested by the structure of the desert Tabernacle (also reflected in the Jerusalem Temple): singing in the outer court, in the inner court, the service of the Word, a chorus may be used in place of a psalm, or the chorus maybe taken from a psalm. A contemporary *Alleluia* may also be wrapped around the reading of the Gospel. There are also contemporary chorus renditions of the creed. In the Eucharist, a contemporary song such as "Holy, Holy, Holy Is the Lord of Hosts" may be sung as the Sanctus. Then, during the reception of the Eucharist, contemporary songs may be sung as people come forward to receive bread and wine. While there is no universally set pattern of singing, a pattern that is often sung during the reception of bread and wine is one that starts with the death of Christ (e.g., "O, The Blood of Jesus"), then moves to the resurrection (e.g., "He is Lord"), then to a more prolonged time of communion with songs of relationship and intimacy (e.g., "As the Deer Panteth for the Water"). Finally a song of great eucharistic joy may be sung, such as "He Is Exalted." The dismissal may be marked by a worship song of going forth into the world, an animated procession, and the words of dismissal as a shout.

While that description indicates where contemporary songs would be included in the liturgy, it is normally true that liturgical convergence practice would not use contemporary choruses at all these places in a single liturgy. An eclectic use of music that includes hymns, psalms, and chant may incorporate choruses at only one or two places each week—and not at the same place from week to week.

The Value of the Contemporary Chorus

Like any other musical genre, the quality of the contemporary chorus covers the spectrum from very poor to very good. The earlier choruses based on Scripture are the best. Choruses written by local musicians for immediate use are usually throwaway choruses that seldom capture the imagination and prayer life of the worldwide movement.

The better choruses provide the congregation with an easy-to-sing prayer response to confession, Scripture reading, and eucharistic reception. They express the longings of the heart and release the felt experience of the worshiper. Another value is in the contemporary sound, though many choruses maybe sung accompanied by the quiet sound of the guitar or in the mystery of the voice only.

In today's world of deeper and deeper subjective experience, these choruses, rightly used in traditional blended or liturgical worship, can create an atmosphere in which the worshiper is enabled to get past the objective and intellectual side of faith to feel the experience of being at worship.

A good resource book for the contemporary chorus is *Renew! Songs and Hymns for Blended Worship*. Many denominations have recently released their own supplemental books of choruses and related materials.

17

Living in the World[1]

EVANGELICAL CHRISTIANITY HAS OFTEN attempted to show its antithesis to the values of the culture by developing a pledge. Almost every evangelical college is characterized by its rules against "smoking, drinking, dancing, and playing cards." This emphasis on trivia misses the main point of Christian separation. To be separate from the world means to conduct our lives in a Christian way. To do this sets us in antithesis to the values of the culture.

To understand this more clearly, let's look at the biblical roots of separation. They are three.

The first is that God's children are a distinct group of people in the world. Peter refers to Christians as "a chosen race, a royal priesthood, a holy nation, a people for God's own possession." They are called "out of darkness into His marvelous light." They are "'aliens and strangers" who are called to keep their "behavior excellent."[2]

The second is a radical commitment to God only. Christians are to have "no other gods."[3] Their God cannot be materialism, sensualism, success, power, or any other worldly god. Only the God of creation is to be served. They are to follow his will and live as "instruments of righteousness to God."[4]

The third is that the Christian lives by the vision of God's kingdom. God's kingdom is both future and present. The future vision is a perfect

---

1. Originally published in *The Post American*, June-July 1974. Used by permission.
2. 1 Peter 2:9–12, NASB.
3. Exodus 20:3.
4. Romans 6:13, NASB.

society. In the ultimate kingdom everyone will live by God's standards, by true values. The present form of the kingdom is simply this: Christians are to live now by the kingdom principles. The Christian is in the world, but does not belong to the world because he lives by different standards and has different goals than the rest of society.

What is the result of taking these three biblical motifs seriously? It brings us into conflict with the system of the world. Paul put it this way: "be not conformed to the world."[5] By this he meant "do not allow yourselves to live by the standards of the world"—greed, selfishness, personal gain, or immorality. But live by those things which are "true, honorable, right, pure, lovely, and of good repute."[6] If we choose to live this way, we will find ourselves opposing the dominant values of society.

In our personal values we are constantly caught in the tension between the desire for power, wealth, recognition, and autonomy as it clashes with the kingdom values of love, compassion, openness, and selflessness. We cannot work or buy or sell or converse with people without participating in the "system-of-the-world." Our conflict is real, unavoidable, inescapable tension between the old order and the new reality by which we are called to live in Christ.

What positive stance does the Christian take toward a world dominated by selfishness, greed, violence, hate, materialism, and injustice? Will the Christian change or alter the direction of society? Will he bring the kingdom of God to earth?

We are led to three biblical notions: the idea of the church as a community of believers; the conviction that this community is the presence of God's kingdom on earth; the belief that in Christ a new humanity is being formed.

In the first place, the testimony of the New Testament is that the church is a true community, a fellowship of believing people. The writer of Acts gives us insight into the earliest Christians who "had all things in common," who sold their property and possessions and "were sharing them with all, as anyone might have need." They were characterized by "one mind" and went from house to house "breaking bread" and took their meals together with "gladness and sincerity of heart."[7] Paul described the church as a "whole building" that was being "fitted together" and "growing into a holy temple in the Lord . . . being built together into

5. Romans 12:2, KJV.
6. See Philippians 4:8, NASB.
7. Acts 2:44–47, NASB.

a dwelling of God in the Spirit."[8] To him, Christians were "one body," clothed with Christ in whom "there is neither Jew nor Greek, neither slave nor free man, neither male nor female"; for all are "one in Jesus Christ."[9] The church is an organism of people, not an organization, or denomination, or hierarchy, not a building, or a program, but people who by faith belong together to Jesus Christ. The role of the Christian in society is not to organize for the promotion of justice but to be a network of people who act as "salt of the earth," "light of the world."[10]

This role of the Christian as "salt and light" undergirds the concept of the church as the active presence of the kingdom of God on earth. As Christians, we are called to "act out" the future kingdom now. We are to be God's kingdom on earth. We are to have an influence on society. We are to live as the distinct community of God's people shaping and patterning our lives according to "kingdom principles."

As such, the church (the body of believers) is a new humanity, a "third force" in society. This collective community of Christians strives to be more Christlike in every aspect of life. This new community of believers acts as a new culture within the old culture. The culture of man is confronted with the culture of God. The principles of evil are confronted by the principles of righteousness. And in this sense there is always a witness to the ultimate kingdom of God in the midst of life. This witness is "salt" because it restrains evil and witnesses to the fact that all human striving stands under the judgment of God, and will some day be exposed for what it is, and destroyed.

The restoration of the true humanity is the key to the church's witness. A Christian family living in a distinctive Christlike style not only exposes the grievous decadence of disintegrated family life, but also points with healing toward the possibilities of new life. A Christian laborer, business person, doctor, or teacher, who dares to live and speak in a truly Christian manner is a force with which few can reckon. A community of believers who live by Christian principles and exercise their prerogative to influence standards of justice in their neighborhood are making the presence of the kingdom felt. Positive, creative, cultural reconstruction is accomplished wherever God's will is obeyed. The person who is in Christ takes seriously his role in culture as the "salt" and "light"

---

8. Ephesians 2:21–22, NASB.
9. Galatians 3:26–28, NASB.
10. Matthew 5:13–16, NASB.

of the world. Consequently, the Christian cannot withdraw from life and meet God in some secret spot where the soul practices a personal religion apart from the issues of life. The fact that he is a new person is determinative for his whole existence. He dare not make a separation between the secular and the sacred. To him, the calling to be the new person is in all of life—at home, at work, with his friends, in his habits and desires, in his role in the community. So the key to the Christian witness in culture lies in the restoration of the true humanity in a community of believers who practice the presence of the kingdom of God.

Valuable insights are gained from examining the message of the prophets. Basically, the prophet is a member of God's Old Testament community, who, like the believers of the New Testament, were God's chosen people on earth. (Although Israel was organized as a theocracy, it was only the real believers within the nation that constituted the true community of God. The same is true today. Not all members of the visible church are members of the community of God.) The community, in the Old and the New Testaments, is made of those people who serve the Lord by their faith, their worship, and their obedience to his revealed will. They are the ones who have been given the responsibility to witness to the righteousness, justice, and love of God. It was out of this community that the prophet emerged to speak the word of God to the nation, to call people to repentance, faith, and obedience. The prophet was not only the spokesman for God, but also of the community. He interpreted the group faith and spoke its far-reaching implications into the heart of the nation and its people. From the prophets, we learn our role in society. First of all, the prophet never shrank from preaching to the nations. Because of their perversion of justice, their indifference to the plight of the needy, their exploitation of the poor, their immorality and their indifference to God, Amos declared that God would destroy them and "Spare them no more."[11] The community of God in the twentieth century is also represented by those of prophetic vision who proclaim the judgment of God against society for its moral, social, legal, and personal sins. Today's prophet cannot fear the charge of being unpatriotic or unsympathetic with his nation. As a spokesman for God, he stands above the culture in which he finds himself. As God's mouthpiece, the Christian in today's world is called to speak out against national wickedness of every sort and call people to repentance and obedience. But it is incumbent upon the community of

---

11. Amos 8:2, NASB.

Christ in the world to bring a positive as well as a negative witness into society. Positively, as a community of the new humanity, Christians are to exemplify how God wants all men to live. In obedience to the will of God, the Christian community is to be a people of love, forgiveness, repentance, holiness, and faith. They are to manifest the future kingdom by living in obedience to God's kingdom of truth, justice, righteousness, and love.

A second prominent note in prophetic preaching is the theme of injustice in the social order. Exploitation, cruelty, and injustice in the nation always aroused the intense anger of the prophets, who went beyond the pious phraseology of principles to the bold task of making people uncomfortable with specifics. Micah, for example, spoke with anger against the large landholders who flourished at the expense of the owners of small holdings. He protested against the greed of these men because it contradicted the demand of God for justice. Shocked at their disregard for personal and social values and their lust for power, Micah proclaimed the judgment of God against them.[12]

Men who were involved in business and trade, then as now, were tempted to exploit and dehumanize their fellow men in order to get rich. So dedicated were they to the pursuit of gain that they despised and profaned the holy days of Israel, trampled on the needy and destroyed the poor. Isaiah denounced them by crying, "He looked for justice, but behold, bloodshed; for righteousness, but behold, a cry of distress."[13] Even the religious leaders and rulers of Israel participated in the corruption of society. Called to uphold law and justice and righteousness, Israel's leaders are described by Micah as those who "hate good and love evil."[14] They "abhor justice and twist everything that is straight"; they "build Zion with bloodshed and Jerusalem with violent injustice"; they "pronounce judgment for a bribe, her priests instruct for a price, and her prophets divine for money," charges Micah.[15] Even though they talk piously and say, "Is not the Lord in our midst? Calamity will not come upon us."[16] Nevertheless Micah warns that "Zion will be plowed as a field, Jerusalem

---

12. Micah 2:1–3.
13. Isaiah 5:7, NASB.
14. Micah 3:2.
15. Micah 3:9–11a, NASB.
16. Micah 3:11, NASB.

will become a heap of ruins, and the mountain of the temple will become high places of a forest."[17]

A third theme of prophetic preaching is the position taken against sensuality. The unrighteous are "heroes in drinking wine, and valiant men in mixing strong drink; who justify the wicked for a bribe, and take away the rights of the ones who are in the right."[18] Because of their irresponsibility toward society they "do not pay attention to the deeds of the Lord, nor do they consider the works of his hands."[19] Wine, claims Hosea, has taken away the "understanding" of God and has resulted in the worship of a "wooden idol" and departure "from their God."[20]

The issue, then as now, is that the man who seeks the sensuous life denies by his passions and attitudes the claim of God over his life. The positive witness is that God's demand is total. He wants nothing less than the radical dedication of the whole man to the service of God in right living. Anything that stands in the way of the goal of the new man must be shunted aside and put out of one's life.

A fourth emphasis of prophetic preaching focused on the popularity of easy and false religion. Although corruption and injustice was at an all-time high, religion, then as now, was also highly respected. The rulers, leaders and laity of Israel who promoted injustice also promoted the regular services of worship, the rituals of ceremonial law, and the sacrifices. Religion was at an all-time high and the prosperity of the age was generally accepted as the blessing of God flowing from his gratitude with the religious fervor of Israel. But the prophets, seeing through the phoniness of established religion, declared that God hated their religious performances:

> I hate, I reject your festivals,
> Nor do I delight in your solemn assemblies,
> Even though you offer up to Me
> burnt offerings and your grain offerings,
> I will not accept them;
> and I will not even look at the peace offerings of your fatlings.
> Take away from Me the noise of your songs;
> I will not even listen to the sound of your harps.[21]

17. Micah 3:12, NASB.
18. Isaiah 6:12, 22–23, NASB.
19. Isaiah 5:12, NASB.
20. Hosea 4:11–12.
21. Amos 5:21–23, NASB.

The prophets clearly saw the meaning of the popular religion of Israel. They knew that Israel was not really worshiping God—but herself. The prophets went to the root of popular religion. It was idolatrous in nature. The Israelites were using God for their own benefit, they were trying to manipulate him, to insure that he was on their side. Their crass form of religion, like institutionalized Christianity, looks at the worship of God from a purely external sense. As long as they followed the rules, they thought, God would be pleased with them and dole out all sorts of favors. This kind of worship is an abomination to God, because God demands the service of the whole man in dedication to himself evidenced through a concern for righteousness and justice in the land. The prophets, knowing this, always connected the call to repentance, amendment of one's ways, and a concern for justice as God's desire in contrast to the popular religion. So Amos, like the other prophets, ends his condemnation of phony religion and cries out, "Let justice roll down like waters, and righteousness like an ever-flowing stream."[22]

The prophetic message (one which should be preached today) was directed, as we have seen, against the culture of the day. But we miss the whole point of prophetic preaching if we see it as a negative message delivered for the purpose of dividing the disobedient from the person genuinely intent on living out God's will. Instead, the thrust of the prophetic proclamation is positive. It is a call to action, a call to repentance, a call to renewal and change through a commitment of life to the will of God. The person who takes this preaching seriously and determines to live by its word will be, without even working at it, a witness to the kingdom of God.

Christianity is about living in the world. Let me conclude with an excerpt from a second century document (*The Letter to Diognetus*) that summarizes what it means for a Christian to live in the world.

> For Christians cannot be distinguished from the rest of the human race by country or language or customs. They do not live in cities of their own; they do not use a peculiar form of speech; they do not follow an eccentric manner of life. This doctrine of theirs has not been discovered by the ingenuity or deep thought of inquisitive men, nor do they put forward a merely human teaching, as some people do. Yet, although they live in Greek and barbarian cities alike, as each man's lot has been cast, and follow the customs of the country in clothing and food and other

---

22. Amos 5:24, NASB.

matters of daily living, at the same time they give proof of the remarkable and admittedly extraordinary constitution of their own commonwealth. They live in their own countries, but only as aliens. They have a share in everything as citizens, and endure everything as foreigners. Every foreign land is their fatherland, yet for them every fatherland is a foreign land. They marry, like everyone else, and they beget children, but they do not cast out their offspring. They share their board with each other, but not their marriage bed. It is true that they are "in the flesh," but they do not live "according to the flesh." They busy themselves on earth, but—their citizenship is in heaven. They obey the established laws, but in their own lives they go far beyond what the laws require. They love all men, and by all men are persecuted. They are unknown, and still they are condemned; they are put to death, and yet they are brought to life. They are poor, and yet they make many rich; they are completely destitute, and yet they enjoy complete abundance. They are dishonored, and in their very dishonor are glorified; they are defamed, and are vindicated. They are reviled, and yet they bless; when they are affronted, they still pay due respect. When they do good, they are punished as evildoers; undergoing punishment, they rejoice because they are brought to life. They are treated by the Jews as foreigners and enemies, and are hunted down by the Greeks; and all the time those who hate them find it impossible to justify their enmity.[23]

---

23. "Letter to Diognetus."

18

Easter: Reliving the Mystery[1]

MONTGOMERYVILLE BAPTIST, A VENERABLE stone church with several huge maples in front and a sprawling cemetery behind, sits proudly on the south side of Pike 309. Rumor has it George Washington once worshiped there.

For most people it is a typical evangelical Baptist church. But for me, it is special—my father was the pastor, and it was there I worshiped as a teenager.

Worship from Sunday to Sunday was quite typical—a few hymns, prayers, Scripture reading, and a sermon. But at least twice a year Christmas and Easter worship leaped out of second gear into overdrive. I remember Easter especially.

Easter was not simply a single day at Montgomeryville. It always included at least Palm Sunday, Good Friday, and Easter Sunday itself. What made these days memorable was the style of worship. We moved out of the usual verbal communications alone to act out the events.

I have long since forgotten the sermons, but I can still remember marching with a palm in my hand, standing before the large, wooden cross, and getting up early for the open-air sunrise service before an empty tomb.

This dramatic re-enactment of the death and resurrection of Christ was done out of instinct as though we knew Marshall McLuhan was right: "The medium is the message." When we not only told the story but acted it out, the message took on new life.

---

1. Originally published in *Christianity Today*, March 21, 1986. Used by permission.

Years later, when I began to study worship, I discovered that our acting out of the Easter events at Montgomeryville was rooted in traditions that go back to the early church. Traces of those traditions are found in the New Testament.

Easter in the early church

In the church of the first centuries after Christ, every Sunday was a "little Easter." The Easter season itself (not unlike that at the church of my childhood) was a special event in which the living, dying, and rising of Christ was not only told in words, but acted out in a participatory drama.

The earliest evidence of an Easter celebration in the New Testament is found in the words of Paul written to the Corinthian community about AD 55: "Christ our Passover has been sacrificed for us."[2] The clue to how Easter may have been celebrated in the primitive Christian community is found in the word *Passover*, for the earliest Christians were Jews.

Jewish worship passed two emphases on to early Christian worship: First, worship was rooted in an event. The Passover service, for example, celebrated the exodus, when God brought the Israelites out of Egypt and made them into his people. Second, celebrating that event in worship made it contemporaneous—the original power of that event evoked feelings among contemporary worshipers similar to the response of the original participants in the event. The event was celebrated and made contemporary by telling the story and acting it out.

It was natural that the early Christians would adopt a worship style similar to the Jewish one. For example, early Christian worship was built around Word and table—a two-fold way of enacting revelation (God spoke) and incarnation (God became one of us). Dramatic re-enactment was especially seen at the table where the action of taking, blessing, breaking, and giving the bread and taking, blessing, and giving the cup re-enacted the Lord's last supper. The idea of acting out the full story sprang from the nature of the Lord's Supper, where the actions were as important as the words.

Perhaps the best insight into Easter worship as story told and acted out comes from the writing of a woman named Egeria. Her *Diary of a Pilgrimage* contains a firsthand account of Easter in Jerusalem in the late

---

2. 1 Corinthians 5:7, NASB.

fourth century. The diary, together with liturgies from that period, provides us with an inspiring picture of Easter in the early church.

In those days, preparation for Easter began seven weeks before the date. There was an emphasis on personal identification with the suffering of Jesus. These ancient Christians were convinced that the resurrection could not be adequately experienced without traveling the way of death themselves. They desired to fulfill Jesus' admonitions of Mark 10 in a literal way by taking up the cross and going up to Jerusalem with him.[3] They wanted to drink of the cup that he drank,[4] and to be baptized with his baptism.[5] (Our Lord's forty-day fast in the desert suggested the forty days of Lent.)

While this forty-day experience emphasized fasting and prayer, it was not done in the spirit of legalism or ritualism. The intent was to prepare for Easter by reliving the mystery. Fasting and prayer were not ends in themselves—they led the participants into a deeper experiential appreciation of the mystery of salvation through a subjective identification with Christ. By hearing the Word and by acting it out—not just for a day, but over a period of time—the message took hold more firmly.

Holy Week

According to Egeria, what we call Holy Week was known as the "Great Week"[6] in fourth-century Jerusalem. This week of the climactic events of the arrest, conviction, crucifixion, death, burial, and resurrection of Christ is the most extraordinary week in the Christian calendar, the week in which the redemption of the world happened, in which the re-creation of the world began.

Egeria describes the day-to-day events of the Great Week:

- On *Palm Sunday*, all the Christians assembled at the top of the Mount of Olives. Grasping palms and branches in their hands, they sang, "Blessed is he who comes in the name of the Lord,"[7] as they walked slowly to the church in Jerusalem. The bishop of Jerusalem, symbolizing Christ, was in the midst of the crowd. When night fell,

---

3. Mark 10:33.
4. Mark 10:39.
5. Mark 10:39.
6. Egeria, *Diary of a Pilgrimage*, 103.
7. Matthew 23:39, NASB.

evening prayers were celebrated, concluded by a prayer in front of a cross erected for the occasion.[8]

- On *Monday*, they continually sang hymns and antiphons, and read passages from the Scriptures appropriate to that day in Holy Week. Egeria reports that these readings and songs were continually interrupted with prayers.[9]

- On *Tuesday*, they did the same except for this: "The Bishop takes up the book of the Gospels, and while standing, reads the words of the Lord which are written in the Gospel according to Matthew at the place where he said 'Take heed that no man deceive you.'"[10]

- On *Wednesday*, everything was done as on Monday and Tuesday except that the bishop read the passage where Judas went to the Jews to set the price they would pay him to betray the Lord.[11] Egeria reports that "while this good passage is being read, there is such moaning and groaning from among the people that no one can help being moved to tears in that moment."[12] (This, and similar comments throughout her account, suggest the powerful effect that re-enactment can have on the worshipers' feelings.)

- On *Thursday* evening, Communion was celebrated. Then all went home to eat their last meal until Easter, and later returned to worship all night as a way of re-enacting the Gospel accounts of Thursday night. "They continually sing hymns and antiphons and read the Scripture passages proper to the place and to the day. Between these, prayers are said."[13]

- Early on *Friday*, after worshiping all night, the Christians proceeded to Gethsemane, where they read the passage describing the Lord's arrest.[14] Egeria reports that "there is such moaning and groaning with weeping from all the people that their moaning can be heard practically as far as the city." They then went to the place of the

---

8. Egeria, *Diary*, 104–5.
9. Egeria, *Diary*, 106.
10. Egeria, *Diary*, 106.
11. Matthew 26:14ff.; Mark 14:10ff.; Luke 22:3–6ff.
12. Egeria, *Diary*, 107.
13. Egeria, *Diary*, 108.
14. Matthew 26:36–56.

cross where the words of Pilate were read.¹⁵ Then the bishop sent the crowd home to meditate, instructing them to return about the second hour so that everyone would be "on hand here so that from that hour until the sixth hour you may see the holy wood of the cross, and thus believe that it was offered for the salvation of each and every one of us."¹⁶

- On *Friday night*, they acknowledged the cross as the instrument of salvation. A cross was put on a table and the people passed by "touching the cross and the inscription, first with their foreheads, then with their eyes; and after kissing the cross, they move on."¹⁷

- On *Saturday*, worship was conducted at the third and sixth hours. After nightfall the Easter vigil was held.¹⁸ Although Egeria says little about this service, we know from other sources that it was a dramatic re-enactment of the resurrection. It included a service of light that celebrated Christ as the light of the world, and the annual baptismal service in which people were baptized into Christ's dying and rising. (The early church practice of baptism by immersion was a graphic enactment of burial and resurrection.) And the glorious service that occurred on Sunday morning (after the all-night vigil) celebrated the resurrection of Christ through readings, antiphons, preaching, and the Eucharist.

Consider the involvement, the total immersion in the death and resurrection of their Lord that the worshipers must have experienced. For weeks they had prepared for this service. Then, throughout Holy Week, they had been exhausted by the intensity of following after the events in Jesus' life that led to his death. Now, after another night of vigil and anticipation, the moment of Jesus' resurrection came. Because these people had entered the tomb with him, they were able to experience his resurrection—in a way that would never happen apart from the dramatic journey they had taken.

Finally, Egeria tells us that Easter did not end on Easter day. It was followed by eight days of celebration.¹⁹ The worshipers' fast was over.

15. Matthew 27:2–26; Mark 15:1–15; Luke 23:1–25; John 18:28, 19:16.
16. Egeria, *Diary*, 110.
17. Egeria, *Diary*, 111.
18. Egeria, *Diary*, 114.
19. Egeria, *Diary*, 117.

They identified no longer with death, but with resurrection and life. For eight days the Christians gathered in worship. These festive services were in sharp contrast to the sober preparations for the Passion. They extended the resurrection side of Easter even as fasting had prepared for the crucifixion.

Traditions for today

For us today, the principle of re-enactment can guide the development of Easter traditions in our local churches. First, regaining a full tradition of Easter—one that stretches back forty days through Lent and forward fifty days to Pentecost—will help us mark time Christianly. Frozen foods, central heat, electric lights, and other modern marvels have robbed our lives of their daily and seasonal rhythms. A week in the office in bleak January is indistinguishable from a work week in budding April.

But this is hardly the biblical experience of time. Biblical time is marked by weekly and seasonal feasts and fasts and by a history full of significant events and signs of hope. In Holy Week the world leans into the future when Christ will return to establish his kingdom over all the earth. Thus, this week of weeks not only celebrates the past, but anticipates the future. It is the source from which all time proceeds.

Second, when we act out Easter as well as tell about it, we employ means of communication that both build on the strengths and repair some of the damage of the television age.

One strength of the television age is the restoration of visual communication. We remember what we see and hear so much better than what we merely hear. Of course, the written word will never and should never become passé, but the communications revolution of the twentieth century is restoring visual and action-oriented communication to its rightful place.

The curse of television has been to encourage passive attitudes and short attention spans. We have become content to sit and watch a stream of thirty-minute sit-coms and thirty-second commercials rather than to become engaged with ideas or to build relationships (as we do when we invest hours in a challenging book or practice the art of conversation—or even play parlor games).

But participatory worship, especially the re-enactment of Easter and the other great Christian events, can help fight passivity and restraint and restore fervent faith.

We can enhance our worship by rediscovering the power of dramatic participation. Drama is no substitute for preaching and teaching. But it is another way of proclaiming the message. It not only says, it does. And it draws us into action. Dramatic participation in worship, like my adolescent memories of Montgomeryville Baptist Church, has staying power.

19

From Modern to Postmodern: Worship Changes During the Twentieth Century[1]

Introduction

THE INTENT OF THIS writing is to present and evaluate the changes that have taken place in worship during the twentieth century, with general reference to the Protestant church, and particular emphasis on the Free Church tradition.

There has been very little thoughtful engagement with worship in the Free Church tradition from which we can draw. For example, the study of worship as a biblical, historical, and theological discipline has been neglected in the Free Church seminary curriculum. Worship has been relegated to the practical department as if it were only a matter of skill. To further complicate the study of Evangelical worship, worship has been defined almost exclusively as music. While music courses and degrees have proliferated and a musical history can be written, the same cannot be said for a theologically-driven understanding of Free Church worship.

This divorce between the academic study of worship and the emphasis on worship as music makes the evaluation of Free Church worship difficult because there appears to be no biblical or theological standard against which Free Church worship may be evaluated. The study of Free Church worship is thereby reduced to a history of preaching, a history of music style, a history of form, or a history of the relationship between

---

1. Originally published in *The Southwestern Journal of Theology*, Summer 2000. Used by permission.

worship and culture. While all these histories are important academic inquiries, this study will concentrate primarily on the relationship between worship and culture and treat matters of preaching, music, and form only tangentially as they may bear on the subject at hand.

I. Free Church Worship 1750–1960

In the last two hundred years Free Church worship has interacted with two cultures. Both the Enlightenment, the dominant culture, and the Romantic era, a subculture of the Enlightenment, have played significant roles in shaping worship in the Free Church tradition.

Rene Descartes, father of the Enlightenment, found his place in intellectual history because of his famous dictum "I think therefore I am." Descartes argued for the authority of reason, the autonomy of the individual, and the ability to arrive at provable propositions through the use of the empirical methodology based on observation and analysis.

Both before and immediately after Descartes's life, culture was going through the revolution from the medieval worldview to what has come to be known as modernity. The cosmological revolution shifted the understanding of the world from the moral cosmology of the medieval church to the radical and worldview-changing cosmology of the Newtonian world machine. The world, it was argued, is subject to laws that function just like a machine. Consequently, there was an epistemological shift from revelation to knowledge attained through reason, experience, and science. God's revelation was subsequently put under the scrutiny of this new methodology, and biblical and historical criticism were born.

While some Free Church pastors paid little attention to the intellectual trends of the time, others, particularly seminary professors, set out to discredit the modern attack on Scriptures and defend the Bible. Graduates who studied under these professors took the battle out of the classroom into the church, turning worship into a time for teaching right truth. While churches continued to sing, read Scripture, pray, and occasionally celebrate the Lord's Supper, the high point of worship was the sermon. This approach to worship reflects the strong emphasis on knowledge that derived from the culturally forming influence of the Enlightenment. This sermon-centered pedagogical approach to worship has endured into the twentieth century and is still found in many churches today.

A second influence on worship in the modern world derives from the influence of the Romantic era. The Romantic era of the nineteenth century was a vigorous and intentional attack on rationalism by those who were committed to knowledge through experience and intuition. At the same time that William Wordsworth and Samuel Coleridge were leading the attack against the Enlightenment emphasis on reason, a whole new approach to the faith and its worship was erupting in the work of the new evangelists—Charles Wesley (1707–1788), John Wesley (1703–1791), George Whitefield (1714–1770), and, in America, the work of Charles Finney (1792–1875).

Like the Romantics, the evangelists had little regard for rational intellectualism. For them, it was a waste of time to defend the Bible against the critics. They insisted the Bible did not need to be defended as much as it needed to be believed and acted on. For these evangelists, the central message of the Bible is that man is a sinner who needs to trust in Jesus and be born again. For them, the Wesleyan experience of a heart "strangely warmed" and a testimony that "he saved *me, even me*" was significantly more important in the ultimate sense of the word than reasons for the faith.

These evangelists engendered a whole new approach to worship, based on experience and an emotional way of knowing. The evangelistic service which they held in the fields and marketplaces was now transferred to numerous local churches by their earnest followers. It was this flame of evangelism that spread across America in what James White the calls "frontier worship." While some of the "heady" churches shifted to this new radical approach of evangelistic worship, most churches that adopted the model of worship evangelism were new-start churches that were founded all across America by the numerous itinerant evangelists. In this style of worship, the threefold pattern of "singing, preaching, and inviting" took hold in the great majority of free churches.

These two approaches to worship—one shaped by the Enlightenment and its emphasis on reason and the other shaped by Romanticism with its emphasis on experience—were locked into a silent battle at the beginning of the twentieth century. Throughout the twentieth century, in spite of all the changes that have occurred in culture and in worship, these two approaches to worship still exist.

Traditional Free Church worship, forged out of the Enlightenment and taking an educational approach to worship, continues with some changes to the Free Church worship model of 1870:

- Choral call to Worship
- Invocation
- Hymn of Worship
- Devotional Scripture Reading
- Hymn of Devotion
- Principal Prayer
- Hymn of Preparation
- Sermon
- Prayer
- Final Hymn
- Benediction

Evangelistic worship from the Romantic era, with some slight changes, continues with the threefold pattern of:

- Singing
- Preaching
- Invitation

A hybrid model has also appeared in which some churches have dropped the invitation but continue the twofold pattern of singing and preaching, with preaching geared toward educating God's people rather than evangelizing the sinner. The hybrid model is more common in the northern states, whereas the evangelistic model is more frequently found in the southern states.

Evaluation

How are we to evaluate the pedagogical, revivalistic, and hybrid models of worship? First, by comparison to Reformation worship with its emphasis on the worship of God, the focus of modern Protestant worship shifts to a preoccupation with self. The emphasis on self is evident in the insistence of "knowing" and "experiencing." In sermon-oriented worship, worship has accomplished its goal if the worshiper has gained new insights. In revivalistic worship, worship has accomplished its goal if it results in conversions.

Free Church worship planners ask "what should worship accomplish?" Their answer is that worship should teach the saint or save the sinner. But biblical worship asks, "What does worship represent?" A study of Revelation 4–5 shows us that worship represents God's saving action in Jesus Christ through re-presentation. When our worship proclaims and enacts God's saving deeds culminating in Jesus Christ, it does have the effect of forming the saint and transforming the sinner. However, the motivating factor of our worship planning is neither personal knowledge nor experience, but a signification of God's saving action in Jesus Christ that we remember, proclaim, and enact to the glory of God.

II. The Cultural Disruption and Worship Changes Between 1960 and 1990

Cultural analysts recognize a huge shift that began to take place in American culture immediately after World War II. The nation turned its attention away from matters of war to national concerns such as economic growth, education, the emergence of middle-class America, and the shift from an industrial to an information-based society. Sociologist Francis Fukuyama points out in his book *The Great Disruption* that during this time of change (1960–1990) a great disruption occurred in the social values of the Western world. His hypothesis is that "just as economies... were making the transitions from the industrial to the information era" there were also "negative social trends" that "reflected weakening social bonds and common values holding people together in Western societies."[2] These two movements were so intricately held together that "with all the blessings that flow from a more complex, information-based economy, certain bad things also happened to our social and moral life."[3] For example Fukuyama asserts: "The culture of intensive individualism, which in the marketplace and laboratory leads to innovation and growth, spilled over into the realm of social norms where it corroded virtually all forms of authority."[4]

This rebellion against authority was uniquely expressed in the culture of the 1960s where the "breaking of the rules becomes, in a sense,

---

2. Fukuyama, *Great Disruption*, 5.
3. Fukuyama, *Great Disruption*, 5.
4. Fukuyama, *Great Disruption*, 5.

the only remaining rule."[5] The 1960s initiated the "forward looking generation"[6] in which the insights of the past were regarded as inferior to the social revolutions that, it was believed, were creating a better future.

The church and its worship were directly affected by these cultural changes. Just as society in general was calling into question the authorities and traditions of the past, a new group of revolutionaries rose up in the ranks of the church to introduce new ways of being the church and new ways of doing worship that were regarded as more culturally relevant.

In brief, two significant changes have taken place. The first is the shift toward a more culturally-relevant, subjectively-oriented approach to worship in the Pentecostal, Charismatic, and praise and worship traditions. The second is a more objectively-oriented approach to worship in the Catholic and mainline church traditions, which included a renewal of the arts. The following brief review of these movements and their manifestations between 1960 and 1990 will help us interpret and understand the movements since 1990 that are propelling the Free Church traditions in new directions in the twenty-first century where it corroded virtually all forms of authority.

Subjective Worship

The Rise of the Pentecostal Movement

The Pentecostal movement traces its origins to the Holiness movement of the nineteenth century and to its roots in the spirituality of John Wesley. Culturally, it is the earliest of the movements toward a more subjective worship. Edith Blumhofer[7] writes, "Because they dealt in verities that touched the deepest human emotions, they regarded tears, groans, vocal praise and audible individual prayers as appropriate, even necessary, in corporate and individual praise."

This American Pentecostal movement traces its origin to 1906, to the outburst of speaking in tongues, and to this day regards tongue

---

5. Fukuyama, *Great Disruption*, 14.

6. Fukuyama, *Great Disruption*, 14.

7. Edith Blumhofer was a professor of history at Wheaton College from 1999 to 2017. She wrote extensively about American religious history and Pentecostalism. Dr. Webber did not specify the source(s) of these quotations.

speaking as the manifestation of the reception of the spirit. Its worship is characterized by the unique experience of "singing in the Spirit."

This happens as a congregation moves from singing a worship song into sung expressions of individual praise. Singing in the same key and moving among several basic chords, individuals express their feelings in words meaningful to them. The music may seem to flow from one individual to another, the voice of one occasioning another's participation until many are involved.

According to Blumhofer, the original approach to Pentecostal worship changed after 1960 as they "abandoned the musical vocabulary through which they had once understood and expressed the meaning of their religious experience." By the late 1960s singing "occurred only at stated times in the service," and Pentecostal worship became influenced by styles of worship common to Charismatic and praise and worship churches. Consequently, "with the acceptance of praise choruses came a turn toward the charismatic practices like standing for long periods at the beginning of services, lifting up hands, and repeating the same choruses." Pentecostals lost their unique approach to worship and began to assimilate styles of worship emerging in the Charismatic and praise and worship churches.

The Charismatic Movement

The unique character of the Charismatic movement is its emphasis on "the power of God and the manifestation of miraculous and revelatory gifts of the Spirit, especially tongues and prophecy." While this movement became quite prominent during the 1960s and 1970s, its origin is traceable to an early time. For example, the Christian cell movement of the late 1940s and 1950s was already emphasizing the free use of charismatic gifts as well as healing and "body ministry." The term *charismatic* was probably first used at the fourth international convention of the Full Gospel Business Men's Fellowship International (FGBMFI) held in Minneapolis on June 25–29, 1956.

It was during the 1960s that the Charismatic movement began to find increasing acceptance in both traditional Protestant and Catholic churches. In the late 1960s a yearly Charismatic conference was held at Notre Dame University in South Bend, Indiana. Thousands of both Catholic and traditional Protestant Christians came to these conferences and returned to their denominations and local churches to spread the charismatic experience.

The heart of the charismatic experience has always been its worship, and within its worship, the manifestation of the gifts. D. L. Alford[8] has written that "freedom in worship, joyful singing, both vocal and physical expressions of praise, instrumental accompaniment of singing, and acceptance of a wide variety of musical styles are all characteristic of this renewal" and that "it is not unusual to find charismatic worshippers singing, shouting, clapping hands, leaping, and even dancing before the Lord, as they offer him sincere praise and thanksgiving." By the end of the 1980s charismatic worship was well established in America and around the world. In the meantime a third movement with some similarity to both the Pentecostal and charismatic approaches to worship emerged, the Praise and Worship movement.

The Praise and Worship Movement

The origins of the Praise and Worship movement are generally associated with the revival that took place among the hippies of the 1960s. As the hippie movement began to dissipate, many hippies moved to the beaches of southern California with the hopes of reviving the movement or at least keeping it going.

These children of the Sixties, as noted by Chuck Fromm of Maranatha! Music, focused on a "strange new figure—the counter cultural anti-hero, enemy of authority, committed free thinker, impassioned free lover, obsessive researcher." These anti-hero figures were "standard bearers of a new consciousness" and were found in every discipline, but nowhere were they more prominent than in the music of the new rock culture. These anti-hero, counterculture, rock-crazed kids were touched by the gospel and spawned a new countercultural church and worship that has reached around the world.

During the final years of the sixties, outreach movements to these young people sparked what came to be known as the "Jesus Movement." National attention was immediately focused on this movement, the outbreaks of thousands of conversions in major cities (especially the West

---

8. D. L. (Delton) Alford is a music director in the Church of God and professor of music at Lee University. He has written several books and articles about music in Pentecostal and Charismatic churches. Dr. Webber did not specify the source(s) of these quotations.

Coast), the rise of coffee houses, the emergence of new youth culture churches, and of course, the rise of new forms of Christian music and a new pattern of worship.

The epicenter of the Jesus Movement appears to be Calvary Chapel in Costa Mesa, California. In 1968 the church, pastored by Chuck Smith, was a small community of 150 people. Today the church averages more than 20,000 people in its weekly services and has spun off more than 300 daughter churches, some of them with congregations of over 5,000 people.

Tommy Coomes, the leader of a rock group known as LoveSong, was a key player in the emergence of the new music and the emergence of a pop instrumentation that included electric guitars, keyboards, and various percussion instruments. This secular rock and roll band was earning its way in bars and nightclubs. Under the leadership of Tommy they lived communally and experimented with drugs and Eastern mysticism. But Tommy, who was looking for God, was invited to visit Calvary Church at Costa Mesa, California. He and four members of the band were converted. They then began to write new songs from the Scripture (especially the Psalms) and were soon invited to play their songs at Calvary Church. They subsequently went on the road and performed their songs in churches and schools throughout the states. By the mid-1970s they had inspired dozens of other groups as well as hundreds of other writers and musicians who spawned a whole new genre of music and worship. A new industry known as Contemporary Christian Music (CCM) also emerged, as well as specific organizations such as Maranatha! Music, Integrity-Hosanna, Mercy Publishing, and a host of smaller ministries that contributed to the worldwide spread of the Praise and Worship movement.

Evaluation

While these three movements have captured worldwide attention and have been received enthusiastically by many church leaders, an awareness is beginning to emerge that the subjective approach to worship is not adequately rooted in a biblical and theological understanding. Critic Henry Jauhiainen, a Pentecostal minister, writes: "A serious defect . . . is the lack of intense, in-depth biblical and theological reflection upon the nature of worship. As a result, worship tends to be a means to an end, whether that be church growth, personal fulfillment, or the defeat of God's enemies. Worship tends to become a utility or a self-absorbing experience.... Pragmatism wins over theology; that which attracts and holds a crowd is seen as that which God endorses."

Jauhiainen makes a number of observations about this new movement, observations that are becoming widespread as more leaders are beginning to agree with his basic criticism stated above. He voices four themes worth noting:

1. The need for worship to correspond to truth. Because worship and faith share a common hermeneutic, what is done in worship should harmonize with our teaching. For example, when worship is triumphalistic, it detracts from the essential message of humility and the daily need for God's grace and mercy.
2. The need for worship to recover its christological focus. We fail, Jauhiainen insists, to declare "the total redemptive story" in our praise and worship churches.
3. The need to recover a true sense of mystery in worship. We are not called, he insists, "to gather around mystical experience . . . but the mystery of God incarnate."
4. We need to rediscover the essence of the kingdom of God in our worship. We worship, he insists, as an "eschatological people" and not merely as a people who believe in eschatology.

In brief, contemporary worship has become primarily instrumental. We want our worship to "do something." Worship, we believe, should empower the believer, save the sinner, heal the wounded, and grow the church. Instrumental worship, like the Enlightenment or Romantic-influenced worship, asks the wrong question. Worship is not an instrument of the church, but the signification of what God is all about in the history of the world. The mission of God to the world is to rescue the world through Jesus Christ. When we actively hear and consciously live in this truth proclaimed and enacted by the church, all we want worship to accomplish will be accomplished: the sinner will be saved, the saint will be edified and healed.

We turn now to the second stream of worship renewal in the twentieth century that is making an impact on the shape of worship in the Free tradition, the Catholic and mainline renewal.

Objective Worship

Catholic Worship Renewal

During the rise of the Praise and Worship Movement among the Jesus people, a parallel movement of worship renewal was taking place in the Roman Catholic Church. *The Magna Carta* of this reform movement was the *Constitution on the Sacred Liturgy*, which was issued on December 4, 1963. When the document was announced as the first publication of the Reform Council, Vatican II, Pope Paul VI said that because it was "treated before others, in a sense it has priority over all others for its intrinsic dignity and importance to the life of the Church."

Liturgical reform in the Catholic Church was based on the recovery of biblical theology and the study of patristic resources. Worship renewal focused primarily on Jesus Christ and his priestly ministry in the church. A new emphasis was placed on the nature of worship as the historical recitation of God's saving deeds culminating in Jesus Christ in whom and through whom the understanding of the future of history in the consummation was anticipated. Equally important to the Catholic renewal was the recovery of the biblical and early church structure of worship, the four-fold pattern of worship. This recovery resulted in the restoration of the biblical notion of the assembly, a new emphasis on reading Scripture and preaching, a revived interest in the patristic practice and understanding of the Eucharist, and an emphasis on the mission of the church in the world as sent forth to do God's work in the world. *The Constitution on the Liturgy* stressed the importance of the role of the lay people in worship by calling for "fully conscious and active participation" of all the people, the restoration of lay leadership, and the rethinking of music and the arts, the Christian year, and the sacraments.

Many Catholic churches in the United States followed the trends of pop culture and introduced folk, jazz, and even rock Masses. The substance of the Mass as well as its structure described above remained intact by the requirements of the universally determined rubrics and the watchful eye of the bishops, but the style of the Mass became contemporary in many churches. Since the late 1980s, there have been new moves by the pope as well as leading bishops to restore dignity and transcendence to the Mass and move it away from its overdependence on intimacy and familiarity.

Worship Renewal in the Mainline Church

Worship renewal in the Roman Catholic Church made an immediate impact on the mainline churches. The practices of worship in the churches birthed in the sixteenth century were quite diverse. However, since the late 1960s the emphasis in the mainline church has turned toward a more common approach to worship based on the early church resources rather than the differences that resulted from the Reformation.

This trend is most clearly demonstrated by the World Council of Churches' document on *Baptism, Eucharist and Ministry* and the accompanying service known as the Lima Liturgy. Between 1970 and 1990 every mainline denomination has produced new liturgical books and resources that demonstrate a similarity in "almost all areas of liturgy, including the Eucharist, Christian initiation, calendar and lectionary, daily prayer, and other services such as ordination, marriage, the funeral and a wide range of pastoral liturgies."

Liturgist James White, a Methodist and professor of worship in the liturgical graduate program of the University of Notre Dame, published a "Protestant Worship Manifesto" in which he called for twelve reforms in traditional Protestant worship. These included the recovery of Eucharist in every Sunday celebration, the restoration of sacramental action, the recovery of the Christian year, a renewed interest in the arts, and the introduction of courses in worship in seminary education.

While these changes occurred in every mainline denomination and thousands of local churches, the same leaders who initiated these changes acknowledged by 1990 that something was still lacking and that the changes for the most part had failed to make an impact on the experience of worship in most local churches. For example, Eleanor Kreider writes "there is unease. People in every Christian group are aware of inadequacies in their corporate worship. Something, they sense, is incomplete."

The Rise of the Arts

The arts, except for music, never played a highly important role in Protestant worship until after the 1960s. However, the resurgence of the arts in worship gained its impetus from the *Constitution on the Liturgy* and from the worship practices of the Pentecostal, Charismatic, and praise and worship communities.

Following the Roman Catholic initiative in art and environment, Protestant mainline churches have paid new attention to the architectural space of worship and to the environmental setting of worship, particularly to the environment for services of the Christian year. There is also a new interest in the use of media to make worship more visual and engaging of the sense of sight. Philip Griffith III captures this new interest in art when he writes "art as it speaks to us today in our worship . . . makes present the reality of our Creator and Redeemer."

Evaluation

How are we to evaluate the contribution of the more objective trend in the Roman Catholic and mainline church? The contribution they have made to worship renewal in the twentieth century is primarily in the area of early church studies. They have asked us to return to the biblical and historical sources of worship, to recover the four-fold pattern of worship, to celebrate the Table more frequently, to celebrate the Christian year, and to pay attention to the role of music and the arts in worship.

Nevertheless, the worship renewal engendered by the research into early church worship and promoted in the Catholic and mainline Protestant churches has come under recent criticism. There is a general recognition among liturgical scholars in both the Catholic and mainline world that, as Frank Senn has stated in his monumental work *Christian Liturgy Catholic and Evangelical*, the worship renewal envisioned "has not been implemented in America."

While research into the origins of Christian worship has given us valuable insight into the form and meaning of worship, the general criticism of the contributions of the research is that it lacks spirit and intention. Our worship must be "in Spirit and in truth." Good worship necessitates a believing and intentional community. When personal faith is lacking, truth can be expressed as dead formalism.

However, the impact of the research done in the Catholic and mainline churches is already beginning to filter into the worship of the Free Church tradition. Therefore, as we face the twenty-first century, Free Church worship is at a crossroads. The changes that may propel Free Church worship in a new direction have become increasingly evident since 1990.

III. 1990 and Beyond: The Shape of Worship in a Postmodern World

We have seen that Free Church worship has followed the curvature of culture. The focus on worship as "knowledge," "experience," and the instrumental understanding of worship have dominated the practice of worship in the twentieth century. But what of the future?

By the 1990s it became clear that the modern worldview, fueled by the Enlightenment with its emphasis on reason and the Romantic era with its emphasis on experience, had fallen apart. These two movements presupposed that life was characterized by meaning and that history was progressing toward a Golden Age. People of the Enlightenment lived by the narrative of science and believed industry and technology would eventually birth the "American Dream" for everybody. This "doctrine of progress," based on the nineteenth-century dogma of evolution, was to carry the human family from its humble origins out of chance to a new and grand state of being. This Enlightenment narrative has persisted with the Boomer generation, those people born between 1946 and 1961. But for many Generation X (1961–1981), and especially for the millennial (1981–) youth, the promises of the past have been irretrievably broken and the secular metanarrative is dead. We now live in a postmodern culture.

Postmodern Culture

Today's young people have inherited a culture that is secular, atheistic, and nihilistic. This world is "postmodern" in the sense that it is "after" the idealism of the Enlightenment and the Romantic Era. But the "after Modernity" does not yet have a name or face. However, there does seem to be a change that is currently taking place.

Francis Fukuyama in *The Great Disruption* writes that "the evidence is growing that the Great Disruption has run its course and that the process of renorming has already begun."[9] Religion, he claims, will play an important part in the renorming of society, but it will not be like the religion of the pre-1960s. It will be "less an expression of dogma" and more of the "community's existing norms and desire for order." People will come to faith because of their "desire for community." In this context

---

9. Fukuyama, *Great Disruption*, 271.

people will "return to religious tradition," they will "repeat ancient prayers and reenact age-old rituals . . . because they want their children to have proper values."[10] Just as society is returning to tradition, there is a parallel movement among Christians to recover their identity with the past and to restore ancient ceremony and ritual within worship.

Worship in the Postmodern Culture

While the content of Christian worship is countercultural, we may find points of contact with people influenced by the postmodern world. Briefly, there are at least five cultural revolutions through which a worship that signifies the truth about life can be communicated. First, the religious revolution from secular humanism to a supernatural view of life has created a cultural climate in which a biblical supernaturalism may flourish. Second, the historical revolution, which at one time focused attention toward preoccupation with the future and the doctrine of evolutionary progress, has now resulted in a new interest in the past. The research of Catholic and Protestant liturgists of the twentieth century has retrieved the past for the present. Third, the philosophical revolution has shifted our emphasis from reason to mystery. A central feature of authentic worship is the mystery of God incarnate "for us and for our salvation," as the creeds of the church universally attest. Next, the communication revolution has shifted from a verbal/print-oriented form of communication to a more symbolic way of communicating through immersion in a participatory event. Finally, the shift from the autonomous individualism of the Enlightenment toward the desire for community has opened the door for the church to be a welcoming community in a world that is hostile and unwelcoming.

This worship envisioned for a postmodern world is not self-focused as in either Enlightenment or Romantic-influenced worship, nor is it instrumental as in late twentieth- century worship. Rather, it is worship that signifies God's truth in Jesus Christ through proclamation and enactment. This God-focused worship will have as by-products of its central focus growth in knowledge, new depth of authentic experience, and transformed lives.

---

10. Fukuyama, *Great Disruption*, 279.

Conclusion

What does Free Church worship currently look like in the context of this cultural change? The current and most popular response of current worship is, to use a phase from liturgist Marva Dawn, a "dumbing down." This market-driven approach to worship focuses on entertainment and the immediacy of experience. Like the revivalistic and experiential worship of the nineteenth and twentieth centuries, pop worship of the postmodern world continues to be self-focused. This emphasis on self has all but lost the true vision of worship which proclaims and enacts what God has done for the world through Jesus Christ. We are therefore driven to ask: What may authentic worship look like in a postmodern culture?

The place to begin thinking about authentic worship in a postmodern world is to break with the undue emphasis on personal and cultural relevance and return to truth. We may start with the conviction that Christians are "resident aliens," as Stanley Hauerwas and William Willimon have so aptly stated. We do not live by the broken narrative of the scientific worldview nor do we live by the "chaos" of the postmodern world. We live out of another story, the story of Israel and Jesus.

This story is not known in our postmodern, North American world. It was also not known in the pagan Greco-Roman world. But Christians told the story in personal encounters and in the communal setting of their worship. This story is not about me and my experience (although it does have an experiential dimension). It is the story of God in the world. It is the story of God creating, the story of humanity rebelling against God, the story of God entering time, space, and history in the incarnation to rescue the world, the story of the hope of the new heavens and the new earth.

This is the story that worship remembers, proclaims, enacts, and the future that worship anticipates. This story, which sweeps from creation to consummation, stands in antithesis to all other stories of the post-modern world and informs our worship. Worship that ignores this story and delivers only pieces of it or seeks to make it a means of a mere spiritual experience will fall short of truth and ultimately of relevance. What is relevant about worship is not this or that insight or experience, but the restoration of a vision of the world that sees the world and all its problems in the light of the historical event of Jesus (*anamnesis*) and the eschatological hope of the church (*maranatha*).

This brief survey of worship and culture in twentieth-century Free Church movements shows that Protestants have generally followed the curvature of culture in their approach to worship. This is no longer possible nor is it desirable in the postmodern world. The most relevant position we can take in a postmodern world is to be anti-cultural in our worship. Instead of postmodern nihilism and nothingness, we offer the true story of the world in Jesus Christ. Instead of antipathy toward the past and fear of the future we offer a connection with both the past and the future. Instead of autonomous and lonely individualism we offer a genuine community of loving people who gather every week to ritualize the meaning of the world, who enter into a new story that re-enchants the world and puts hope in the God who has acted decisively to renew and restore the created order. The task that lies before the church is to signify this message as it builds bridges to a world sensitive to the supernatural, in need of historical connection, reawakened to mystery, and in search of community.

20

The Road to the Future Runs Through the Past: Reviving an Ancient Faith Journey[1]

CHURCHES IN NORTH AMERICA are feeling the effects of vast cultural changes. With increasing secularization, the concept of a Christianized society has undergone a long, slow, hard death, and Christians live amid principalities and powers in an increasingly alien culture. Postmodernism asserts that no single metanarrative can speak to an understanding of the world, and the resulting relativism of belief and practice surrounds us. Since 9/11, an awareness of personal vulnerability has opened many to spirituality, mostly of New Age variety. The church's future depends on its ability to come to terms with these changes in our postmodern, secular-but-still-spiritual society, while bearing witness to its conviction that it has an authentic spirituality and a unique story, a true interpretation of existence.

In this climate of change and challenge, several models or forms of church coexist. Some churches, shaped by their response to World War II, continue to serve the idea of a Christianized society. Their approach to ministry is that of caretakers. Pastors keep the machinery going. These churches practice mass evangelism. Worship is sermon-driven. Spirituality is keeping the rules. Education is the accumulation of knowledge. Youth work is program after program. Some of these traditional churches flourish, but many are in decline.

Other churches have been shaped by the revolution of the 1960s. They are innovative, follow the business model, and use slick marketing.

1. Originally published in *Vision: A Journal for Church and Theology*, Institute of Mennonite Studies, Fall 2003. Used with permission.

Their pastors are their CEOs. Worship is primarily music-driven, half an hour of contemporary song followed by a sermon. Spirituality focuses on the therapeutic, stressing that a Christian can live the good life. Evangelism is seeker-oriented. Education is Christianity 101. Youth work happens around retreats. This pragmatic model has challenged the established church. Using church growth principles, these megachurches flourished in the eighties and nineties. Now their future is uncertain.

Newer churches bump up against the relativism of postmodernity. They embrace a missional self-understanding. Their approach to ministry is shaped by the servanthood of Jesus. Worship moves toward the ancient emphasis on Word and Table. Spirituality also seeks to revive older traditions. Evangelism is a journey into faith and discipleship. Education focuses not on the accumulation of facts but on spiritual formation. Youth work concentrates on prayer, Bible study, and social concerns. Twenty-somethings predominate in the Emerging Church; these start-up groups are featured on websites.

These emerging churches seek to work with cultural change. Seeing the impact of globalization, they strive to be multicultural and multi-generational. Breaking with an evolutionary philosophy of history, they affirm that the road to the future runs through the past. Questioning the religious rationalism of the Enlightenment and its impact on forms of ministry, these churches embrace mystery. Repudiating the isolation of individualism, they seek the experience of Christian community. Recognizing the effects of technological change, they foster an interactive approach to Christian faith, worship, and formation.

The Journey to Jesus

Because I am convinced that the church must replace superficial evangelism with a discipleship that forms new believers and incorporates them fully into the life of the church, I have adapted a third-century model of evangelism and Christian formation into a process called Journey to Jesus.[2] I assume that our culture is primarily pagan, that Christian witness in this context cannot take for granted that people understand the Christian faith. The spiritual path I have laid out happens in the church and is especially connected to worship. Like the early church pattern, it includes a time to evangelize, then to disciple, then to spiritually form,

---

2. See Webber, *Journey to Jesus* and *Ancient-Future Evangelism*.

and finally to assimilate into the church. It is based on a study of biblical texts that deal with Christian formation, and it includes life-changing rituals in which participants renounce evil and embrace the transforming power of Jesus Christ.

This process assumes, as the early church did, that we live among the principalities and powers. It teaches that Christ, by his death and resurrection, has overcome the powers of evil and will at the end of history rescue creation from the clutches of evil. As envisioned by Isaiah and in the revelation to John, Christ's shalom will rest over the entire created order. In the meantime, in its worship and in its way of life, the church is called to witness to the overthrow of the powers. The church is therefore the womb in which new Christians are conceived, birthed, and guided into a lifelong relationship with God. The process is a long obedience in the same direction.

The four stages of the process use the language of seeker, hearer, kneeler, and faithful, all terms used in the early church. I believe the church best marks this process of birth and growth and maturation with rituals. I have adapted the rituals to fit the believers' tradition of faith formation. However, I have maintained the sequence of the early church, which practiced adult baptism as the culmination of the process.

Evangelize the seeker. The first step in the journey to Jesus is to bring a person to the place of initial conversion. Sociologist Rodney Stark argues that early Christianity grew largely because of conversions that took place in the context of immediate social networks of family, friendship, working relationships, and neighborhood witness.[3] The statistics of the American Church Growth Institute testify to the ongoing power of this relational approach to bringing people to faith. Seventy-nine percent of people the Institute surveyed came to faith through interaction with a friend or relative.[4] One-on-one mentoring relationships can provide opportunity to talk about Gospel stories presenting who Jesus is, what he did, and how his death and resurrection are the source for transforming life. Mentors may bring seekers to church, where the hospitality of God's people and the proclamation of Christ in worship intensify their interest in faith.

---

3. Stark, *Rise of Christianity*.

4. The remainder came to faith through a pastor (6 percent); Sunday school (5 percent); walk-ins (3 percent); outreach programs (3 percent); special needs (2 percent); visitation (1 percent); crusades (0.5 percent).

When seekers are ready to follow Jesus, they make a public confession of faith, which includes a rite of renunciation of the powers of evil and affirmation of allegiance to Jesus as Lord.

Disciple the hearer. At the 1999 International Consultation on Discipleship in Eastbourne, England, more than 450 Christian leaders from around the world met to address the problem of conversions that fail. They bemoaned the fact that the church seems to be a mile wide but an inch deep. They urged congregations to develop ways to disciple new Christians. The second step in the journey to Jesus helps new converts learn what it means to be a disciple: what does it mean to be the church; what does it mean to be at worship; how does one pray with Scripture?

At the end of this stage, when new Christians are ready, they celebrate the rite of covenant. As in the early church, this rite is a commitment to proceed to baptism. Candidates step forward to reaffirm faith in Christ by writing their names in the book of the covenant. The whole community looks on and celebrates by singing "Alleluia" as each candidate's name is recorded.

Spiritually form the kneeler. For the next six weeks, the candidate—now known as a kneeler—prepares for baptism by learning how to deal with the principalities and powers. To live in baptism is to identify with the death and resurrection of Jesus. The Christian answer to the powers is to live in our baptism, daily dying to sin and rising to the new life of the Spirit that is in Christ. During this period, candidates learn the Apostles' Creed and the Lord's Prayer. Through these primary sources, one learns the content of belief and to whom and how to pray.

The ritual that follows this instruction is baptism, the rite par excellence of conversion. In this rite one renounces the powers of evil and submits to a new identity, is baptized into Christ to live on in the pattern of death and resurrection.

Assimilate the faithful. When the converted have been baptized, what remains of their initial discipleship journey is incorporation into the full life of the church. A seven-week study of biblical passages is geared to helping new members discover their calling to work, to the care of creation, to the poor and needy. They also discover their gifts and offer them to the life of the church.

This stage has no one-time rite of passage. Instead the rite of Communion offers continuous nourishment. At the Table, God meets believers again and again to confirm their faith in truth and to nourish them with the body and blood of Christ. The initial journey to Jesus has been completed. Converts are ready to be involved in the church, continuing to grow even as they now mentor others in the faith.

Concluding Thoughts

The six-month process I have summarized may begin and end at any time, but some may find it meaningful to order it around the Christian year. On Pentecost Sunday, commission the evangelists of your community to make a connection with one person in their social network, and begin the conversation described in part one. On the first Sunday of Advent, celebrate the rite of conversion. Then lead new converts through the next stage during Advent, Christmas, and Epiphany. On the first Sunday of Lent, celebrate the rite of covenant. During Lent, introduce new converts to the discipline of spirituality summarized in part three. Baptize them at the great Easter vigil on Saturday night of Holy Week, or in the Easter Sunday service. During the seven weeks of Easter assimilate new converts into the full life of the church.

The journey to Jesus model is not a quick fix. Getting started may require a small group of committed people who go through the process themselves, and then begin to invite unchurched people into it, until it expands to include the whole church and those beyond it in the process of discipleship. This paradigm is new, but it draws on early church resources, because we too live in a world that is pagan. This model has the potential to revolutionize the twenty-first-century church, as it did the church of the Roman world almost two thousand years ago.

21

Symposium on Witnessing Through Worship

WHEATON COLLEGE, KEYNOTE ADDRESS, JUNE 12, 1987

A COUPLE OF YEARS ago I was traveling back from Chicago, where I had a speaking engagement, and I did something that I rarely do. I turned on the radio. Now, you're saying to yourself, "Why would Bob Webber very seldom turn on the radio?" I think the reason is probably because at that particular time, all of my children, four of them, were ranging between the ages of thirteen and nineteen. Ever have four teenage kids in your home? Every time they walk in the door, they just simply walk right over to the stereo and turn it on. They open the car door and the radio is on before the door is slammed shut. So whenever I'm traveling any place I say to myself if I'm alone, "Good. Silence." I don't want to hear a thing.

But on this particular occasion I decided to turn on the radio and I'm not sure why, but I'm glad that I did, because there was a psychologist from Harvard who was talking about meaning in life, and he said there are three things that give meaning to life. First of all, he said, we derive meaning in life from love and the relationships of those people who love us, and we love them. I thought about my own relationships of love and my family and extended family, and I said to myself, "Indeed, that's true. That brings meaning to my life." Then he said we derive meaning from our work, and I thought to myself, "That's really true. I love my work. It's not something that I have to do, or something that I just have to endure. I can't believe that people actually pay me to teach." My students will sometimes say the same thing. But work brings meaning to my life. And then the third thing he suggested is that meaning to life comes through re-creation or recreation, and I thought to myself of the larger context of my social life and physical activities that brought recreation to my body and to my spirit, and I said to myself, "Indeed, that also brings meaning to my existence."

So there you have it. Meaning comes from love, meaning comes from work, and meaning comes from our recreation. But then he said, "After I wrote the article suggesting that meaning is derived from these three things, I sat down and I really began to think through what I had said, and I came to the conclusion that there is one more source, a very significant and vital source, for meaning." I pricked up my ears because I thought to myself, "What else could he be referring to?" And he said just what I wanted him to hear, although I really did not second guess him, he said, "Meaning in human existence is derived from worship." Now I think the question that we're attempting to ask today is what kind of worship gives meaning to human existence? The answer that I want to give to that and expand upon, hopefully through all the activities that we're going to do today, is to say that the kind of worship that gives meaning to human existence is the kind of worship that is, in a sense, a witness to the meaning of human existence. And the witness to the meaning of human existence is to be found in the story of the Christian faith, the living and the dying, and the rising again of Jesus Christ.

Now I want to speak to four principles that provide meaning in worship and speak to the meaning of human existence, and these are the four principles that have been established in the renewal of worship that is taking place in the twentieth century. As you all know, we are living in a time of incredible upheaval in the whole of life and in the whole of the world in which we live. And in the context of all of the changes that are taking place, there are some very significant changes that are taking place in the life of the church, and particularly in the life of worship, and there has been in this century what we call the liturgical renewal. Out of this liturgical renewal, scholars have been able to identify four principles that are applicable to every single worshipping community. These four principles are applicable to the Catholic community, to the Orthodox community, to every one of the Protestant communities, to the Evangelical communities, and to the Charismatic community. Now you're saying, "Wow, these must be some four principles if they're applicable to all these groups." Let me set them forth briefly and then we will interact with regard to these four principles today.

The first principle is this: worship celebrates Christ. Now let me try to define Christ and celebration just briefly. The Christ that I'm speaking about here is the biblical, historical, orthodox Jesus. I'm not speaking of a Jesus who is just simply a human person, a Jesus who is a window to the Father, a Jesus who is a unique human being, a Jesus who is an example of humanity. He is all of that, but the Jesus that I'm speaking about that we celebrate and worship is more than that, because the Jesus that I'm speaking about that we celebrate and worship is what we may call the cosmic Christ, the Christ who reconciles all things. The Apostle Paul speaks about this Jesus. In Colossians he says that "in him all things are created; in him all things exist; and through him all things are reconciled." So we're talking about the Jesus of history, who is the center of human existence, the one in whom the living and dying and rising again of all of history is to be understood. Now, I want to speak about the word *celebration*. What does it mean when we celebrate this Jesus Christ, the living and the dying and the rising again of Jesus Christ? I want to try to define that word *celebration*, because I think it's a key word to understanding what we do in worship. There are three things that are important about celebration.

First, a celebration is always rooted in an event, a past event. Second, a celebration makes the past event become contemporaneous. Third, the means by which that past event is made contemporaneous is through story and drama. Now, let me try to give you an example here, and then I'll apply this to worship. My oldest son will be twenty-two in August. I can still remember the day when that rascal was born. You know, there's something special about bringing a child into the world, but there seems to me to be some special memory attached, I think, to the time when that first child is brought into the world. I remember when we took him home from the hospital, I was at Covenant Theological Seminary at the time, and I was so proud. I was so full of joy that I had fathered this child, and I put this little rascal into my arms and I walked into the seminary. I walked up to the president and I said to him, "Meet my son John."

At that particular point, the president was unimportant. What was important was this kid John. And I walked over to the librarian whom I nicknamed Squeaky Shoes, because she always squeaked through the library with her crepe sole shoes, and I said to her, "Meet my son John." And I saw some fellow students: "Meet my son John." Now, when John was one and two and five and ten and eleven and last summer twenty-one, you know what I did at his birthday celebration? I told and acted out the story again. "John, remember when I brought you home?" He answered, "Okay, Dad. Twenty-one times is enough. No more."

But why did I do that? Because I was celebrating an event. We were celebrating his birth twenty-one years ago, and we were making the celebration of his birth and the telling and acting out of the story contemporary. We were bringing it into the context of that celebrating community, so that within the context of that celebrating community we experienced once again the joy of bringing a life into the world. Now, let's apply that to worship. In this application, let me say this is true of both Old Testament worship and New Testament worship. Worship is rooted in an event. When we worship, we celebrate an event that took place 2000 years ago. Two thousand years ago, as the Apostle Paul tells us, God was in Christ reconciling the world to himself. And when we worship, we take that event, which was historical, and we bring it down through the corridors of history and within the context of the worshiping community. The meaning of that event becomes alive within the context of those people who are reenacting that story and telling it again. Worship celebrates Christ. We tell and act out the meaning of human existence in the living and dying and rising again of Jesus Christ. Now, let me say, by way of an aside, that that's the definition of worship that the liturgical renewal of the twentieth century is essentially working with. It can be stated in a number of different ways.

But it is essentially this. I'll summarize it: the definition of worship is to tell and act out the living and the dying and the rising again of Jesus. And in doing that, that historic event, which is unrepeatable, becomes present in power in the context of the worshiping community to form us and to shape us after the image of Jesus. Now, there's a major implication, which I don't have time to develop here, but I'll just simply mention it, and that is that this understanding of worship lies behind the all-important issue of the order of worship. Because, you see, if worship means to tell and act out the Christ event, then somehow the order of worship itself must do it. It must tell it. It must act it out. Now, because I am limited to thirty minutes, I'll not expand on that, but maybe sometime today we'll be able to discuss that a little bit. Now, let me go to the second principle of worship. It is this: it's a very simple principle. In worship, God speaks and acts. Now, what we're talking about here is the divine side of worship. Worship is not just something that we do from a human perspective. There is a divine side of worship. There is a presence of God in worship. God is speaking and acting.

A scholar by the name of Mowinckel, an Old Testament scholar speaking of Old Testament worship, which would also be applicable to New Testament worship, says that in worship something happens, that the purpose of worship is to create life. Therefore, we can say that in worship our relationship with God is established, maintained, repaired, and transformed. Something really happens in worship. Now, worship is in a sense what I want to describe here as a divine drama. A number of years ago I went to Jim Young, who is the director of theater here at Wheaton College, and said, "Jim, does worship have a script?" That's the wrong question to ask Jim, if you have only five or ten minutes, because he just exploded. And a couple of hours later I walked away with the sense that indeed worship does have a script. But let me summarize for you what he said. Indeed, worship does have a script. Worship is like a drama, but he said it's not a tragedy. It's a comedic drama. And I said, "Well, what do you mean by that?" He said in a tragedy—and this is generally true of drama that is tragedy—there's never any resolution to the conflict.

We also discussed at that particular time the play *Waiting for Godot*. I remember perhaps one of the most vivid illustrations that I've ever heard where the conflict never ends, because one time an English professor decided that he was going to discuss *Waiting for Godot* with his students. He said come to class on Friday, prepared to discuss the play. After the bell rang [for the start of class], a student runner ran into the class and he said, "The professor has asked me to inform you that he has a long distance telephone call and he'll be a little bit late, but wait." About fifteen minutes later another student ran in and said, "You won't believe this, but the professor has been interfered by something and he will be here really soon, so please just wait." And then a third runner came in, and you know what happened? The bell finally rang, the class was over and the conflict had not ended because the professor never came, just as *Waiting for Godot* never ends. Jim Young said, "It seems to me that a lot of our worship is just that. We never have any resolution to the conflict, and there's a sense in which this kind of worship may be just intellectual worship, worship that's cerebral that really doesn't touch us with the meaning of human existence, sends us out into the world to grit our teeth and to hang on, with no sense that the conflict of the world has been resolved." But he said in a comedy, the conflict of the world is always resolved, or the conflict in that play is always resolved.

And so worship is in a sense a drama in which the divine activity of God, in solving the conflict of the world, is told and acted out. Now, let me give you a couple of examples of this. Because I think that in worship properly understood, the conflict appears again and again and again, and the resolution to the conflict appears again and again. Worship is generally understood to have four parts to it. Preparation, service of the word, service of the table, and the dismissal. Now, let me give you an example from the preparation. For the most part, the preparation and the various ways in which the preparation is accomplished within the context of worship is modeled on Isaiah chapter 6, and you remember that passage. Isaiah is lifted up into the heavens and he sees God seated on the throne, and he hears the angels singing holy, holy, holy, the whole Earth is full of your glory. And you recall what he says: "I am a man of unclean lips." Now, that's an incredible tension that you experience.

In the presence of the transcendent God, the one who is wholly other, the one who is holy and righteous, and all of a sudden when we stand in the context of that God, we see ourselves for what we are, sinners. That's conflict. Historically, in the preparation, there is some kind of absolving of our sinful status, a reminder that when in Christ we are forgiven, and that God sees us through Jesus Christ. And then we're ready to hear the Word. Now, there are many different ways to do that, but that's something I think that's worth talking about today. Then we hear the Word. But the word is another presentation of the conflict, because the read and preached Word really has to do essentially with the dualistic conflict that we find within the context of this world, the conflict that Paul so often speaks of, that we wrestle not against flesh and blood, but against principalities and powers, and that's the fundamental conflict of the universe.

But the Apostle Paul says God was in Christ, reconciling the world to himself, and there's the resolution to the conflict. And so that somehow within the context of the reading and preaching of the Word of God, that conflict needs to be expressed and we need to be brought into resolve. Now, traditionally in the historic liturgy, that resolution is expressed in the transition from the service of the Word to the service of the table in the kiss of peace. The kiss of peace is a wonderful expression of the peace of God, which essentially says that because Jesus Christ in all that he has done has established peace between the Father and his creation, there is now peace between the people of God. And the kiss of peace is in a sense a kind of glimpse into the eschatological shalom, the peace that will rest over this whole world, and when we pass the kiss of peace, there's a sense in which we're saying to everybody that the conflicts of this world are not the ultimate and final word that's written over history, but the ultimate and final Word that is read over history, is the shalom of God, which will reign over this earth after his coming again.

The table is also a conflict. You have exposition in the taking of the bread and wine, and in the Eucharistic prayer, the prayer of Thanksgiving. But when the bread is broken, a very dramatic point in our worship, it's that conflict that appears again, because Christ's body was broken and his blood was shed for the sake of the salvation of the whole world. And we say, "Christ our Passover is sacrificed for us, hallelujah," and we receive the bread and we take it into our mouth and we bite it hard and we claim that the conflict is over. And we take that wine and we let it run down our throats and we claim that the conflict is over, and then we are sent forth in peace to live our life out in worship in the world. Now, all of that relates to the second principle that in worship God speaks and acts, and thus the proclamation that the conflict has ended is experienced by us through Word and table, through song and prayer, and a number of other ways in which we could talk about.

Now, the third principle is that we respond to God and to each other. Again, it's a very simple principle. It's the human side. When we talk in terms of the divine side, the divine action, the divine presence, we need to acknowledge that there is also a human response to that divine presence, because if the divine presence really becomes truly there, really, *really* there in the context of Christian worship, how can we sit passively? So the presence of the divine breaks through the barriers of passive worship and calls upon us to become actively engaged in an encounter with the saving and healing presence of the reality of the living and the dying and the rising of Christ that becomes present and is formed within the context of that worshiping community. Now, let's talk briefly about how that happens.

First, let me say that if this is true that there is that sort of dialectic between the divine and the human that is happening there, then worship—I'm going to use a very strong word here—has to be dialogic. It *has* to be dialogic. I don't know about you, but I've gotten to the place where I just feel so antsy in a passive worshiping community, where all I do is sit, watch, stand up to sing a hymn, and throw some money in the plate. There's got to be more response than that, because worship is a dialogue and the pattern of it is that God speaks, God acts, we respond to the speaking, we respond to the acting. Now, how do we do that? How does that happen? Well, first of all, let me say that it seems to me that there needs to be the rediscovery of a kind of acclamation of response.

One of the things that's happening today in some quarters of worship renewal is that people who want to become more dialogic, churches that want to become more dialogic, are writing out long statements. The pastor or the worship leader will make a long statement, then the people will make a long statement in response. And let me say that there is something that is too intellectual about that. It's something that is too cerebral about that. Say the historic acclamations are always short, not something you have to read from the bulletin, but something you just simply say arises from the heart. The Amen. You know, we need to restore the Amen at the appropriate places within the context of worship. We need to restore something as simple as "thanks be to God." Now, when Mel read the Scripture today and he said, "This is the Word of the Lord," I don't know why I didn't say this. I was just playing the passive role again. I should have leaped from my chair and said, "Thanks be to God!" Right? Hey, good. The crowd is waking up.

So the Amen, the thanks be to God, the Hallelujah. One of the things that I think we're going to hear today from Dana and Sue Talley is about the Hallelujahs and the responses of the early church, sometimes wordless responses, which are absolutely marvelous ways of responding to the divine presence and the divine action within the context of worship. I think the Black Church is a better model of worship for us than what many of us do. This leads me to also remember that when Egeria, who wrote a diary of her travels in Jerusalem, said that as she walked by the church during the Easter season, when the mystagogy was occurring within the context of the Christian community—that is when they were explaining to them the meaning of what happens at the table with the early Christians called the Eucharist—she said that yards away from the church she could hear shouts of the people within the context of that Christian community. So I think we need to figure out ways to break through passive worship and make worship dialogic once again.

Now, the second thing that I want to say about this third principle that we respond to God and to each other is that worship is a rehearsal of our relationship to God. Worship is a rehearsal of our relationship to God. Now, if you go back to that first principle, then in worship we celebrate

Christ, and the second principle that in worship God speaks and acts, what we are doing within the context of worship, as I've indicated is telling and acting out the meaning of human existence by telling and acting out the living and the dying and the rising again of Jesus Christ. Now, if that is true, then every single act of worship is, in a sense, a rehearsal of our relationship to God.

I don't know about you, but when it comes time for worship on Sunday, this old sinner is in desperate need of being present in that community and hearing the Word of the Lord again. And I carry into the worship experience, as I'm sure you do, the burdens and problems of life. And I come in and I'm sort of out here when worship begins. But as worship proceeds, it becomes increasingly more intense for me, and by the time we get to the Sanctus, "Holy, Holy, Holy, the whole Earth is full of your glory," there's just something that happens that kind of draws me right into the Spirit of Christ, and I become present once again to my initial experience of conversion, and I'm touched by the reality of the Jesus Christ, who is present to save me and to heal me.

One of the things I find that's interesting out of the worship renewal that's happening in the twentieth century is that there is a unique recognition that Jesus touches us in an unusual way at the table of the Lord. And many Christian churches now, in recognition of that, are asking their people not only to come forward and to receive the bread and wine, but are recognizing that at that particular point there is an intensification of the presence of Jesus, and suggesting then that those who are in need of prayer for emotional reasons or physical reasons or other reasons just slip by after they receive the bread and wine, stand before an elder or some other celebrant who is nearby, and receive from him the anointing of oil. I find that that's a wonderful experience to receive the bread and the wine and then to walk over to this person and have them put the oil on my forehead and name of the Father, the Son and the Holy Spirit, and to clasp my head and to pray for those things that I struggle with in my life. And we can do that in worship because Jesus is there, he's really, really there, present to touch us and to heal us and to forgive us and to bring us into union with the body of Christ and into union with himself. So we break through passive worship when we respond to the divine presence that is there.

Now, the fourth and final principle, and I'm going to say this one quickly, because I see that I've pretty much taken the thirty minutes that belongs to me, is this: all creation joins in worship. Now, let me be very,

very brief about this. There's a statement by a Roman Catholic theologian by the name of Teilhard de Chardin, which I like, and it is this, "Because of creation, and even more because of incarnation, there is nothing profane for those who know how to see." Now, what that essentially means is that all of creation bespeaks, not only the creative activity of God, but is capable of bespeaking the redemptive activity of God. And I think that we need to explore those ways in which the creation may be put to redemptive use. I'll just make a couple of illustrations here and then close.

First of all, I think we need to recover the theology of time, because that's part of creation. When we think in terms of organizing the time of our worship around Advent and Christmas and Epiphany and Lent and Holy Week and Easter and Pentecost, we are, in a sense, through time itself, allowing time to tell the story of the meaning of human existence rooted in Jesus Christ.

Second, we need to take a look at our space, and we need to ask ourselves the question, "How does this space speak of redemption? How does the furniture within the space, the pulpit, the table, the baptismal pool or font? How does the placement of them, the placement of the body of Christ around these pieces of furniture, these symbols of God's activity and history, how do they bespeak redemptive activity?" And then we're going to hear a lot today about music. I really think that music is one of the most important vehicles for the renewal of worship. And I would like to also suggest such things as the recovery of liturgical dance, color, drama, but time will not permit me to talk about those or to make comment on them.

So let me conclude with this one statement. I want to go back to that story that I began with. Meaning and life comes from love, from work, from recreation, and from worship. When I first began to think about that, I said to myself, "There have been some times in my life when not one of those was a source of meaning." And I think that if all of us sit down and think about it, we would probably find some dark spots in our existence in which none of those seem to be working. And then I said to myself, "There have been times in my life when all four of those have been in place. What a high."

And then I concluded that life would be okay if only two were in place. But one of the ones that I think desperately needs to be in place, and we need to think about this in terms of the people of our congregations, is that it is our responsibility, it is our calling in the life of the church, to make certain that at least all of the people in our congregation have at least one thing that gives them meaning, and that's the worship that we do in the life of our congregation, because if that misses, and that doesn't give them the worship, it will take away, at least if our evaluation is right, at least 25 percent of that which gives meaning to human existence.

22

Enter His Courts with Praise: A New Style of Worship Is Sweeping the Church[1]

A NEW STYLE OF worship has been spreading throughout North America and other parts of the world in the last several decades. While this worship approach is described by a variety of names, the one that seems to be gaining most acceptance is "Praise and Worship" (P&W). I want to explain what this style of worship is and how it may affect traditional worship in the future.

Where Did It Originate?

I cannot pretend to have specific insight into the details of the rise of P&W. Nevertheless, by looking at the broad landscape, we can pick out some trends that came together to create this contemporary form of worship.

These trends include the perception some people have that traditional worship forms are dead. Along with that conviction goes a concern for an immediacy of the Spirit, a desire for intimacy, and a persuasion that music and informality connect with people of a post-Christian culture.

One of the earliest expressions of these trends was the rise of testimonial music through the leadership of Bill Gaither in the early sixties. Songs such as "He Touched Me," "There's Something About That Name," "Let's Just Praise the Lord," and "Because He Lives" touched many lives

---

1. Originally published in *Reformed Worship Journal,* June 1991. Used with permission.

and opened people up to a new genre of music. At first these were performance songs, but soon they became congregational: people sang along or at least joined in on the refrain. A second expression of these trends came in the late sixties on the West Coast (and all over the world) in the form of a new expression of the Spirit known as the Jesus Movement. A major emphasis of this movement was the singing of praise choruses, some of which were written and sung right on the spot. Tommy Coombs, president of Maranatha! Music and a contemporary songwriter in this genre of music, was converted in the early days of the Jesus Movement. He tells of his search for God in the sixties, of wandering here and there with his guitar, singing secular songs and taking dope. All the while, he was looking for God.

One day someone invited him to attend a service at Calvary Chapel in Costa Mesa, California. According to Tommy, when he walked into that service and heard the music of the Jesus People, he said immediately, "Here is where God dwells—here I will find God." Soon Tommy Coombs became a writer of P&W music, a leader in a form of music worship that brought Tommy and thousands of others who were wandering in the desert of meaninglessness and drugs into a relationship with Jesus Christ.

Since those early days in the late sixties and early seventies, this form of music and the style of worship it has engendered have developed into a new worldwide approach to worship. According to Chuck Fromm, chief executive officer of Maranatha! Music, "It became legal to sing in worship what was not published in a hymnbook."

Characteristics of P&W

While the P&W tradition may be complicated in terms of its historical origin and spread in North America and beyond, the movement itself is not difficult to describe.

First, P&W is a post-Enlightenment expression of worship. Since the eighteenth century, Western thought has been influenced by the Enlightenment's rationalistic and scientific explanations of our existence. Worship influenced by the Enlightenment is essentially cerebral, appealing to the mind and to the intellectual side of our beings. It is "left-brained." In contrast, P&W touches the affective side of the person. It is "right-brained," reaching into the feelings and emotions of the human personality. However, it is not correct to dismiss it as merely emotional worship or as worship lacking in content or biblical precedent.

Indeed, a second characteristic of P&W is that it seeks to recapture the lost element of praise found in both Old and New Testament worship. It stands in the tradition of the Talmud, saying "Man should always utter praises, and then pray." Praise God first and foremost, then move on to the other elements of worship, say the leaders of P&W.

Distinguishing Praise from Worship

A major feature of the P&W movement is its tendency to distinguish praise from worship. Judson Cornwall, a P&W leader and author of more than a half-dozen books, addresses the distinction between praise and worship in his book *Let Us Worship*.

Cornwall argues that the Scriptures present praise as something different than worship, and he cites Psalm 95 as a good example of this distinction. In the opening verses, the psalmist invites praise: "O come, let us sing unto the Lord: let us make a joyful noise to the rock of our salvation. Let us come before his presence with thanksgiving, and make a joyful noise unto him with psalms."[2] Only then, after praise has been offered, does the psalmist invite worship: "O come, let us worship and bow down: let us kneel before the Lord our Maker."[3] So Cornwall concludes that "the order is praise first, worship second." [4]

"Praise," Cornwall writes, "prepares us for worship"; it is a "prelude to worship." Praise is not an attempt to get something from God; it is a ministry that we offer to God. We offer praise for what God has done— for God's mighty deeds in history and continued providential presence in our lives.

While we praise God for what he has done, we worship God for who he is. The one extols the acts of God, the other the person and character of God. Cornwall makes this distinction between praise and worship clear: "Praise," he writes, "begins by applauding God's power, but it often brings us close enough to God that worship can respond to God's presence. While the energy of praise is toward what God does, the energy of worship is toward who God is. The first is concerned with God's

---

2. Psalm 95:1–2, KJV.
3. Psalm 95:6.
4. Cornwall, *Let Us Worship*, 143.

performance, while the second is occupied with God's personage. The thrust of worship, therefore, is higher than the thrust of praise."[5]

The Temple Sequence

The order of the service, the movement from praise to worship, is patterned after the Old Testament tabernacle and temple movement from the outer court to the inner court and then into the Holy of Holies. All of these steps are accomplished through song. The song leader (or the worship leader, as she or he is more often called) plays a significant role in moving the congregation through the various steps that lead to worship.

He or she begins with choruses of personal experience or testimony, such as "This is the Day" or "We Bring Sacrifices of Praise into the House of the Lord." These songs center on praise, are all upbeat in tempo, and relate to the personal experience of the believer. They are songs that often mention "I," "me," or "we." In the Tabernacle typology, during this first step the people are still outside the fence that surrounds the Tabernacle. They cannot worship until they come through the gates into the Tabernacle court.

So that's what takes place in the second step: the mood and the content of the music shift to express the action of entering the gates and coming into the courts. Here the song leader leads people in songs that express the transition from praise to worship. These are songs of thanksgiving, such as the Scripture song from Psalm 100: "I will enter his gates with thanksgiving in my heart/I will enter his courts with praise" or "Come let us worship and bow down, let us kneel before the Lord our God, our Maker."

This second step is explained by Cornwall: "It is a matter of bringing them from a consciousness of what has been done in them and for them (testimony) to who did it in and for them (thanksgiving). The procession through the Eastern gate into the outer court should be a joyful march, for thanks should never be expressed mournfully or negatively. While the people are singing choruses of thanksgiving, they will be thinking both of themselves and of their God, but by putting the emphasis upon the giving of thanks, the majority of the thought patterns should be on their God. Singing at this level will often be a beginning level of praise, but it will

---

5. Cornwall, *Let Us Worship*, 146.

not produce worship, for the singers are not yet close enough to God's presence to express a worship response."[6]

The third step, into the Holy of Holies, brings the believer away from herself into a full, conscious worship of God alone. No longer is the worshiper thinking about what God has done, but rather of who God is in person and character. A quiet devotion hovers over the congregation as they sing songs such as "Father, I Adore You," "I Love You, Lord" and "You Are Worthy." In these moments of worship "the emotional clapping will likely be replaced with devotional responses of upturned faces, raised hands, tears, and even a subtle change in the timbre of the voices." For when there is an "awareness that we have come into the presence of God, we step out of lightness with sobriety."[7]

John Chisum, vice president of worship resources at Starsong Communications in Nashville, describes the third phase of the sequence as an experience of "the manifest presence of God." He says this experience does not differ greatly from the liturgical experience of the presence of Christ at the Lord's table. "In this atmosphere," he claims, "the charisma, or gifts of God are released." And "just as many throughout the history of the church have experienced physical and spiritual healing while partaking of the body and blood in the elements of the table of Christ, so many today are tasting of special manifestations of the Holy Spirit in worship renewal as He inhabits, i.e. settles down, makes His home and abides, in the praises of His people."

Variations

While the tabernacle/temple order of worship is quite prominent in Praise and Worship churches, it is not the only order or sequence of song. For example, I recently visited the Vineyard Church in Anaheim, California, a church that fits into the broader category of the P&W tradition of worship. Here I experienced a slightly different variation of the progression that brings a worshiper into God's presence.

Vineyard Church worship begins with an invitation phase, which is like a call to worship. Songs of invitation such as "I Just Came to Praise the Lord" may be sung with clapping, swinging the body, and looking at other worshipers—smiling and acknowledging their presence.

---

6. Cornwall, *Let Us Worship*, 156.
7. Cornwall, *Let Us Worship*, 157.

In the next movement, the engagement phase, the people are brought closer to God, and their songs are addressed to God, not to one another. A good example may be "Humble Yourself in the Sight of the Lord."

The song leader then moves the people into the adoration phase. In this phase of worship the broad range of pitch and melody that characterized the previous phases is exchanged for the smaller range of music and the more subdued tone of songs such as "Jesus, Jesus, There's Something About that Name" or "Father, I Adore You."

Next the congregation is led into the intimacy phase, which is the quietest and most personal phase of worship. Songs such as "O Lord, You're Beautiful" and "Great Are You, Lord" are personal statements of an intimate relationship directed from the believer to the Lord. As these songs are sung, people become highly intense and lose themselves in the ecstasy of the moment. During this phase of the worship service that I attended at the Vineyard Church, people stood with heads and hands turned upward and eyes closed as they sang these songs of what John Wimber calls "love-making to God." Some people, especially in the front rows, were kneeling or even prostrate on the floor during this "quiet time."

The final phase of the Vineyard worship progression is a closeout song, a song that helps the people move out of the experience of being transfixed on God to prepare for the next phase of the service, the time of teaching.

Praise, Worship, Teaching, Prayer, Ministry

It is common in the P&W tradition of worship to distinguish between the various acts of a typical service. The most significant distinction is that of praise from worship, as described above. Other acts in the service include the time for teaching, the time for intercessory prayer, and the time for ministry.

Because most P&W churches are informal, the various acts of the service are done in an informal way. For example, while teaching is fairly straightforward, it may end with a time of brief feedback or discussion (depending on the size of the congregation).

Intercessory prayer may also be informal. The idea of the traditional pastoral prayer may be replaced by a prayer circle. I took part in such a circle when I visited the Church on the Way in Van Nuys, California, where Jack Hayford is the pastor. There were more than three thousand people in the congregation (one of four services). When the time for prayer came, Pastor Hayford asked all the people to form into "prayer circles." I turned around to find myself in a circle of four people.

As we clasped hands, one of the four said "Are there any prayer requests?" The young woman to my right immediately said, "Please pray for me; my husband left me this week." We all laid hands on her and prayed for her in her time of distress. I wondered how many other people were experiencing a community of immediate support as we did in those few minutes of prayer. My guess is that many did.

After prayer, many churches may enter a time of ministry. I once attended a charismatic Lutheran church that sent people into various rooms where people gifted with ministry for particular needs were laying hands on each other and praying for the hurt and broken lives that came for a touch from the Master's hand. I thought what was being experienced there was very meaningful, ministering in a powerful way to the people of God.

The Presence of Praise and Worship in Traditional Congregations

Broadly speaking, traditional churches have responded to the spread of P&W in three ways.

First are those churches that have not responded at all—perhaps because they are not consciously aware of the P&W tradition. These congregations may have heard one or two P&W-style songs and be vaguely aware of the existence of such a style of worship in nontraditional churches, but for the most part they are impervious to P&W.

Second are those congregations who are more aware of the P&W tradition but are indifferent to it or actively dismiss it, arguing that it is "too superficial" or "too charismatic."

The third set of traditional churches are not only aware of P&W and its relevancy to a post-Enlightenment culture but also seek to integrate this new approach to worship into the local church.

I have experienced the third attitude in both liturgical churches (including Episcopal, Lutheran, Roman Catholic) and traditional, non-liturgical churches (most mainline Protestant denominations, including Presbyterian and Reformed bodies).

Traditional worship is characterized by four movements: Entrance, Word, Table, and Dismissal. Traditional congregations who adopt all or part of the P&W tradition integrate it into this four-fold movement in a variety of ways.

I think, for example, of an experience I had at St. Bartholomew's Episcopal Church in Nashville. There, the traditional prelude was replaced by Gathering Songs (songs of praise), supported by a full band of drums, guitars, and a synthesizer. As people entered to take their seats and assemble for worship, they sang high praise choruses such as "We Bring the Sacrifice of Praise." After a traditional prelude/processional, call to worship, invocation, and confession of sin, the congregation sang more praise music, especially music that reflected the thanksgiving of entering into the inner court. Later, during communion, the congregation sang choruses as people were receiving the laying on of hands and anointing for healing. The congregation sang songs that expressed an intimate relationship with God, songs such as "Father, I Adore You," "I Love You, Lord," and "I Lift My Voice to Worship You." People were kneeling, some with hands raised, all with a sense of what John Chism calls "the manifest presence of God."

Traditional, nonliturgical churches also integrate P&W music into their services. I have worshiped in mainline churches in which the entire prelude and processional follow a pattern of choruses and hymns that express the journey from the outer court into the inner court. For example, David Stout, Pastor of the Lakeview Community Church (RCA) in Rochester, New York, sent me a bulletin showing how he integrates praise music into the opening of worship. While he follows a fairly typical Reformed approach to God, he opens the order to allow praise songs.

The worship of the newer, creative, contemporary churches such as Willow Creek Community Church in suburban Chicago, now the second largest church in the USA and the church that is setting a pattern for many independent congregations, also uses praise music. In a recent visit to the midweek Believers Worship at this church, I experienced an effective use of these choruses. After a five-minute period of silence, in which each of us meditated on a psalm intended to help us come into contact with the dislocations in our lives, we sang choruses such as "He Is Able." The songs we sang assured us that whatever problem we faced, God was able, in the midst of that problem, to be our God. Through these choruses—which praised God as the God of all of life—the congregation was relocated in God.

After worship, the worship leader shared some responses he had received from the congregation. One man told him, "I needed that—my wife left me this week"; another said, "That really spoke to me—I just learned my business is going bankrupt." There's apparently a message in these choruses which, if properly used, brings healing and relocation in the lives of people. These praise songs connect with where people are in a chaotic world.

Assessing P&W

P&W is concerned with the heart. In a recent conversation, Chuck Fromm of Maranatha! Music related the rise of P&W to a saying of St. Francis: "St. Francis told us that a laborer works with his hands, a craftsman with head and hands, and an artist with head, hands, and heart," said Fromm. "The praise and worship tradition has brought the heart back into worship because of the work of the artists."

Certainly the heart has been and continues to be engaged in many liturgical and traditional nonliturgical services of worship. Nevertheless I agree with Chuck Fromm. Because worship has been intellectualized and geared primarily toward the mind, it has become dull and lifeless in many churches. While many people like it this way and even derive meaning from what others consider dead and dull, our young people are fleeing to a worship that touches the heart and engages the senses.

P&W recognizes that the media is the message. For some the pipe organ and classical music represent the message of a God who is transcendent and mysterious. But for others, the guitar, the synthesizer, and the drums, the media of their own culture, represent a God who is immanent, a God who wants intimate fellowship with the church. For them this style of music and worship brings immediacy, relevancy, and an engaging participation.

So which style should dominate? Each congregation will have to decide what to do about P&W. Some will ignore it. Others will resist it. And others will incorporate it into traditional worship. What I see in the future is a convergence of worship traditions, a convergence of the liturgical, traditional nonliturgical, and the Praise and Worship tradition. It does not seem to me to be an either/or, but a both/and.

What a convergence service will look like is dependent on the way the traditions are brought together. When good preaching and good music and the festivity of the Lord's Supper are all brought together, our congregations may discover a richness and fullness to worship that one tradition without the benefit of the others does not seem able to achieve.

The future of worship lies, then, not in the repudiation of this or that tradition, but in a mining from all the traditions—a convergence of worship traditions that recognizes the gifts of God given to the people of God who worship in ways different than our own.

23

The Future Direction of Christian Worship[1]

THIS PAPER SEEKS TO determine how the contemporary study of worship in the biblical and historical tradition has affected worship in the local church. The following renewal movements and biblical and historical studies provide information and insight: (1) the Constitution on the Sacred Liturgy of Vatican II; (2) the liturgical movement within mainline churches (illustrated by the new books on worship and the World Council of Churches text Baptism, Eucharist and Ministry); (3) the renaissance of the arts with an emphasis on music, art and architecture, environmental art, drama and dance; (4) the rise of the Charismatic movement with its recovery of biblical charisms, and (5) the emergence of the praise and worship tradition of worship. The observations of this article are drawn from the study and experience of the author and are meant to serve as a reflection upon the future direction of worship as it is now being shaped by biblical and historical studies.

An advertisement for St. Gregory Nyssen Episcopal Church in San Francisco attracted my attention for it asserted, "We follow an early church model of worship with full congregational participation and involvement."

A visit to this church proved the advertisement was true, for this church had a highly participatory and engaging style of worship. The congregation first gathered around a large table at the east end of the church. There we practiced the "Alleluias" we were to sing in the service. Worship then began with an entrance hymn in which we all processed in a dance movement to the worship space for the service of the Word.

1. Originally published in *Ex Auditu*, 1992. Used with permission.

After completing the entrance rites, we sat facing each other and listened to the Word of God read from a lectern flanked by African flags. After each Scripture reading a Tibetan gong was rung, and as its sound passed through the room, we meditated on the words we had heard. After the sermon, which was preached sitting down (an ancient custom), the congregation was invited to respond. One by the one the people stood and responded. Some asked questions and received an answer. Others spoke of needs met or awakened. Still others spoke of how God had spoken to them through the sermon or how God was present in their life struggles. After the service of the Word we processed with congregational dance back to the table. Standing around the table we passed the peace of Christ, gave thanks over the bread and wine, partook, and then sang and danced around the table. Finally, a benediction was given and then bread, cheese, and fruit were brought to the table for all to eat and enjoy.

A similar experience occurred at Christ's Church in Nashville, a large Pentecostal church that is moving toward the worship of the early church. Every Sunday morning this church celebrates a special Eucharist during the Sunday school hour for those wishing to participate. On the first Sunday of every month the entire congregation celebrates the Eucharist.

The service of the Eucharist began with spirited singing—hymns, choruses, psalms, and songs particular to the Pentecostal tradition. The singing was followed by a time of prayer during which we gathered in small circles, held hands and prayed for each other. We then heard and responded to two Scripture readings, which were followed by a brief sermon. Then the pastor called the people to gather around the table of the Lord. Again we sang and sang. The pastor led us through a confession of sin using the Book of Common Prayer and then asked if anyone present was in need of healing. Several people came and knelt for the anointing with oil and the laying on of hands by the pastor. The congregation then received the bread and wine while songs of resurrection and exaltation were sung. As we left we greeted each other with the peace of Christ.

I have described two Christian traditions on opposite ends of the Protestant spectrum, one a liturgical church and the other a Holiness Pentecostal church. Yet both of them have moved from the particular style of their tradition to a new style, a style that has numerous common elements. This phenomenon, which is happening in nearly every denomination and all around the world, can be explained by three interrelated statements:

1) Churches of nearly every tradition are discovering the worship of the biblical and historical traditions, particularly the model which emerges from the time of Justin.
2) Churches of nearly every denomination are discovering each other and are recognizing that elements of worship preserved in other traditions are relevant to today's worship.
3) What is happening is the convergence of worship traditions.

Since "convergence" worship is both a present trend and a possible future direction of worship, this paper will address six areas in which the convergence of traditions is taking place.

1) A restoration of the event orientation of worship
2) A restoration of the fourfold order of worship
3) A restoration of music and the arts as vehicles of communication
4) A restoration of the Evangelical nature of the Christian year
5) A restoration of sacrament as encounter with Christ
6) A restoration of the relationship of worship to the outreach ministries of the church

A Restoration of the Event Orientation of Worship

Scholars of worship agree that biblical worship is directed toward God in acts that extol God's character. For example, the Gloria in Excelsis Deo, or a hymn such as "Praise Ye the Lord the Almighty, the King of Creation" or a praise chorus such as "Father We Adore You" proclaim God's worth. But there is another side of worship that has been lost to most Protestant traditions until lately. That is the conviction that worship remembers the mighty saving deeds of God. It is this biblical conviction that underlies convergence worship and which this paper will explain, expand, and illustrate. This "event orientation" of worship is the foundation of a very old and yet very new understanding of worship.

If a Jewish person were asked, "What is the most significant event in Jewish history?" or, "What event defines you and gives shape to your existence in the world?", the answer would be, "the exodus." In the exodus God acted for Israel, and brought Israel up out of its bondage to Pharaoh. It is where God entered into relationship with Israel and constituted

Israel as a special and unique people bound to God on the basis of a covenantal relationship.

Consequently, Israelite worship recalls the exodus and looks forward to the promised land. As this true story is rehearsed again and again in various ways, God is praised for his faithfulness. Remembering the faithfulness of God, the people are to live out this story, allowing its hope to shape their personal and corporate lives.

If a Christian were asked, "What is the most important event in human history?" the answer will be, "the Christ Event." That is where God acted for us. In this event God delivered us from the bondage to the evil one and made us his people. God entered into covenant with us and we with him. Consequently our worship recalls this event. It brings the presence of Christ to us and continually shapes and molds us into the people of God.

This conviction that the person of Christ and his work is central to worship is what Robert Taft calls a "fundamental principle of New Testament theology."[2] In Jesus the Christ all salvation history has been recapitulated and made personal. In him the entire Old Testament with all of its signs, symbols, and rituals has been fulfilled. He, Jesus, is the new creation, the new Adam, the new Paschal Lamb, the new covenant, the new circumcision, the new manna, the new temple, the new sacrifice, the new priest, the new Sabbath rest. He is the eternal Word of God, the All in All, the Alpha and the Omega, the first and the last, the beginning and the end. Consequently, true worship or service is nothing other than the life, death, and resurrection of Jesus Christ through whom and by whom the power of evil is overthrown and the restoration of all things is established.[3]

Worship then is primarily *anamnesis*. It is to live in the memory of the Christ event. This *anamnesis* is not a mere intellectual recollection, but a living into and a living out of the death and resurrection of Jesus. Worship is a life lived into the pattern of the death and resurrection of Jesus. We are to continually bring to death the old person and be raised to the new person shaped by the Spirit.

Consequently, the liturgy we celebrate when we gather to worship recalls the death and resurrection of Jesus. But this is not a mere representation of history; it is not the mere telling of a story. Rather, we make

---

2. Taft, *Liturgy of the Hours in East and West*, 334.
3. See Taft, *Liturgy of the Hours in East and West*.

anamnesis. The Christ who overcame evil, overcomes evil again. And in making our memory again we are seized by that power, released once again from the bondage of evil, and made free to be raised into the new life of the Spirit. We are, as it were, joined into Jesus. His definitive victory over sin is repeated within each of us and within his body collectively until he comes again.

This concept of *anamnesis*, which remembers the victory of Christ over evil, is not only a biblical understanding of worship, but also a historical and contemporary understanding. For example, one finds this theme in the eucharistic prayer recorded in *The Apostolic Tradition*:

> And when he was betrayed to voluntary suffering
> that he might destroy death,
> and break the bonds of the devil,
> and tread down Hell, and shine upon the righteous,
> and fix the limit, and manifest the resurrection,
> he took bread and gave thanks.[4]

In contemporary times, this theme of *Christus Victor* is clearly recovered by the Roman Catholic Constitution on the Sacred Liturgy. The Constitution speaks of the message of Christianity in these words:

> Christ has freed us from Satan's grip and brought us into the Paschal mystery of Christ: they [those who believe in Christ] die with him, are buried with him, and rise with him.[5]

In sum, contemporary worship is in the process of being restored to a biblical and historical understanding and practice of worship. This is a worship practice which represents Jesus Christ through re-presentation, a worship that tells and acts out the living, dying, and rising of Christ, a worship that celebrates Christ's victory over evil, the certain doom of Satan, and the promise of a new heaven and a new earth.[6]

A Christ-centered worship—which is event-oriented worship—can never be static and merely intellectual because what happens in worship is an actual and real communication of the power and saving benefit of the life, death, and resurrection of Christ. Worshiping churches recognize that every gathering of worship is ultimately a gathering for praise and thanksgiving for the overthrow of evil by God in Christ. This victory

---

4. See Jasper and Cuming, *Prayers of the Eucharist*, 22.
5. See *Constitution on the Sacred Liturgy*.
6. See Revelation 4 and 5.

not only happened two thousand years ago, but it happens today in the lives of people who bring to worship their own struggles against that evil which shatters relationships, oppresses the poor, and brings constant dislocation into life.

Christians confess that the event of Christ is the source of meaning and purpose. The promise of salvation and its fulfillment evoke passionate and heartfelt praise and thanks, especially for those aware of their own brokenness and the healing that Christ brings into their lives. For this reason, worshiping churches are returning to the biblical focus of worship—a celebration of the work of Christ characterized by a spiritual immediacy that touches people where they are. In this event-oriented worship, God breaks in and becomes present to touch our lives and create us anew.

A Restoration of the Fourfold Order of Worship

A second feature of convergence worship is the restoration of the biblical and early church model of the order of worship. For example, the description of Christian worship in Acts 2:42 gives us an insight into the order of primitive worship. They devoted themselves to the Apostles' teaching and fellowship, to the breaking of bread and the prayers.

In this description we are introduced to the two central institutions of worship through which Christ is proclaimed and remembered: the *kerygma* and the breaking of the bread.

The earliest accounts of Christian worship tell of worship in the synagogue and worship in homes. Synagogue worship focused on Scripture while home worship was ordered around the breaking of the bread. In these two institutions of worship, we find the origins of both the service of the word and the service of the table. Allow me to take you back to the first century so that you can experience worship as it may have happened among early Christians. Imagine for a moment that you are a first-century Christian living in AD 40, ten years after the resurrection. What is it that you see, feel, and experience in both synagogue worship and home worship?

When you enter the synagogue, you greet your friends and neighbors and then sit down to prepare yourself to hear the Word of the Lord, the Old Testament Scriptures, which is the only Scripture you know. The synagogue contains all the symbols of your rich history, and you gaze on them in preparation for worship. You remember that the building itself, which faces toward Jerusalem, is a symbol of God's promises to Israel and of the coming of the Messiah—a promise fulfilled, you believe, in the person of Jesus.

Your eyes then move to the front of the building and settle on the ark that houses the written records of God's activity in your history. You note the veil protecting the scrolls in the ark and the seven-branched candlestick (menorah) with its flickering flame. These symbols remind you of the presence of God in the history of Israel as well as here in this place. Your eyes now turn to the bema, the raised reading platform in the middle of the synagogue. Here the Scriptures will be read, the prayers said, and the Scriptures explained. Again, you recall how the Scripture and its proclamation symbolize the presence of God. You know that this God of the Word who becomes present through the reading of the Scripture actually became present in Jesus of Nazareth, the man crucified and proclaimed by many to be the Messiah.

Now you look at the seat of Moses. Soon a rabbi will sit there. He will expound the Scripture and enter into debate about this Jesus of Nazareth. You know that the rabbi who will speak today does not believe Jesus is the Messiah. For him, the symbols of the synagogue and the Scripture have not yet been fulfilled; the Messiah is still to come. He does not see in the symbols the same things you see. He sees the old; you see the new. And in the discussion of Scripture after the rabbi's explanation, other Christians will challenge his interpretation for in it they, too, see the new and not the old.

Soon synagogue worship is over. As usual the worshipers have debated over the Christ, and some hard feelings have resulted. Family, friends, and neighbors are divided over the issue. So you look forward to the celebration of the New Covenant in the house where the Christians now meet.

You enter the house, greeting your friends with enthusiasm. It is good to be among those who will not be debating about Jesus. You know that together you will experience his presence in worship.

The house meeting begins with a meal, a love feast in which the Jewish prayers are prayed. These prayers, which you have heard in your home all your life, will be changed slightly to express the conviction that Jesus Christ is the Messiah. As you gather with others in the home, your eyes fall on the rich variety of food set on the table around the bread and wine.

Before you eat, the host in the tradition of Jewish prayers raises a cup filled with wine. He prays, "We give you thanks, our Father, for the holy vine of David, your servant, which you have made known to us through Jesus, your servant." You and the others respond, saying, "To you be glory forevermore." The wine is passed around, and you drink some. A similar prayer is said over the bread, and it, too, is passed around and eaten. You then, along with everyone else, eat your meal, talking, laughing, and enjoying the company of other believers.

After the meal, the leader may lead the congregation in psalm singing. An Old Testament passage or two may be read and discussed. Or perhaps an apostle may be visiting, and tell stories about Jesus, interpreting his death and urging you to live a life pleasing to the Lord.

Then come the prayers, after which the leader will say, "*Maranatha!*," which means "Our Lord, come." These words signal the beginning of a brand new rite, a thanksgiving offered to God the Father for the Son and for the new life that comes through his death and resurrection. You will say new prayers connected with the bread and wine. These elements were once symbols of food for the body, but now they are symbols of food for the soul as well. By participating in this offering of bread and wine, you know that you are participating in Christ's death and resurrection. Christ died to destroy the power of evil, and you participate in his death by allowing the power of his death to come into your life and put to death the evil that you struggle with. Just as Christ's resurrection was a resurrection to a new life, you surrender to the power of the resurrection in your own life. You allow God to release the Spirit of joy, peace, long-suffering, kindness, goodness, faithfulness, gentleness, and self-control within you. This is not only the thanksgiving of the church, but yours too. It is your Eucharist, your offering of thanks to God the Father.

In this imaginary depiction of early Christian worship (one must recognize the imaginary description of early Christian worship as scholarship cannot reduplicate it exactly) we are introduced to the biblical precedent for both the service of the Word and the service of the table.

In spite of scholarly inability to reduplicate the details of early Christian worship, there is consensus regarding the two central acts of biblical and historical worship—Word and table.[7] As time progressed, the early Christians developed acts of entrance and acts of dismissal in worship. Consequently, historical worship is divided into four movements: (1) we

---

7. See Webber, *Worship Old and New*.

enter into God's presence; (2) we hear God speak; (3) we celebrate at God's table; and (4) we are dismissed.

A glance at the revised prayer and service books of our time—Catholic, Anglican, Lutheran, Presbyterian, Methodist, United Church of Christ, Disciples, Evangelical Covenant, and many bulletins in Evangelical, Holiness, Pentecost and Charismatic churches will readily show the recovery of this fourfold pattern of worship.

What lies at the bottom of this recovery is not merely the restoration of a particular order, but a shape of the liturgy (to use Gregory Dix's phrase), a shape which allows for *anamnesis*. For in this shape the story is told and enacted, making the death and resurrection of Christ the pattern of our personal and corporate life in the world.

A Restoration of Music and the Arts as Vehicles of Communication

The concept of using the arts in worship is grounded biblically in the incarnation. A theology of the incarnation says that God, the immaterial one, became present in this created world in a material, tangible way. What this means for the arts is that the divine chooses to become present through creation: through wood, stone, mortar, color, sound, shape, form, movement, and action. Christians are not Gnostics who reject the body, the material, and the tangible. To do so would be to reject the incarnation. Christians affirm the created order because God affirmed the creation in the incarnation. Therefore, we need to set the creation free to speak redemption through the use of the arts in worship.

The arts are important because, like the incarnation, they communicate. The arts are the language of the intuition; they provide a poetic, imaginative way of supporting and enhancing the "text" of worship, the gospel. Communication through the arts is being recovered in Protestant services because Protestant worship is suffering from verbal overdose. Protestants have felt the need to explain everything as though verbal communication is the only legitimate form of communication. Protestants are learning to trust the arts—to see, touch, smell, and hear what they have to say. The arts are an active symbol, a visible word, a visual speech. They can and do speak. They can be used by the Spirit to communicate. But worshipers must learn to hear what the arts are saying, to befriend them, to let them live, worship with us, and serve as a vehicle for our praise.

Environmental Art

Environmental art is, first and foremost, the space in which we worship and, second, the furniture, hangings, and symbols with which we fill it. And this environment can indeed enhance and enliven the worship experience. Convergence churches are increasingly concerned about the space in which they worship.[8]

Frank Lloyd Wright reportedly said, "We shape our environment and then our environment shapes us." This axiom is particularly true in worship. For example, one growing church first met in a very small space where people were close together. The space generated a feeling of warmth, hospitality, and community. But then the church built a much larger space that distanced the people from each other and from the action of worship. Soon the people who had once shared a sense of community began to reflect the coldness and distance of their worship space. There is a liturgical correlation between space and the hospitality of the people who worship there. A church that meets in a cold and uninviting space, yet maintains a warm and hospitable community feeling, is rare. Space speaks. It is a visible word, a form of communication that speaks in subliminal ways.

Marshall McLuhan is famous for saying "the medium is the message."[9] This truth is expressed in a building being planned by Irvine Presbyterian Church, a convergence church in Irvine, California. Before planning their new sanctuary, the building committee spent time studying the theology of worship and liturgical space. They wanted to know, "What do we want our space to say?" Like McLuhan, they were convinced that the medium in which worship is done needs to support the action of worship, not fight it.

Unfortunately, the space in many churches works against worship renewal because the space is designed for worship that is either evangelistic or given to lecture style. For this reason, many Protestant churches have a front "stage" or "platform" with a pulpit, three chairs, a choir

---

8. See White, *Art, Architecture and Liturgical Reform*; and Kennel, *Visual Arts and Worship*.
9. See McLuhan, *Understanding Media*.

behind, a piano to the left, and an organ to the right. This space is good for listening and watching, but it does not support the current recovery of a worship that is dialogic and participatory.

Irvine Presbyterian Church turned its back on an evangelistic, pedagogical, or entertainment space and designed a space for worship that fits our participatory age, a space that sets people free to worship. The building committee planned their worship space around three themes—God's being, God's works, and God's people, and wrote a paper explaining the theology of liturgical space to the congregation. God's works, the committee's paper pointed out, are creation, redemption, and eschaton. The conviction that creation glorifies the Lord and proclaims God's splendor and power led them to feature natural materials in their worship space. Natural light and living plants serve to remind the worshiper that the whole universe is the sanctuary of the living God.

Because of their belief that Scripture reading, preaching, and the sacraments proclaim God's acts of salvation, these people concluded, "the furniture and fixtures relating to the preaching of the Word and the administration of the sacraments must be imbued with gained significance and occupy a place of prominence in the chancel." Because the eschaton is the promise that one day earthly worship will be joined with heavenly worship, the sanctuary "needs to express the glory of the kingdom, the unity of the church in heaven and earth, and the hope of eternal life."

Finally, the committee turned its attention to the space for the people, the community of worship. Because this is a "house of worship," they wrote, the space should not resemble "a lecture hall or auditorium" but should "foster a mood of prayerfulness and meditation rather than one of chattering conviviality." Consequently, "the seating will be gently arched so that we are aware of each other's presence, but not so much that we are distracted from worship." And because they gather in community to serve others, they added, "Our sanctuary should inspire us to live our lives in service to the Lord."

Not all churches that seek worship renewal have the luxury of building a new space. Nevertheless, attention needs to be given to the existing space. How can the space be modified so that it works for worship renewal and not against it? Many churches have refurbished their space by rearranging the seating in a semicircle, by placing both table and pulpit in prominent places, and by using appropriately placed banners, wall hangings, or Christian symbols. These touches add a sense of being connected with God's whole church as well as a feeling of warmth and hospitality.

Ultimately, a church has to wrestle with the relationship between space and its understanding of worship. Space does communicate. It can communicate warmth, hospitality, awe, reverence, and remembrance of God's action in history. Space can also evoke praise, worship, silence, and hope. There is no single correct or effective style. All these emotions can be evoked in a stately cathedral or in a building that is quite contemporary. More and more churches throughout the world are paying attention to how God encounters us through space and are becoming intentional in the way they use space for worship.

Music

Once we have created the space in which we worship, we are to fill it with the action of worship and with those sounds and movements which speak of our encounter with God. While it is possible to worship without the arts, modern worshipers are acutely aware of how important the arts are to worship. The arts are the wheels upon which the text of worship moves. They lift worship from an enslavement to words and set worship free to happen through action and symbolism.

A great deal is happening in music and worship today. Space does not permit the exploration of the shift from choir to cantor, a study of the various genres of music, or a discussion of the return of hymn festivals, the restoration of psalm singing, the emergence of a new hymnology, the restoration of ancient hymns, the birth of new praise choruses, or the use of Taizé music. I will concentrate, therefore, on the mix of musical styles in worship, a mix that expresses the full recovery of biblical and historical music in worship.[10]

The mixing of music styles is a phenomenon found all over the world. What I mean by the mixing of musical styles is that renewing churches are becoming aware of styles of music from other traditions and discovering how their worship is enriched by music from other traditions and cultures. For example, we usually associate stately hymns with liturgical churches. But now Catholic, Orthodox, Anglican, and Lutheran churches are singing the contemporary choruses we usually associate with the praise and worship tradition. Such choruses are being used especially at Communion.

---

10. See Day, *Why Catholics Can't Sing*; Funk, ed., *Sung Liturgy*; Hustad, *Jubilate!*; Hatchett, *Guide to the Practice of Church Music*; Westermeyer, *Church Musician*; Winter, *Why Sing*; and *Bishops Committee on the Liturgy*.

At the same time, Charismatics and praise and worship tradition people are beginning to discover the ancient hymn as well as some of the new hymns that are currently being introduced into worship. For example, Pentecostal worship leader Calvin Johansson has written several books urging Pentecostals and charismatics to recover the historical tradition of music.[11]

Perhaps what is being experienced by the church is the full recovery of music in worship as expressed by Paul in Ephesians 5:18-19, "Be filled with the Spirit, as you sing psalms and hymns and spiritual songs among yourselves, singing and making melody to the Lord in your hearts."[12]

Drama

Because worship recalls the living, dying and rising of Christ, it is a "kind" of drama. That is, like drama, worship is characterized by exposition, conflict, and resolution. The exposition is the gospel story. The conflict is the underlying cosmic conflict between good and evil and the resolution is the experience of the victory of Christ over evil.

One may see this matter of exposition conflict and resolve in the Eucharist. The Eucharist itself is a dramatic exposition of the gospel story. Through the words and actions of the breaking of bread the conflict between good and evil is vividly proclaimed and portrayed. And in the giving of the bread and wine with words such as "the body of Christ, the bread of heaven" and "the blood of Christ, the cup of salvation" with the accompanying response of "amen," the resolution is experienced through the experience of the overcoming power of Jesus and the saving and healing benefit he brings to the worshiper.

For this reason it is important to learn the script of worship. Learning the script sets the worshiper free to enter into the drama and play his or her part with full attention to the meaning of worship. More and more people in liturgical churches memorize their worship and people in non-liturgical churches are learning to be aware of the underlying script and movement of their worship.

---

11. Johansson, *Music & Ministry*.
12. Ephesians 5:18-19, NRSV.

Dance

Dance, like music, art, or drama, must complement the text and never dominate it. Like the other arts, it should never be a performance, but a visual and physical expression of the text it accompanies.[13]

In the context of a discussion of the propriety of dance in worship, I witnessed a woman dancing as she brought bread and wine to the Communion table. Her dance was to the hymn "Break Thou the Bread of Life." Although this hymn was originally meant for the preaching of the Word, this woman used it effectively at the bringing of the bread and wine. While the people sang, she served the text. She provided hand and body motions that effectively portrayed the bringing and the breaking of the body. What was important about this dance is that it allowed the people to visualize and feel the Word; her dance expressed what they were about to do. She did what dance and any art should do in worship—she served the text. Through the medium of movement, she allowed us to participate in the meaning of communion in a way that went beyond the limitations of the verbal text.

Another kind of dance has been introduced by many Charismatics, and that is the dance of joy, a participatory dance engaged in by the whole congregation. Recently in the chapel of Wheaton College during International Week, a group of Africans was in charge of the music. African Christians love to dance in worship (sometimes for an hour or more), so these Africans decided they were going to lead the entire student body in song and dance. That is not an easy thing to do in Edman Chapel because the seats are fixed (another point to be aware of in planning worship space). Nevertheless, the worship leaders had all the students stand, and they taught them an African song with movement. I cannot remember a more joyful experience in Edman Chapel! The students continued to comment on how freeing it was to dance to the Lord. This experience demonstrates how dance is a way of expressing and feeling great joy in worship. This is what convergence worshipers are rediscovering—worship as a response of joy to God who through Jesus Christ has redeemed us and set us free.

Much has been left unsaid in this section on the arts in worship. Nothing has been said about banners, textiles, pottery, sculpture, vestments, books, candles, colors, musical instruments, and other matters

---

13. See Adams and Apostolos-Cappadocia, eds., *Dance as Religious Studies*; and Gagne et al., *Introducing Dance in Christian Worship*.

pertinent to worship. Yet these play an important part in the recovery of the arts as well in contemporary worship.

What I have argued is that renewing churches are paying attention to the arts, recognizing that worship itself is an art, and integrating the arts in worship. The churches most sensitive to the arts are churches that give them a servant role in worship. In these churches worship is not arts-driven, but arts-enhanced. What is prominent in worship is the celebration of God's great deed of salvation in Jesus Christ. When the arts serve this message, they serve and assist worship. Through the arts, Christians are finding in their worship new dimensions of praise and thanksgiving. God uses the arts and becomes present to his people in a healing and comforting way as the arts bespeak redemption.

The Restoration of the Evangelical Nature of the Christian Year

Throughout this article we have been exploring the implications of worship as a celebration of the death and resurrection of Christ. Here I wish to show how the Christian year is related to the death and resurrection of Christ.

In his First Letter to the Corinthians, Paul challenges the church to "get rid of the old yeast that you may be a new batch without yeast as you really are. For Christ, our Passover lamb, has been sacrificed. Therefore, let us keep the festival, not with the old yeast, the yeast of malice and wickedness, but with the bread without yeast, the bread of sincerity and truth."[14] Every Sunday when Christians gather to worship, they celebrate the Christian Passover, but this Christian Passover also spans the entire year as an extended feast, a continuous celebration of God's saving deeds in Jesus Christ.

The salvation and healing of God's creatures and the world is brought about by the living, dying, and rising of Christ. Salvation is historical. It arises from specific events in history, not some transaction that takes place outside of time, space, and history. God's work of salvation is in history and through history and will be brought to completion within history. The services of the Christian year take us through the experience of those events of salvation.

Here lies the Evangelical nature of the Christian year: the gospel events that took place in time, space, and history find a tangible place in

14. 1 Corinthians 5:7–8, NIV.

present time. And through this yearly rehearsal of salvation, our spirituality, insofar as we allow, is actually shaped by the story of salvation.

This story of salvation is one of birth, life, death, resurrection, and empowerment. In the services of the church year, worshipers celebrate this pattern of salvation and do so in such a way that their own birth and life, their own pattern of death (brokenness and failure) and resurrection (being raised to new life), and their own Pentecost (empowerment to live in the Spirit) are all lifted up into the pattern of the life and death of Jesus. By celebrating his life, death, and resurrection, worshipers are constantly challenged into the newness of their own lives patterned on his death and resurrection.[15]

The practice of the Christian year brings us into the pattern of Jesus' life. Advent, when we wait for the coming of the Messiah, becomes our own spiritual waiting for the coming of Christ into our own lives. Christmas, which celebrates the birth of the Savior, becomes our own experience of Christ born within us. Epiphany, which rejoices in the proclamation of God's salvation in Christ to the Gentile world (as to the three wise men), becomes our own experience of recognizing Christ. Lent, which recalls the rising up against Jesus and the gathering storm that led to his rejection by his own people and death at the hands of the Romans, becomes a journey into our own sin and rebellion against Christ and a call to renewal. Holy Week, which marches through the last days of Jesus from his triumphant entry on Palm Sunday to his crucifixion, death, and burial, symbolizes our own death to sin. Easter, the great resurrection of our Lord to newness of life, becomes the anticipation of our own resurrection, our new birth. Finally, Pentecost, the celebration of the coming of the Spirit, marks a new gift of the Spirit in our own lives.

Many churches are discovering that the restoration of the evangelical nature of the Christian year is vital to the renewal of worship. The services of the Christian year guide us into an experience of Christ that direct the spiritual pilgrimage of the congregation into an ever deepening relationship with him. The services of the Christian year also constantly remind (*anamnesis*) us of God's saving deeds and provide opportunities for him to touch us with his transforming power.

---

15. See Adam, *Liturgical Year*; L'Engle, *Traditional Season*; Nardone, *Story of the Christian Year*; Talley, *Origins of the Liturgical Year*.

A Restoration of a Sacrament as Encounter with Christ

Contemporary worship renewal is paying new attention to the sacraments, ordinances, and sacred actions of the church. Sociologists and educational specialists are enabling us to see these spiritual acts in new ways. We are seeing these acts as rites of passage for spiritual growth and development. We also recognize them as encounters with Christ, encounters that shape the pattern of our dying and being raised again.

Although there are tensions that exist between various Christian groups and denominations, differences that go back four hundred years to the Protestant Reformation, the contemporary church is finding a common ground where sacramentalists and non-sacramentalists can meet. That common ground is found in the gospel that worship celebrates in sacred actions.[16]

Contemporary Orthodox, Catholic, and Protestant sacramental theology recognizes Jesus Christ as the one primordial sacrament. He and he alone makes us holy and brings us to God. This means that the sacred actions of the church are symbols of divine action. These signs are not ends in themselves or objects of faith, but visible, tangible signs through which worshipers experience a special action of God to save and to heal us. These signs then become for us an encounter with Christ.

Perhaps the most stunning achievement of modern theological convergence on the sacraments is the 1982 World Council of Churches text, *Baptism, Eucharist and Ministry* (*BEM*). In the preface to this work the writers declare:

> In leaving behind the hostilities of the past, the churches have begun to discover many promising convergences in their shared convictions and perspectives. These convergences give assurance that despite much diversity in theological expression the churches have much in common in their understanding of the faith.[17]

The early church's understanding of baptism which is recaptured in BEM is that baptism represents the end of one relationship and the beginning of another. That is the reason baptism belongs in worship. Worship celebrates the victory of Christ over evil, and baptism is an act of relocating one's life from a surrendering to the power of evil to a surrendering

---

16. See Driver, *Magic of Ritual,* and Mitchell, *Meaning of Ritual.*
17. *Baptism, Eucharist and Ministry*, Preface II.

to the power of the Spirit. The one symbol of that action is the rite of renunciation, the spit in the face of the devil.[18]

The symbols of the bread and wine at the table of the Lord are also inextricably bound to the meaning of worship as a celebration of the victory of Christ over evil and of the application of that victory to our own lives. The *BEM* proclaims:

> The church, gratefully recalling God's mighty acts of redemption, beseeches God to give the benefits of these acts to every human being.[19]

The motif that Christ is the victor over sin, or, as Hippolytus puts it, that he died "to shatter the chains of the evil one, to trample underfoot the powers of Hell," is being rediscovered in nearly all the denominations of the world and expressed in their eucharistic prayers. This theme of Christ as victor is set forth not only in the text of the eucharistic prayer but in song, which accompanies that text and in the rites of healing which often occur either as the Eucharist is being celebrated or immediately before or after.[20]

A Restoration of the Relationship of Worship to the Outreach Ministries of the Church

The relationship of worship to the outreach ministry of the church is captured in these words from the *Constitution on the Sacred Liturgy*:

> The Liturgy is the summit toward which the activity of the church is directed; at the same time it is the fount from which all the church's power flows.[21]

Since Vatican II the churches are giving considerable thought to the relationship of worship to evangelism,[22] education,[23] spiritual formation,[24]

---

18. See Murphy Center, *Made, Not Born*; Kavanaugh, *Shape of Baptism*; and Stevick, *Baptismal Moments; Baptismal Meanings*.

19. *Baptism, Eucharist and Ministry*, 11.

20. See Crockett, *Eucharist*; Schmemann, *Eucharist*; Staples, *Outward Sign and Inward Grace*; and Stevenson, *Eucharist and Offering*.

21. *Constitution on the Sacred Liturgy*, 10.

22. See Boyack, *Catholic Evangelization Today*.

23. See Ostediek, *Catechesis for Liturgy*.

24. See Braso, *Liturgy and Spirituality*; and Schreiter, *In Water and Blood*.

work[25] and social ethics.[26] Due to limitations of space my comments will be restricted to the relationship between worship and evangelism.

In recent years some churches have been in the process of recovering the pattern of evangelism of the early church, particularly that of the fourth century.[27] This pattern of evangelism, which was widespread,[28] presupposed a *Christus Victor* view of the world and the church as a mothering and nurturing community. The external rites of the catechumenate ordered internal experience, and the convert passed through various stages of conversion and spiritual maturation.[29]

In brief, evangelism consisted of seven steps which took place over a three-year period (longer or shorter in some places) and was made up of three passage rites and four prolonged stages of development. These seven steps are summarized below:

1) inquiry (a time to encounter the gospel message)

2) rite of welcome (a passage rite into the church)

3) catechumenate (a three-year period of spiritual formation and growth into the understanding of the faith)

4) rite of election (a passage rite of public affirmation of the faith)

5) period of purification and enlightenment (an intensive period of spiritual preparation immediately before baptism)

6) rite of initiation (the passage rite of baptism that brings the convert into the fullness of the church with eucharistic privileges)

7) mystagogy (a period of time to explain the rites the catechumen had undergone and integrate the converted person into the full life of the church).

This ancient form of evangelism is now the object of study in nearly every major denomination of the world. While its present rise is primarily in the liturgical churches, most denominations are addressing how this form of evangelism can be adapted to their own worshiping community. It cannot now be said what will happen in the church as a result

25. See Tabori, *Eucharist and the World of Work*.

26. Empereur and Kiesling, *Liturgy That Does Justice*; Grosz, ed., *Liturgy and Social Justice*; and Willimon, *Service of God*.

27. See Dujarier, *History of the Catechumenate* and *Rites of Christian Initiation*.

28. See Yarnold, *Awe-Inspiring Rites of Initiation*.

29. See Webber, *Liturgical Evangelism*.

of this study, except to say that the adaptation of this ancient form of evangelism holds considerable promise for local church evangelism. This ancient pattern may have the power to bring people not only into Christ, but also into a communal relationship with the church.

Models of evangelism with some similarity to this ancient model are now being found in the seeker service movement. For example, at Willow Creek Community Church in South Barrington, Illinois, the process of evangelism and the nurturing of new Christians follows these seven steps:

1) Every-member evangelism (each member of the church is viewed as an evangelist).

2) Prepare to give a verbal witness (each member learns the art of telling his/her story).

3) The Seekers Service (a place to bring inquiring people who are interested in the Christian faith as a result of steps 1 and 2. These persons are encouraged to remain in the seekers service stage until they have been converted and baptized). Meets Saturday night and Sunday morning.

4) The new community. (Converts are now involved in believers worship where they are nurtured in understanding and growth through Word and Sacrament.) The converts meet Wednesday and Thursday evening.

5) Small groups. Converts are put into a small group situation where they are discipled in the faith.

6) Discernment of gifts. The gifts of new converts are discerned, and they offer these gifts to the body.

7) Stewardship. New converts are trained to be stewards of God's earth, of their time, and of their money.

While the parallels between evangelism and worship with the early church are not exact, they do point to the recognition of the relationship between worship and evangelism, and second to the understanding of conversion as a process of growth and development into Christ and the church.

Conclusion

This paper has attempted to point to the future direction of worship in the local church. The six contours of development stated above are not yet seen in the majority of local churches. Yet, these trends influenced the lives of numerous church leaders, pastors, music ministers, and lay people of the church. A movement appears to be in the making, a movement that has considerable content and spirit, a movement that has the potential to reshape the life of worship and the life of the local church. And this movement is the convergence of worship traditions based on the recovery of biblical and historical studies in worship.[30]

---

30. This paper is a summary of Webber, *Signs of Wonder*. Portions of the book are incorporated in this article with permission of the publisher.

24

A Call to an Ancient-Evangelical Future[1]

Prologue

IN EVERY AGE THE Holy Spirit calls the church to examine its faithfulness to God's revelation in Jesus Christ, authoritatively recorded in Scripture and handed down through the church. Thus, while we affirm the global strength and vitality of worldwide evangelicalism in our day, we believe the North American expression of evangelicalism needs to be especially sensitive to the new external and internal challenges facing God's people.

These external challenges include the current cultural milieu and the resurgence of religious and political ideologies. The internal challenges include evangelical accommodation to civil religion, rationalism, privatism, and pragmatism. In light of these challenges, we call evangelicals to strengthen their witness through a recovery of the faith articulated by the consensus of the ancient church and its guardians in the traditions of Eastern Orthodoxy, Roman Catholicism, the Protestant Reformation, and the Evangelical awakenings. Ancient Christians faced a world of paganism, Gnosticism, and political domination. In the face of heresy and persecution, they understood history through Israel's story, culminating in the death and resurrection of Jesus and the coming of God's kingdom.

Today, as in the ancient era, the church is confronted by a host of master narratives that contradict and compete with the gospel. The pressing question is: Who gets to narrate the world? "The Call to an Ancient-Evangelical Future" challenges Evangelical Christians to restore the

[1]. Originally published in *Christianity Today*, September 1, 2006. Used by permission.

priority of the divinely inspired biblical story of God's acts in history. The narrative of God's kingdom holds eternal implications for the mission of the church, its theological reflection, its public ministries of worship and spirituality, and its life in the world. By engaging these themes, we believe the church will be strengthened to address the issues of our day.

1. On the Primacy of the Biblical Narrative

We call for a return to the priority of the divinely authorized canonical story of the triune God. This story—creation, incarnation, and re-creation—was effected by Christ's recapitulation of human history and summarized by the early church in its rules of faith. The gospel-formed content of these rules served as the key to the interpretation of Scripture and its critique of contemporary culture, and thus shaped the church's pastoral ministry. Today, we call Evangelicals to turn away from modern theological methods that reduce the gospel to mere propositions, and from contemporary pastoral ministries so compatible with culture that they camouflage God's story or empty it of its cosmic and redemptive meaning. In a world of competing stories, we call Evangelicals to recover the truth of God's Word as the story of the world, and to make it the centerpiece of Evangelical life.

2. On the Church, the Continuation of God's Narrative

We call Evangelicals to take seriously the visible character of the church. We call for a commitment to its mission in the world in fidelity to God's mission (*missio Dei*), and for an exploration of the ecumenical implications this has for the unity, holiness, catholicity, and apostolicity of the church. Thus, we call Evangelicals to turn away from an individualism that makes the church a mere addendum to God's redemptive plan.

Individualistic Evangelicalism has contributed to the current problems of churchless Christianity, redefinitions of the church according to business models, separatist ecclesiologies, and judgmental attitudes toward the church. Therefore, we call Evangelicals to recover their place in the community of the church catholic.

3. On the Church's Theological Reflection on God's Narrative

We call for the church's reflection to remain anchored in the Scriptures in continuity with the theological interpretation learned from the early Fathers. Thus, we call Evangelicals to turn away from methods that separate theological reflection from the common traditions of the church. These modern methods compartmentalize God's story by analyzing its separate parts, while ignoring God's entire redemptive work as recapitulated in Christ. Anti-historical attitudes also disregard the common biblical and theological legacy of the ancient church.

Such disregard ignores the hermeneutical value of the church's ecumenical creeds. This reduces God's story of the world to one of many competing theologies and impairs the unified witness of the church to God's plan for the history of the world. Therefore, we call Evangelicals to unity in "the tradition that has been believed everywhere, always, and by all," as well as to humility and charity in their various Protestant traditions.

4. On the Church's Worship as Telling and Enacting God's Narrative

We call for public worship that sings, preaches, and enacts God's story. We call for a renewed consideration of how God ministers to us in baptism, Eucharist, confession, the laying on of hands, marriage, healing, and through the charisms of the Spirit, for these actions shape our lives and signify the meaning of the world. Thus, we call Evangelicals to turn away from forms of worship that focus on God as a mere object of the intellect or that assert the self as the source of worship. Such worship has resulted in lecture-oriented, music-driven, performance-centered, and program-controlled models that do not adequately proclaim God's cosmic redemption. Therefore, we call Evangelicals to recover the historic substance of worship of Word and table and to attend to the Christian year, which marks time according to God's saving acts.

5. On Spiritual Formation in the Church as Embodiment of God's Narrative

We call for a catechetical spiritual formation of the people of God that is based firmly on a Trinitarian biblical narrative. We are concerned when spirituality is separated from the story of God and baptism into the life of Christ and his body. Spirituality, made independent from God's story, is often characterized by legalism, mere intellectual knowledge, an overly therapeutic culture, New Age Gnosticism, a dualistic rejection of this world, and a narcissistic preoccupation with one's own experience. These false spiritualities are inadequate for the challenges we face in today's world. Therefore, we call Evangelicals to return to a historic spirituality like that taught and practiced in the ancient catechumenate.

6. On the Church's Embodied Life in the World

We call for a cruciform holiness and commitment to God's mission in the world. This embodied holiness affirms life, biblical morality, and appropriate self-denial. It calls us to be faithful stewards of the created order and bold prophets to our contemporary culture. Thus, we call Evangelicals to intensify their prophetic voice against forms of indifference to God's gift of life, economic and political injustice, ecological insensitivity, and the failure to champion the poor and marginalized. Too often we have failed to stand prophetically against the culture's captivity to racism, consumerism, political correctness, civil religion, sexism, ethical relativism, violence, and the culture of death. These failures have muted the voice of Christ to the world through his church and detract from God's story of the world, which the church is collectively to embody. Therefore, we call the church to recover its counter-cultural mission to the world.

Epilogue

In sum, we call evangelicals to recover the conviction that God's story shapes the mission of the church to bear witness to God's kingdom and to inform the spiritual foundations of civilization. We set forth this call as an ongoing, open-ended conversation. We are aware that we have our blind spots and weaknesses. Therefore, we encourage Evangelicals to engage this call within educational centers, denominations, and local churches through publications and conferences.

We pray that we can move with intention to proclaim a loving, transcendent, triune God who has become involved in our history. In line with Scripture, creed, and tradition, it is our deepest desire to embody God's purposes in the mission of the church through our theological reflection, our worship, our spirituality, and our life in the world, all the while proclaiming that Jesus is Lord over all creation.

This call is issued in the spirit of *sic et non*; therefore, those who affix their names to this call need not agree with all its content. Rather, its consensus is that these are issues to be discussed in the tradition of *semper reformanda* as the church faces the new challenges of our time. Over a period of seven months, more than 300 persons have participated via email to write the call. These men and women represent a broad diversity of ethnicity and denominational affiliation. The four theologians who most consistently interacted with the development of the call have been named as theological editors. The board of reference was given the special assignment of overall approval.

25

What We've Learned Along the Way: Reformed Worship Through Twenty Years of Liturgical Change[1]

TODAY'S WORSHIP MOVEMENT BEGAN back in the sixties and early seventies from two very divergent sources. First, renewal within the liturgical movement was prompted by the publication of the *Constitution on the Sacred Liturgy*, the first document of Vatican II. On the date of its release (December 4, 1963) Pope Paul VI spoke of worship as "the first subject to be examined [by the Vatican Council] and the first, too, in a sense, in its intrinsic value and in importance for the life of the church." The second worship renewal movement was born in the "Jesus Movement" of the late sixties and early seventies. The leaders of this movement, like Tommy Coombs, actually "found Christ" in worship at what is now Calvary Church in Costa Mesa, California.

It is significant, I think, to note that both the liturgical and contemporary movements, out of opposite histories, recognized the need to prioritize worship as the first thing—or at least, one of the firsts among several equals—that the church must be about. Worship is a first, because it is a source from which the mission of the church in the world proceeds. One may see these two worship movements as a "thesis" and "antithesis," which spawned a "synthesis" or convergence worship movement. Throughout its years of publication, *RW* has served both these movements of renewal.

---

1. Originally published in *Reformed Worship Journal*, September 2005. Used by permission.

Thesis: A Protestant Worship Manifesto

It was scholar James White, professor of liturgy at Notre Dame, who began the crusade to apply the principles of the *Constitution on the Sacred Liturgy to the Protestant Church*. In "A Protestant Worship Manifesto" first published in *The Christian Century* (January 27, 1982), White called the Protestant community to pay attention to the following twelve themes of worship renewal:

1. Worship should be shaped in the light of understanding it as the church's unique contribution to the struggle for justice.
2. The Paschal (Easter) nature of Christian worship should resound throughout all services.
3. The centrality of the Bible in Protestant worship must be recovered.
4. The importance of time as a major structure in Christian worship must be rediscovered.
5. All reforms in worship must be shaped ecumenically.
6. Drastic changes are needed in the process of Christian initiation (discipleship and baptism).
7. High on the list of reforms is the need to recover the Eucharist (Lord's Supper) as the chief Sunday service.
8. Recovery of the sense of God's action in other "commonly called sacraments" is essential.
9. Music must be seen in its pastoral context as fundamentally an enabler of fuller congregational participation.
10. The space and furnishings for worship need substantial change in most churches.
11. No reform of worship will progress far until much more effort is invested in teaching seminarians and clergy to think through the functions of Christian worship.
12. Liturgical renewal is not just a changing of worship but is part of a reshaping of American Christianity root and branch.[2]

---

2. White, "Protestant Worship Manifesto," 82.

As I have recorded these twelve goals set forth by White twenty-three years ago, I've noted, twelve times over, that this particular concern has been and is being addressed by *Reformed Worship*. There is no question in my mind that *RW* has, for twenty years, served the full spectrum of the issues that proceed from worship as a first-order concern of the church.

Antithesis: A Contemporary Worship Manifesto

But what about the contemporary worship movement? Has *Reformed Worship* spoken to the concerns within that body as well? This question is more difficult to answer for two reasons. First, contemporary worship has not evolved in a straight line. It has many permutations within the historic Pentecostal movement, the contemporary movement, and, of course, the Evangelical megachurch movement. And second, *Worship Leader* has been the primary voice of this movement. However, *RW* has also served the contemporary movement by addressing contemporary issues and by encouraging the leaders of the contemporary worship movement to draw from the rich sources of historic worship.

To help you see how *RW* has addressed contemporary worship issues, let me introduce you to a little-known manifesto written by Henry Jauhiainen, pastor of a contemporary Pentecostal Charismatic (yes, they can all be brought together in worship) church in Crystal Lake, Illinois. I asked Henry, a very thoughtful and deep person, to write a contemporary manifesto for the *Complete Library of Christian Worship: Vol. II, Twenty Centuries of Christian Worship*. His comments help put into perspective another side of the ministry of *RW*. He calls the church to seven cutting-edge concerns that bear on contemporary worship:

1. We should see our worship as Christian, occurring within the Pentecostal-Charismatic context—not the reverse.
2. We need to see the vital relationship between Christian worship and Christian truth.
3. We need to maintain the christological focus, the "Paschal Center" of all worship.
4. We need to place our music more purposefully throughout the service.
5. We need to recover a true sense of mystery in Christian worship.

6. We need to rediscover the essence of the kingdom of God in our worship.

7. We need to rediscover a deep sense of our constant need for the grace of God.³

Once again, as I reviewed these contemporary issues of worship renewal, I kept coming back to "*Reformed Worship* addressed that." *RW* has primarily served the Protestant mainline, and its greatest impact has been within the Reformed community, but it has consistently affirmed worship renewal in the whole church and facilitated the renewal of worship and of the church, in every quarter of the body of Christ, including the contemporary movement. In this way *Reformed Worship* has come alongside of the contemporary movement and has encouraged an ecumenical spirit among the churches.

Synthesis: The Convergence Worship Movement

The convergence worship movement has intentionally brought about a synthesis between the liturgical and contemporary worship renewal movements. It has had a number of different permeations and is difficult to track because it is so diverse. The Charismatic Episcopal church is one example of a concerted and intentional effort at convergence. But then, convergence happens in any community that seeks to integrate another tradition into itself. However, as in the areas of traditional and contemporary worship, a manifesto on convergence worship has also been written—Randy Sly and Wayne Boosahda's article in *Twenty Centuries of Christian Worship*. And like the authors of the previously mentioned manifestos, they have laid out a general agenda for convergence churches to follow:

1. A restored commitment to the sacraments, especially the Lord's Table.

2. An increased motivation to know more about the early church.

3. A love for the whole church and a desire to see the church as one.

4. The blending in the practice of all three streams is evident [Liturgical, Charismatic, Evangelical/Reformed], yet each church approaches convergence from a unique point of view.

3. Jauhiainen, "Pentecostal/Charismatic Manifesto."

5. An interest in integrating structure with spontaneity in worship.
6. A greater involvement of sign and symbol in worship.
7. A continuing commitment to personal salvation, biblical teaching, and the work and ministry of the Holy Spirit.[4]

So, has *Reformed Worship* also spoken to the issues of convergence worship? I think so. The breadth of the articles, the concern for historical traditions (especially that of the early church), the open attitude toward a gentle Charismatic spirit, the concern to be Evangelical—all these themes, if not directly addressed in specific articles, underscore the general thrust and tenor of *RW* from its beginning.

In its twenty years of history, then, *RW* has spoken broadly to the entire worship renewal movement—Liturgical, Contemporary, and Convergence.

Future Challenges for Reformed Worship

Here is my "short list" of issues that will shape *RW* in the near future.

1. Consider the new cultural challenge.

Much has happened in culture in the last twenty years. We no longer live in the same world that launched *RW*. Even though many of the "worship issues" remain the same, the culture in which worship must be formed has changed radically. We now live in a post-Christian, postmodern, neo-pagan world. The sharp distinction being drawn between "secularism" on the one hand and a "biblical worldview" on the other hand will result in a worship that is increasingly counter-cultural.

2. Restore the connection of worship with a storied theology.

The demise of "scientific-Enlightenment theology" and the return to the "biblical story" rooted in creation/incarnation/re-creation opens new possibilities for a worship that is rooted more specifically in the story-formed worship of the ancient church—especially for the recovery of a greater sense of mystery and a more intentional use of symbol.

3. Restore the unity between story/worship/spirituality.

Worship and spirituality are both situated in God's story. In recent years worship and spirituality have been separated from a storied theology and moved off into a life of their own, drifting toward a self-focused

---

4. Sly and Boosahda, "Convergence Movement."

narcissism. Worship, instead of being God's story sung, proclaimed, and enacted, has been grounded in the self—what "I" do for God. And spirituality, instead of being an embodiment of God's story in all of life, has turned inward into the journey to self. Only the recovery of God's story as the source of both worship and spirituality can correct the dangerous trend of self-focused worship and spirituality.

These three issues constitute my "short list" that frame, I believe, the future discussion. And I am convinced that *RW* will contribute significant leadership to these new issues, even as it has led in the issues of the past, issues that are still very much with us. Even though many of the "worship issues" remain the same, the culture in which worship must be formed has changed radically. Much has happened in culture in the last twenty years. We no longer live in the same world that launched *RW*.

26

Christ the Victor, Christ the Center[1]

Review of *The Person of Christ*, by David F. Wells, Westchester, IL: Crossway, 1984.

THEOLOGICAL ISSUES RARELY MAKE front-page news. However, when the book *The Myth of God Incarnate* was published in July of 1977, the secular press immediately turned it into a front-page controversy.

John Hick, the book's editor, argued that the notion of God becoming incarnate as man must finally be acknowledged as a myth. The Reformers, he argued, dropped the supernatural concept of the sacraments. The eighteenth- and nineteenth-century theologians dropped the idea of a supernatural Bible. So now, in the twentieth century, the time had finally come to be honest about the last myth—the incarnation.

Hick's heresy illustrates the dilemma of modern theology. Unable to verify in any historical or logical way the supernatural assertions of the New Testament, many moderns have resorted to a mythological interpretation of the life and times of Jesus. Not so David F. Wells, who tackles the tough questions pertaining to a supernatural Christology in *The Person of Christ: A Biblical and Historical Analysis of the Incarnation*.

From the very beginning of Christianity, the bottom line has always been supernaturalism. Thus Wells, professor of theology at Gordon-Conwell Theological Seminary, offers in his book an apology for the supernatural Jesus, and consequently enters into dialogue with all those who reject orthodox theology.

---

1. Originally published in *Christianity Today*, April 5, 1985. Used by permission.

Appropriately, he begins the study of Christology not with an arsenal of texts, but with the Christ event itself and with a description of the cosmic nature of Messiah's work. Christ is, as Paul reports in Colossians, not only the creator—the one in whom all things consist—but the redeemer, the one in whom all things are recapitulated, restored, renewed, and recreated. He, the *Christus Victor*, has destroyed death, trod down the devil, and dethroned the powers of evil. The choice between a mythological Jesus and a historic, supernatural, and cosmic Christ starts here. And the choice one makes, like a stone cast into still water, sends ripples in every direction.

An Excerpt:

> It is abundantly clear from this overview that the New Testament has provided its own categories for interpreting the figure of Jesus, and we do violence to its thought if we supplant them with others more familiar or congenial to us. The Protestant liberals did this, choosing to replace the Kingdom by the category of conventional biography; the Bultmannians are doing it by discounting the human and historic significance of Jesus and eliciting his contemporary meaning through existential verities. In the one case the in-breaking of God with and in Jesus was muted, and in the other the significance of this in-breaking is seen to come, not so much through Jesus, but in each believer. Thus these theologians have developed hermeneutical categories which are reductionistic, and the result is that the real significance of God's action is largely or completely lost.[2]

Faith's Core

Christology is now and always has been the central issue of the Christian faith. When Peter preached his Pentecost sermon, the central theme was that "this Jesus whom you crucified" is Lord and Christ. One of the earliest Christian confessions was "Jesus is Lord." Primitive hymnology such as John 1:1–14 declared that the pre-existent Logos became flesh and manifested the glory of God. And the christological hymn of Philippians 2:1–11 affirms the divine descent into human form and the human ascent into the heavens followed by the exaltation of Jesus.

---

2. Wells, *Person of Christ*, 31.

These liturgical affirmations, which reflected the experience of the earliest Christian communities, soon became the objects of reflection and intellectual inquiry, as well as theological speculation. It was not enough for the church simply to affirm the deity of Christ and the coalescence between the human and the divine. As the faith moved out into the Hellenistic culture, intellectual questions about Christian experience inevitably arose. *How* is Jesus related to the Father? And what kind of language best describes such indescribable matters as the union between the human and the divine in the person of Jesus? This shift from an experiential Christianity to an intellectual Christianity raised—and raises—numerous questions about Jesus' identity that Wells addresses forthrightly from a supernatural perspective.

This orientation on the supernatural Christ does not, however, keep Wells from addressing the proof-texting supernaturalist who does not think theologically. Indeed, Wells is concerned about those Christians who have been stumped by wrong-headed theology. What *do* you say, for example, to clean-cut missionaries from the Jehovah's Witnesses who insist that "Jesus *really* isn't God" because "the New Testament teaches that he's the *Son of God*, the first-born of creation, but not the same essence as God"? Or, what do you say to your neighbor who says, "Oh, I certainly hold Jesus in great respect. Surely he is a window to the Father, the leader of a great humanitarian ideal, the originator of love as the central religious motif. But God? Hardly."

Unfortunately, there are too many supernaturalists who give weak and even heretical answers to these tough questions. For example, a few years ago this reviewer lectured to an Inter-Varsity group at a Midwestern secular university. During a discussion of Christology, a man stood to his feet and insisted he could solve the problem of the relationship between the human and divine in the person of Christ. He proudly announced that "Jesus was a human shell in whom the Logos resided." Because this was the essential argument of Apollinarianism, a heresy of the early church, I retorted with tongue in cheek, "You're a heretic. We ought to burn you at the stake." I later discovered he was the faculty adviser.

This illustration points up still another value of *The Person of Christ*—Wells's methodology. It approaches the christological issue from a biblical, historical, and contemporary perspective, while speaking to a major problem that has plagued Evangelicals since their beginning: the disdain for history and tradition. We tend to leap from the New Testament text to the present, disregarding 2,000 years of history. Cheers for Wells, who does not do that. He painstakingly leads us through the major early church battles, the undermining of supernaturalism in the eighteenth and nineteenth centuries, and into the presuppositions of the modern reformulation of christological thought. Consequently, *The Person of Christ* is not only an example of good methodology, but of solid scholarship.

Wells is no theological sissy. He tackles his thesis with a John Wayne resolve, swaggering into the anti-supernatural town with both barrels blazing, pumping biblical, historical, and theological bullets into his falling targets. And his book is no bus station handout. It is a treatise for the serious student, the thinker. Wells does not tolerate the monosyllabic set who are satisfied with nine-verse tracts.

So get your theological dictionary, your Roget's *Thesaurus*, and discover again that a supernatural Jesus, a supernatural Bible, and a supernatural working of God through the sacraments do indeed belong to a seamless robe.

27

Worship Like You Mean It: Interview with Sally Morgenthaler and Robert E. Webber[1]

YouthWorker Journal: After a big youth rally that's been hyped with pyrotechnics and a full band that practiced for weeks, how do you get students back into authentic worship without the aid of those externals—and keep their praise more than roller-coaster emotionalism?

Sally Morgenthaler: If students aren't experiencing God's presence in any other way than with big, expensive events, they'll assume God's going to go hide somewhere until the next rally comes around.

If you've ever been fortunate enough to witness a Delirious concert, you know the swirling, pulsating lights, smoke, interactive video and the band's incredible musicianship spells awesome. It's unforgettable. Yet if you've been fortunate enough to light one small candle with two or three friends, wait for God in silence and sing a heartfelt confession accompanied by the quiet ripple of an acoustic guitar, you know there's a vast repertoire for this thing we call experiencing God. One of the values we can build into youth is deep interaction with God—a simple here-and-now reality in our spiritual communities.

Robert Webber: First, let's keep in mind there's a new cultural shift taking place with the rise of millennials. A great majority of them are reacting against the loud music and hype often associated with contemporary worship.

---

1. Originally published in *YouthWorker Journal*, July-August 1999. Used with permission.

A key for worship in the regular rhythm of the church is to remember communication in a postmodern world has shifted from verbal explanation to immersed participation in events. The key to good worship is to stay away from entertainment models and return worship to the people. This generation wants to participate with the body and the senses. Thoroughly active and participatory worship will attract and keep our young people.

YWJ: *How do you implement regular worship times in a small group that's never done it consistently before? We've tried several times, but it always seems to die out due to lack of commitment on the part of the musicians or lack of interest on the part of the students.*

Morgenthaler: Maybe the regimentation of a worship time gets in the way. Youth are relationally driven. That's where their motivations are. If you can let worship times emerge out of small group discussion or times of prayer, it may seem more authentic. Also, it could be that our Evangelical definitions of worship—a bunch of praise songs stuck together—needs expansion.

How about paraphrasing Scripture and reading it together? How about, in the context of a small group setting, encouraging your students to dramatize a parable or play some cool, techno music underneath it?

I think a lot of us—adults included—are just plain bored with singing thirty to forty minutes of praise songs. We crave multi-sensory expressions. Why can't we use all the arts to get students to make worship an aesthetic experience that pleases God by engaging their minds, hearts, emotions, and spirits?

Webber: You may have to change your style to a more participatory worship. I use communal gestures: standing, sitting, kneeling, lying prostrate on the floor, prayers of the people, talk-back sermons, passing of the peace, and gathering around the table. You may also anoint with oil and do laying-on of hands. This generation wants an authentic embodiment of worship—and young people are quick and can spot a phony a mile away.

However, when worship is genuine and done *by* them—not to them or for them—they will respond. By the way, passing the peace (if you're not familiar with that term) is based on the first words Jesus said to his disciples in the Upper Room: "Peace be with you." For centuries, Christians passed or spoke his greeting to each other in church between the service of the Word and the Eucharist. It became lost in worship, but recently has been restored.

YWJ: What are the most practical ways to get students involved in actual worship—not just the music part?

Morgenthaler: If you change your model from a praise-song fixation to a fully orbed, aesthetic adoration of God, you're going to need dancers, painters, weavers, sculptors, poets, writers, actors, storytellers, photographers, and digital graphics people. (By the way, there are lots of budding digital daredevils out there. They're working on creative stuff three to four hours a day in their basements—and no one knows!) The arts speak to young people.

Yes, music is part of that; but we've isolated our affective experience of God to one tiny slice of the artistic pie. Worship music often is dictated to us by the worship music industry. I think we can do better. We can write our own music and then expand the expressive vocabulary to tactile, visual, etc. We will be absolutely astonished at the energy that's released in students once they're invited to share their gifts—musical and otherwise.

Webber: Let's go back again to this matter of participation: It's not this person doing an act of worship, such as reading Scripture or offering a prayer; it's the whole congregation doing the worship. Worship is a drama about the meaning of life: The leaders are prompters of the drama, the members of the congregation are the players, and—as Kierkegaard said—"if there's an audience in worship, it's God." We really need a revolution in our understanding of worship if we're to experience what I'm talking about. The notion that worship is a drama that recites and enacts God's saving deeds in history is thoroughly biblical, yet unknown to many of us.

YWJ: Is there some way to develop a farm system for student musicians/vocalists?

Morgenthaler: If you have a band that's first and foremost relationally connected—to each other, to the rest of the group and (this is critical) to non-Christians in your community, musicians will come. They'll not only be attracted to the music, but more importantly to the very real, caring people behind the music. A lot of teens—especially band types—are looking for new families. Your band can become that new family, a new community for students whose lives have been broken apart, students who are at risk and looking for a soft landing.

Webber: The idea of a farm system for students who wish to learn more about worship leading is a terrific idea. I believe youth workers should be proactive in identifying students who have a particular sensitivity to God's moving and Spirit—musical ability is important, but not as important as a heart connected to God. The best way I think you can grow these students into worship leaders is to offer them training.

YWJ: Some youth group leaders have had non-Christian student musicians up front, believing this will change their hearts toward God. Is this wise?

Morgenthaler: Something we have to understand (and this not only applies to musicians, but also to the whole community of students) is that for a generation that values the arts more highly than business, a generation that would rather consume digital content than eat, a generation that would rather stand in line for days to see the latest movie than sleep, the arts are one of our most powerful evangelistic tools.

Now apply that principle to a band situation: Can we make room for the non-Christian, garage band guitarist to play while he or she is in the process of figuring out this God thing? Simple fact: Salvation takes longer in this culture. Rarely do students come to our gatherings and sign on the dotted line the first time. They need to try on faith, to practice doing Christianity with us. They need to develop relationships with us to see if we're for real. Worship is a perfect context for all of that to happen, and the arts can be the conduit into worship.

Now I'm not saying that the majority of your band should be non-Christians or that your worship leader should be a non-Christian. Let's use some common sense. I'm just saying that God works in mysterious ways, and if we wait for people to spout out the right words, to look the way we look, to shed the earrings and tattoos and wear Abercrombie [&] Fitch, we'll probably miss a zillion windows of opportunity. Do we put a premium on accountability? Yes. That's what we do in our families with our kids—they weren't born knowing right and wrong. They learn by doing and watching and participating. Do we teach the in-process seeker what God expects? Absolutely. Again, that's what we do in our own families; but we do it in the context of a small unit—Mom, Dad, brothers and sisters. In the church of the next millennium, the family/small unit will be (to a great degree) groups of artists expressing their God experiences together.

Webber: The kind of worship I'm talking about, the kind that moves you into the presence of God, deepens commitment and fills you with joy requires Christian leadership.

YWJ: How do you gauge whether students are ready to lead worship and what (if any) personal and spiritual requirements should you place on them?

Morgenthaler: Often we've looked at religious criteria (conformity to institutional expectations) rather than spiritual depth (vital relationship with God in Christ) when we choose church leaders. Examples of religious criteria in a student community might be the number of Bible studies they're in, the number and length of personal quiet times, verses and worship songs memorized, etc. While these activities often aid in spiritual development, we all know it's easy and—unfortunately—quite common to go through the motions and not develop greater intimacy with and dependence on Jesus.

Jesus had some harsh words for those religious leaders of his day who tended to concentrate on the visible requirements of faith and ignore matters of the heart—he called them "whitewashed tombs." Clearly God's looking for broken people with "broken and contrite spirits"; people who know that without God's mercy and grace, they can do absolutely nothing of value. These are the kinds of kids we should be watching for and mentoring into worship leaders—not the perfect, popular, squeaky-clean musical prodigies or the self-righteous or religiously conformed. We need to look for tax-collector types who can say, "Have mercy on me, O God, for I am a sinner." Only that kind of person can truly say, "To God be the glory," and then lead others into worship that will transform lives.

Webber: We need to be careful that we don't fall into legalism with requirements for student leaders. You can set up systems such as that, but if it's "come to church three times a week, don't smoke, don't drink," those things don't have a whole lot to do with spirituality. Again, I believe the student worship leader—the one who's the primary person bringing his or her peers into communion with Christ—needs to be a Christian. For the other musicians, particularly back-up players, their roles aren't as central because they're playing instruments only. For them, the issue of personal commitment isn't as crucial.

YWJ: *How do you help a student worship team focus on performing for God and not performing for the group?*

Morgenthaler: We aren't born learning how to worship. In fact, it's our nature to do the opposite (see Romans 1). We have to nurture our teams into the response of worship, and the best way is to adore God deeply together each week and to get involved in each other's life at an intimate level, sharing, confessing, repenting and interceding. We need to practice giving ourselves to God as a small group, not just singing the right notes, playing the right chords or coming up with cool riffs. It's actually much more crucial that we practice redirecting our hearts and letting God cleanse our motivations. Worship leaders have a responsibility to remind team members continually of their higher calling and to speak gently to any prima donna, "look at me" attitudes.

Better than speaking to it, however, is modeling being a worshiper. If the leader and other members of the team are demonstrating true humility and supernatural focus on God, primadonnaism rarely becomes a problem. The neat thing is God is a win-win God. One of the results of intentionally nurturing worshipers within our teams is evangelism. When non-Christian instrumentalists experience God with skin on—God tangibly at work, reshaping and remolding selfish, narcissistic individuals (read: Christians)—they sit up and take notice. They say, "Wow, this stuff is real!"

Webber: Worship leaders need to be intentional. I tell them to reflect on their worship all week long: "Sing it. Hum it. Pray it. Practice it. Get it inside your heart and let it take up residence within you. On the night before you lead worship, throw away all your notes and lead with a sense of abandon." The new generation's worship is shifting from performance to a state of prayer. When you lead worship this way, it will draw the entire congregation into prayerful, intentional, heart-felt worship.

YWJ: *Some find worship through music is an effective part of outreach events; when talking to non-Christian kids, they hear positive responses to the music. Is this a trend?*

Morgenthaler: Music has the ability to access the human soul faster than anything else. This has always been true. When Saul was in the depths of depression, he called on David's musical skills to sooth his spirit and give him a sense of hope and renewed joy. We're now learning that exposure to music early in life helps crucial mental and emotional development.

Is there a new trend in this area? Our whole society—especially those younger than thirty—craves the medicine of music. The percentage of income spent on music purchases has risen dramatically in the past decade. When we apply this trend to the intense spiritual searching that's a fact of life as we round the bend of the next millennium, it shouldn't surprise us that God is harnessing music to tell people he loves them. God is an efficient God and will use the most effective means in any culture to reach the lost. It's a tremendous window of opportunity. Yet I believe God wants us to move beyond music alone and mix in other art forms, as well, which is what MTV has been doing for years. It's also why groups such as Delirou5 have become so popular and effective in telling the old, old story to a new generation.

Webber: We're in the midst of an extraordinary communications revolution that's shifting us from the primacy of print to a focus on the audiovisual. Sound itself—which creates atmosphere—is now viewed as an important communicator. For the kind of worship I propose, sound communicates the various moods of worship—the joy of coming into God's presence, the quietness of confession, the meditative mood of prayer, the joy of the resurrection at the table of the Lord and the sense of going forth to love and serve God.

YWJ: How do you involve all your students in worship when you have a very diverse, multicultural group?

Morgenthaler: What a great situation! Gone are the days when we could be white bread on stage and pretend God was of northern European descent. By 2050, demographic experts tell us Caucasians will be a minority race in America—and it could happen more quickly than that. So how do we involve all colors and backgrounds in student worship? We model diversity on our teams by including women, Latinos, African-Americans, Asians—everybody. It's God's family.

Just as importantly, we should start listening to secular music and incorporating those sounds in our worship writing and arranging, because, folks, the world has become a small place in the past ten to fifteen years. We're mixing Celtic instruments with the Down Under didgeridoo. We're melding Caribbean and Latino rhythms with the sounds of the koto and industrial techno. If you think about it, most contemporary worship music is not contemporary at all. In fact, it's found nowhere else on the planet. It's like we freeze-dried plasticized rock circa 1983 and have been feeding that to people ever since. That's what we consider appropriately Christian—just like we used to consider organ and choral music the only sounds God would hear. No wonder a lot of our students are bored! Our worship music doesn't represent the diversity and incredible variety of their world.

Webber: The future of worship will be multicultural and intergenerational, but there are no gimmicks or tools that have authenticity for multicultural worship. You can read Scripture, pray and sing in different languages; but that's secondary. What this generation longs for is community. If there's genuine love between the cultural groups and a sense that all are worshiping together, that's the key.

YWJ: Should youth leaders lead youth group worship the same way the church's praise and worship leaders do so the students can get adjusted to their styles?

Morgenthaler: Your youth group is a unique community that God continually fashions. Take the freedom God gives you to celebrate that and to create something new and fresh—a style that honors the Almighty and reflects your generation's degree of brokenness, lack of tolerance for slickness and penchant for complete honesty. Sure you can get some ideas, some principles from the worship leaders in the adult services, but God loves a new song (Psalm 40:3). What's more, I sincerely doubt your students want something that's been cloned after their parents' services. They have their own voices, and they want to use them.

Webber: This is a tough question. Many youth don't like current praise and worship with its loud, contemporary instrumentation. What they want is ancient liturgy with a contemporary flair. They want mystery, transcendence, quiet, prayer with the laying on of hands, pageantry, participation, stability, tradition, and authentic embodiment.

This is what one youth worker said at a recent conference: "I tried everything in the book to reach my young people. Finally, I gave up and said, 'We're just going to have a prayer meeting where we can pray for each other and meet each other's needs.' Kids are coming from everywhere—Christians and non-Christians! They sit on the floor, sing, pray and anoint each other with oil."

The point is that we're facing a new day with this new generation. Today's teens don't want fun and games; they want encounters with otherness—encounters that touch their lives with the healing touch of God. This kind of worship is the key to reaching the unchurched and deepening the spiritual commitment of the churched.

Worship is going to change significantly in the new millennium, so we'd better get ready for it now—all of us, youth workers, as well as worship leaders.

Bibliography

Adam, Adolf. *The Liturgical Year*. New York: Pueblo, 1981.
Adams, Doug, and Diane Apostolos-Cappadocia, eds. *Dance as Religious Studies*. New York: Crossroads, 1990.
Augustine, *Against Donatists*, Book 1:14. *The Nicene and Post-Nicene Fathers*, edited by Philip Schaff. Grand Rapids: Eerdmans, 1957.
———. *Against Donatists*, Book 1:15–23. In *The Nicene and Post-Nicene Fathers*, 4:421, edited by Philip Schaff. Grand Rapids: Eerdmans, 1957.
———. *Against Petilian*, Book 3, 9–10. In *The Nicene and Post-Nicene Fathers*, 4:601, edited by Philip Schaff. Grand Rapids: Eerdmans, 1957.
Aulen, Gustaf. *Christus Victor: An Historical Study of the Three Main Types of the Idea of Atonement*. Translated by A. G. Herber. New York: Macmillan, 1969.
Baptism, Eucharist and Ministry. Faith & Order Paper No. 111. Geneva: World Council of Churches, 1982.
Berkhof, Hendrik. *Christ and the Powers*. Scottdale, PA: Herald, 1977.
Bishops Committee on the Liturgy. Washington: United States Conference of Catholic Bishops, ND.
Boyack, Kenneth. *Catholic Evangelization Today: A New Pentecost for the United States*. New York: Paulist, 1987.
Braso, Gabriel M. *Liturgy and Spirituality*. Collegeville, MN: Liturgical, 1971.
Caird, G. B. *Principalities and Powers: A Study in Pauline Theology*. London: Oxford University Press, 1956.
Calvin, John. *The Institutes of the Christian Religion*. Translated by Henry Beveridge. Grand Rapids: Eerdmans, 1997.
Camus, Albert. *The Myth of Sisyphus*. Translated by Justin O'Brien. New York: Knopf, 1955.
Clement. *The Instructor*, Book I, 6. In *The Ante-Nicene Fathers*, compiled by A. Cleveland Coxe, edited by Alexander Roberts, James Donaldson, Philip Schaff, and Henry Wace, 2:20. Grand Rapids: Eerdmans, 1971.
Cornwall, Judson. *Let Us Worship*. South Plainfield, NJ: Bridge, 1983.
Crockett, William P. *Eucharist: Symbol of Transformation*. New York: Pueblo, 1989.
Cyprian. *On the Unity of the Catholic Church*, 6. In *The Ante-Nicene Fathers*, compiled by A. Cleveland Coxe, edited by Alexander Roberts, James Donaldson, Philip Schaff, and Henry Wace, 5:423. Grand Rapids: Eerdmans, 1971.
Day, Thomas. *Why Catholics Can't Sing: The Culture of Catholicism and the Triumph of Bad Taste*. New York: Crossroad, 1990.

Dix, Gregory, and Henry Chadwick, eds. *The Treatise on the Apostolic Tradition of St. Hippolytus of Rome.* Ridgefield, CT: Morehouse, 1992.
Driver, Tom F. *The Magic of Ritual: Our Need for Liberating Rites That Transform Our Lives and Our Communities.* San Francisco: Harper & Row, 1991.
Dujarier, Michael. *A History of the Catechumenate: The First Six Centuries.* New York: Sadlier, 1979.
———. *The Rites of Christian Initiation: Historical and Pastoral Reflections.* New York: Sadlier, 1979.
———. "A Survey of the History of the Catechumenate." In *Becoming a Catholic Christian*, edited by William J. Reedy, 19–38. New York: Sadlier, 1981.
Egeria. *Diary of a Pilgrimage.* Translated and annotated by George E. Gingras. New York: Newman, 1970.
Empereur, James L., and Christopher G. Kiesling. *The Liturgy That Does Justice*, Collegeville, MN: Liturgical, 1990.
Erikson, Erik H. *Childhood and Society.* New York: W. W. Norton, 1950.
Esslin, Martin. "The Theatre of the Absurd." *The Tulane Drama Review* 4, no. 4 (May 1960) 3–15. https://doi.org/10.2307/1124873.
Fowler, James. *Stages of Faith: The Psychology of the Human Development and the Quest for Meaning.* San Francisco: Harper & Row, 1981.
Fukuyama, Francis. *The Great Disruption: Human Nature and the Reconstitution of Social Order.* New York: Free Press, 1999.
Funk, Virgil C., ed. *Sung Liturgy: Toward 2000 A. D.* Washington: Pastoral, 1991.
Gagne, Ronald, et al. *Introducing Dance in Christian Worship.* Washington: Pastoral, 1984.
Grosz, Edward M., ed. *Liturgy and Social Justice: Celebrating Rights, Proclaiming Rights.* Collegeville: Liturgical, 1989.
Harnack, Adolf von. *What Is Christianity? Lectures Delivered in the University of Berlin during the Winter-Term 1899–1900.* 2nd ed. Translated by Thomas Bailey Saunders. New York: G. P. Putnam's Sons, 1908.
Harmless, William. *Augustine and the Catechumenate.* Collegeville, MN: Liturgical, 1995.
Hatchett, Marion J. *A Guide to the Practice of Church Music.* New York: The Church Hymnal Corporation, 1989.
Howard, Thomas. *The Liturgy Explained.* Harrisburg, PA: Morehouse, 1981.
Hustad, Donald. *Jubilate! Church Music in the Evangelical Tradition.* Carol Stream, IL: Hope, 1981.
Irenaeus. *Against Heresies*, Book 2:22, 4. In *The Early Christian Fathers*, translated by Henry Bettenson. Oxford: Oxford University Press, 1969.
———. *Against Heresies*, Book 4:38, 2–3. In *The Early Christian Fathers*, translated by Henry Bettenson, 68. Oxford: Oxford University Press, 1969.
Jasper, R. C. D., and G. J. Cuming. *Prayers of the Eucharist: Early and Reformed.* New York: Oxford University Press, 1980.
Jauhiainen, Henry. "A Pentecostal/Charismatic Manifesto." In *Twenty Centuries of Christian Worship*, edited by Robert E. Webber, 337–40. Nashville: Star Song, 1994.
Johansson, Calvin M. *Discipling Music Ministry.* Peabody, MA; Hendrickson, 1992.
———. *Music & Ministry: A Biblical Counterpoint.* Peabody, MA: Hendrickson, 1984.

Johnson, Maxwell E. *The Rites of Christian Initiation: Their Evolution and Interpretation.* Collegeville, MN: Liturgical, 1999.
Justin Martyr. *First Apology.* In *The Ante-Nicene Fathers*, compiled by A. Cleveland Coxe, edited by Alexander Roberts, James Donaldson, Philip Schaff, and Henry Wace, 1:183. Grand Rapids: Eerdmans, 1971.
Kavanaugh, Aidan. *The Shape of Baptism: The Rite of Christian Introduction.* New York: Pueblo, 1978.
Kennel, LeRoy. *Visual Arts and Worship.* Newton, KS: Faith & Life, 1983.
Lasch, Christopher. *The Culture of Narcissism: American Life in An Age of Diminishing Expectations.* New York: W. W. Norton, 1991.
L'Engle, Madeleine. *The Traditional Season.* San Francisco: Harper & Row, 1977.
Lee, Peggy. "Is That All There Is?," by Mike Stoller and Jerry Leiber. Track 1 on *Is That All There Is?*, Capitol Records, 1969.
"Letter to Diognetus." https://www.ccel.org/ccel/richardson/fathers.x.i.ii.html.
McLuhan, Marshall. *Understanding Media: The Extensions of Man.* New York: McGraw-Hill, 1964.
Minear, Paul S. *Images of the Church in the New Testament.* Philadelphia: Westminster, 1960.
Mitchell, Leonel L. *The Meaning of Ritual.* Wilton, CT: Morehouse-Barlow, 1977.
Morrison, Clinton D. *The Powers That Be: Earthly Rulers and Demonic Powers in Romans 13:1–7.* Naperville, IL: Alec R. Allenson, 1960.
Murphy Center for Liturgical Research. *Made, Not Born: New Perspectives on Christian Initiations and the Catechumenate.* Notre Dame: University of Notre Dame Press, 1976.
Nardone, Richard M. *The Story of the Christian Year.* New York: Paulist, 1991.
Nichols, Adrian, O. P. *The Art of God Incarnate: Theology and Symbolism from Genesis to the Twentieth Century.* New York: Paulist, 1980.
"Nobel Prize: Kyrie Eleison Without God." *Time* 94, no. 18 (October 31, 1969). https://content.time.com/time/subscriber/article/0,33009,839114-1,00.html.
The Orthodox Liturgy: Being the Divine Liturgy of S. John Chrysostom and S. Basil the Great according to the use of the Church of Russia. Translated by Patrick Thompson, London: Fellowship of Saint Alban and Saint Sergius, 1939.
Ostediek, Gilbert. *Catechesis for Liturgy: A Program for Parish Involvement.* Washington, DC: Pastoral, 1986.
Otto, Rudolph. *The Idea of the Holy.* Translated by John W. Harvey. London: Oxford University Press, 1958.
Piaget, Jean. *Structuralism.* Translated by C. Maschler. New York: Basic Books, 1970.
Quebedeaux, Richard. "Rise of the Left-Wing Evangelicals." *New Oxford Review* 45, no. 3 (March 1978) 10–15.
Schlier, Heinrich. *Principalities and Powers in the New Testament.* New York: Heider & Heider, 1961.
Schmemann, Alexander. *The Eucharist: Sacrament of the Kingdom.* New York: St. Vladimir's Seminary Press, 1988.
Schreiter, Robert J. *In Water and Blood: A Spirituality of Solidarity and Hope.* New York: Crossroads, 1988.
Second Vatican Council. *Constitution on the Sacred Liturgy.* Council of Catholic Bishops, 1963. https://adoremus.org/1963/12/sacrosanctum-concilium.

———. "Constitution on the Sacred Liturgy." In *Documents on the Liturgy, 1963–1979: Conciliar, Papal, and Curial Text*, edited by the International Commission on English in the Liturgy. Collegeville, MN: Liturgical, 1982.

Sly, Randy, and Wayne Boosahda. "The Convergence Movement." In *Twenty Centuries of Christian Worship*, edited by Robert E. Webber, 131–41. Nashville: Star Song, 1994.

Staples, Rob L. *Outward Sign and Inward Grace: The Place of the Sacraments in Wesleyan Spirituality*. Kansas City, MO: Beacon Hill, 1991.

Stark, Rodney. *The Rise of Christianity: A Sociologist Reconsiders History*. Princeton: Princeton University Press, 1996.

Stevenson, Kenneth. *Eucharist and Offering*. New York: Pueblo, 1986.

Stevick, Daniel B. *Baptismal Moments; Baptismal Meanings*. New York: The Church Hymnal Corporation, 1987.

Tabori, Fabio. *The Eucharist and the World of Work*. Translated by Matthew J. O'Connell, Collegeville, MN: Liturgical, 1990.

Taft, Robert. *The Liturgy of the Hours in East and West*. Collegeville, MN: Liturgical, 1986.

Talley, Thomas J. *The Origins of the Liturgical Year*. New York: Pueblo, 1986.

Tertullian. *On Baptism* In *The Ante-Nicene Fathers*, compiled by A. Cleveland Coxe, edited by Alexander Roberts, James Donaldson, Philip Schaff, and Henry Wace, 3:669–70. Grand Rapids: Eerdmans, 1971.

———. *On Martyrdom*, I. In *The Ante-Nicene Fathers*, compiled by A. Cleveland Coxe, edited by Alexander Roberts, James Donaldson, Philip Schaff, and Henry Wace, 3:693. Grand Rapids: Eerdmans, 1971.

Vander Hart, Ruth. "The Seeker Service: A New Strategy for Evangelism." *Reformed Worship*, Calvin Institute of Christian Worship, 23, March 1992. https://www.reformedworship.org/article/march-1992/seeker-service-new-strategy-evangelism.

Ware, Timothy. *The Orthodox Church*. Baltimore: Penguin, 1963.

Webber, Robert E. *Ancient-Future Evangelism: Making Your Church a Faith-Forming Community* Grand Rapids, Baker, 2003.

———. "Are Evangelicals Becoming Sacramental?" *Ecumenical Trends*, 16 (March 1985) 36–38.

———. "A Call to an Ancient-Evangelical Future." *Christianity Today* 50, no. 9 (September 1, 2006) 57–58. https://www.christianitytoday.com/ct/2006/september/11.57.html.

———. "Behind the Scenes: A Personal Account." *The Orthodox Evangelicals: Who They Are and What They Are Saying*, edited by Donald G. Bloesch and Robert E. Webber, 16–39. Nashville: Thomas Nelson, 1978.

———. "Bring Them In: Three Models for Evangelism Through Worship." *Reformed Worship*, Calvin Institute of Christian Worship, 23 (March 1992). https://www.reformedworship.org/article/march-1992/bring-them-three-models-evangelism-through-worship.

———. "Christ the Victor, Christ the Center." *Christianity Today* 29, no. 6 (April 5, 1985). https://www.christianitytoday.com/ct/1985/april-5/books.html.

———. "Church Buildings: Shapes of Worship." *Christianity Today* 25, no. 14 (August 7, 1981) 18–20. https://www.christianitytoday.com/ct/1981/august-7/church-buildings-shapes-of-worship.html.

―――. "A Critique of Popular Evangelical Christianity." *New Oxford Review* 46, no. 8 (October 1979) 6–10.

―――. "Easter: Reliving the Mystery." *Christianity Today* 30, no. 5 (March 21, 1986) 16–18. https://www.christianitytoday.com/ct/1986/march-21/easter-reliving-mystery-experiencing-drama-unites-us-with.html.

―――. "Ecumenical Influences on Evangelical Worship." *Ecumenical Trends* 19 (May 1990) 73–76.

―――. "Enter His Courts with Praise: A New Style of Worship Is Sweeping the Church." *Reformed Worship Journal*, Calvin Institute of Christian Worship 20 (June 1991). https://www.reformedworship.org/article/june-1991/enter-his-courts-praise-new-style-worship-sweeping-church.

―――. "Ethics and Evangelism: Learning from the Third-Century Church." *The Christian Century* 103, no. 27 (September 24, 1986) 806–8. https://www.religion-online.org/article/ethics-and-evangelism-learning-from-the-third-century-church.

―――. "Evangelism and Christian Formation in the Early Church." *Reformation & Revival Journal: A Quarterly for Church Renewal* 13, no. 4 (Fall 2004) 79–94, https://biblicalstudies.org.uk/pdf/ref-rev/13-4/13-4_webber.pdf.

―――. "From Jerusalem to Willow Creek: A Brief History of Christian Worship." *Leadership Journal* 13, no. 70 (1992) 121–29.

―――. "From Modern to Post-Modern: Worship Changes During the Twentieth Century." *Southwestern Journal of Theology* 42, no. 3 (Summer 2000) 5–21.

―――. "The Future Direction of Christian Worship." *Ex Auditu* 8 (1992) 113–28.

―――. "Is Our Worship Adequately Triune?" *Reformation & Revival Journal: A Quarterly for Church Renewal* 9, no. 3 (Summer 2000) 121–29. https://biblicalstudies.org.uk/pdf/ref-rev/09-3/9-3_webber.pdf.

―――. *Journey to Jesus: The Worship, Evangelism, and Nurture Mission of the Church*. Nashville: Abingdon, 2001.

―――. "Let's Put Worship into the Worship Service." *Christianity Today* 28, no. 3 (February 17, 1984) 52. https://www.christianitytoday.com/ct/1984/february-17/speaking-out-lets-put-worship-into-worship-service.html.

―――. *Liturgical Evangelism: Worship as Outreach and Nurture*. Ridgefield, CT: Morehouse, 1992.

―――. "Living in the World." *The Post American* 3, no. 5 (June–July 1974) 26–28.

―――. "Narrating the World Once Again: A Case for an Ancient-Future Faith." *Criswell Theological Review* 3, no. 2 (Spring 2006) 15–29.

―――. "Praise and Worship Music: From Its Origins to Contemporary Use." *Pastoral Music* 27, no. 3 (February-March 2003) 21–23.

―――. "The Road to the Future Runs Through the Past: Reviving an Ancient Faith Journey." *Vision: A Journal for Church and Theology* 4, no. 2 (Fall 2003) 15–20. https://press.palni.org/ojs/index.php/vision/article/view/541/484.

―――. *Signs of Wonder: The Phenomenon of Convergence in Modern Liturgical and Charismatic Churches*. Nashville: Abbott Martyn, 1992.

―――. "The Silence of God." Wheaton College Chapel, transcript from audio recording. Wheaton, IL: Buswell Library Archives & Special Collections, November 5, 1969.

―――. "The Tragedy of the Reformation." Wheaton College Chapel, transcript from audio recording. Wheaton, IL: Buswell Library Archives & Special Collections, October 24, 1974.

———. "The Trinity." Wheaton College Chapel, transcript from audio recording. Wheaton, IL: Buswell Library Archives & Special Collections, October 13, 1980.

———. "What Is Liturgical Evangelism?" In *Celebrating Our Faith: Evangelism Through Worship*, 1–15. San Francisco, Harper & Row, 1986.

———. "What We've Learned Along the Way: Reformed Worship Through Twenty Years of Liturgical Change." *Reformed Worship Journal*, Calvin Institute of Christian Worship, 77 (September 2005). https://www.reformedworship.org/article/september-2005/what-weve-learned-along-way-reformed-worship-through-twenty-years-liturgical.

———. *Worship Old and New*. Grand Rapids: Zondervan, 1982.

Wells, David F.. *The Person of Christ: A Biblical and Historical Analysis of the Incarnation*, Westchester, IL: Crossway, 1984.

Westermeyer, Paul. *The Church Musician*. San Francisco: Harper & Row, 1988.

Wheaton College Archives and Special Collections. https://archives.wheaton.edu.

White, James F. "A Protestant Worship Manifesto." *The Christian Century* 99, no. 3 (January 27, 1982) 82.

White, Susan J. *Art, Architecture and Liturgical Reform*. New York: Pueblo, 1991.

Willimon, William H. *The Service of God: How Worship and Ethics Are Related*, Nashville: Abingdon, 1983.

Winter, Miriam Therese. *Why Sing: Toward a Theology of Catholic Church Music*. Washington: Pastoral, 1984.

"Worship Like You Mean It: Interview with Sally Morgenthaler and Robert E. Webber." *YouthWorker Journal*, July-August 1999. https://www.youthworker.com/worship-like-you-mean-it-interview-with-sally-morgenthaler-and-robert-webber.

Yarnold, Edward. *The Awe-Inspiring Rites of Initiation: Baptismal Homilies of the Fourth Century*. Middle Green: Great Britain, 1972.

Yoder, John Howard. *The Politics of Jesus*. Grand Rapids: Eerdmans, 1972.

www.ingramcontent.com/pod-product-compliance
Lightning Source LLC
Chambersburg PA
CBHW030823230426
43667CB00008B/1356